OF PILGRIMS AND FIRE

OF PILGRIMS AND FIRE

When God Shows Up at the Movies

Roy Anker

William B. Eerdmans Publishing Company
Grand Rapids, Michigan / Cambridge, U.K.

Published 2010 by

Wm. B. Eerdmans Publishing Co.

2140 Oak Industrial Drive N.E., Grand Rapids, Michigan 49505 /

P.O. Box 163, Cambridge CB3 9PU U.K.

Printed in the United States of America

15 14 13 12 11 10   7 6 5 4 3 2 1

Library of Congress Cataloging-in-Publication Data

Anker, Roy M.

   Of pilgrims and fire: when God shows up at the movies /

   Roy Anker.

      p.   cm.

    ISBN 978-0-8028-6572-4 (pbk.: alk. paper)

    1. Religion in motion pictures. 2. Supernatural in motion pictures.

    I. Title.

PN1995.9.R4A55   2010

791.43′682 — dc22

                          2010027778

www.eerdmans.com

To the members of CALL,

    seers and cineastes of the first order

Contents

Acknowledgments

Almost every book has behind it generous people who in many different ways nurture its best parts. The people in the English Department at Calvin College like movies almost as much as they love writing and books; hanging out with them is always a deep pleasure. Among them, Jane Zwart, Jennifer Holberg, and Gary Schmidt provided wonderful help in attacking the clunkiness of my prose. And it is impossible to overstate the support and great good humor of my family, especially Ellen, with her limitless patience and zest. In their passion and insight, many students have added greatly to my own understanding of film. Most of all, special gratitude goes to the members of CALL, the Calvin Academy of Lifelong Learning, to whom this book is dedicated—as kindly and profound a group of cineastes as ever brightened the dark of a theater.

Of Pilgrims and Fire

Pilgrims

As Yoda would no doubt put it, pilgrims all we are — whether we know it or not, like it or not. Strangely enough, that old notion of what constitutes humanness still has a lot of "grab," and not just because of John Wayne's famous movie greeting, "Howdy, Pilgrim." Movies fade, truths persist.

What was both catchy and memorable about Wayne's greeting was that it included everyone in that fellowship of pilgrims, every stranger-wayfarer he came across. Out there on the vast emptiness of the frontier, it seemed especially apt, though the same greeting fits the present well enough, perhaps even more so, especially for those wandering souls searching for paths in urban jungles and suburban sprawl. For all our techno-dazzle in getting around quickly via cars and planes, not many people anywhere — in the church or outside it — seem to have much of a sense of where in fact they're headed and why.

The term "pilgrim," of course, has within it a whole anthropology, a view of what makes humans tick deep down. We theorize about what people most desire, though "desire" is perhaps too tame a word for what propels us all: the word "crave" perhaps moves closer to the core, so thirsty and determined are we to find some fulfilling magic as we move from one thing to another. After all, every human creature searches, albeit unconsciously, for a destination that promises meaning and welcome, a "true" place that sates the self and soothes the rest-

1

less soul. "Then longen folke to go on pilgrimage," says the great medieval taleteller Geoffrey Chaucer.

In the Middle Ages, the pilgrim journeyed, often in the company of others, to visit a shrine or holy site, some place that commemorated some manifestation of the divine. The hope was that the place itself still possessed some residue of that original holy manifestation (*hierophany*, as scholars of religion put it). Think of Canterbury, or the shrine at Lourdes, to which many still travel for its healing presence. The impulse to journey in search of a potent, magical, holy something has not changed, though destinations certainly have. In the vast smorgasboard culture of postmodernity, that destination could be just about anywhere — from a rock concert to Wrigley Field to Las Vegas to Disneyland, or, more likely, the shopping mall or golf course. And today's pilgrims often transport themselves not on foot or donkey but on a Harley or in a Bimmer or by jet. And their rewards? Well, those transported pilgrims arrive in a rush for a buzz or a thrill, anything that relieves the humdrum of the ordinary. Whatever the particulars, the pattern of North Americans rushing about hither and yon for this or that raises the question of where we all are headed and for what. For what are we "longen"?

Light

The best and most ancient image for the pilgrim's destination is light, and light comes in manifold forms, small and large, from glimmers to fireworks to dangerous, all-consuming blazes. In its most fundamental physical utility, light illuminates the darkness, showing us where in the world we are and providing a bit of safety from those predators who see in the dark. In this world at least, light comes from fire, and when harnessed, fire gives not only light but heat, thus banishing cold and death — for the time being. In one of its more benign manifestations, fire cooks food. It is no wonder, then, that light is associated with so many diverse intellectual, emotional, and social "goods." Knowledge, truth, joy, delight, love, kindness, solace, intimacy, reconciliation, and beauty — naming just a few of the most important goods.

Light comes from fire, whether this-worldly or metaphysical, mundane or religious. When we are lost in the cold and darkness, especially religiously, there's nothing we crave as much as a mere flash that might give some direction and maybe also some warmth. There is also Light with a capital *L,* light that is in some measure divine, transcendent, salvific, or redemptive. In the theologies of the West, it is this divine Light that provides for all these other "goods." And this Light also comes in many forms and intensities, ranging from flickers and flashes to blazing radiance in rainbows and transfigurations. In the Jewish and Christian traditions, light is a central metaphor for all that is most important to humans and also a manifestation of God's own self. The Old Testament has its pillars of fire, burning bushes, glowing faces, and chariots of fire; in the New Testament, Jesus is characterized as a refining fire, a bold and scary claim. These images emerge from Judaism and Christianity and later spread to Islam. Perhaps the most famous — and central — statement in all of Christianity is Jesus' simple claim, in the Gospel of John: "I am the Light of the world" (John 8:12). Similar examples appear in the other major world religions. Indeed, what pilgrims most journey toward is the Light, that which illuminates, warms, shows the way, and brings us to recognize fellow pilgrims.

Stories

We see the pilgrim's search for light most clearly in the stories we love to hear, read, and see: from the narratives of sports, *American Idol,* and politics to dramas of *Lost, The Passion of the Christ,* and *A Field of Dreams.* Stories have a peculiar power, both to evoke curiosity and to deliver meaning, hope, despair, remorse, love, and so on. Humanity's appetite for stories is insatiable, because stories are deeply pleasurable. Within the human's relentless curiosity, though, the most urgent question of all is the one about what will happen to one's own self, fragile and mortal, and for what reasons and purposes it will happen. That is the deep mystery to which stories speak. People generally seem to be wired that way, whether from a survival instinct or as a trace of the "image of God" lingering within them. Simply put, we love stories, and not just as illustrations of larger, abstract truths. Stories themselves have a depth of appeal and cogency that math and philosophy never will. Stories entice and compel and, if told well, convince. Even *The Scientific American* has pursued this question, concluding finally that "the safe, imaginary world of a story may . . . have a unique power to persuade and motivate, because [stories] appeal to our emotions and capacity for empathy" (9/18/2008).

Most stories are really very simple. The late novelist John Gardner once observed that there are really only two kinds of stories: a stranger comes to town, or someone goes on a trip. Someone comes, or someone goes — both are pilgrims — and then change and the unexpected happen. Stories have always focused on conflicts between people, fate, and the gods, and they typically move through chaos to some sort of resolution, sometimes ending in the sorrowful mess of the tragedies and sometimes in the stable and safe societies of the comedies. The larger questions about stories have centered on how compelling they are in depicting the human predicament: How truthful are they in what they portray about human circumstances, and how effectively do they deliver that portrait? The arts, then, labor toward that end of continually shedding light on what we and our world are really like.

Stories work to tell us what the world and the creatures in it are like, providing maps, if you will, of the terrain of human experience: why people do what they do, what's likely to happen, what evil looks like, what ultimately matters most, and what we can generally expect from life in a human skin. That's true in nursery rhymes, and it's true in the grim realism of renowned novelists such as Philip Roth and J. M. Coetzee. And this grimness is easy enough to pull off, given its proximity to real life in which soldiers die, towers fall, and love fails.

In fact, the pervasiveness of tragedy, the inescapable given of the human predicament, means that perhaps the greatest challenge for all the arts — movies included — is how to deliver light — however we may define that — convincingly. In life after the Fall, we have plenty to be grim about, despite the human tendency to prettify things. Most people recognize when stories turn into wish fulfillment or happy talk, though they may still draw much pleasure from them — and even some hope. However, hope, faith, and love, as Saint Paul names them, are generally a hard sell, especially if one pays attention to the tragic news about human life. Nevertheless, an unquenchable human hope persists, seemingly inscribed in our human DNA. As novelist and apologist Frederick Buechner puts it, the news is always bad before it is good.

Movies

There is perhaps no artistic medium that relies so much on "light" to find Light as film does, especially with its ever-greater technological storehouse of cinematic sorcery. At its most rudimentary level, the movie camera "catches" light and the projector "shines" light on a reflective, iridescent screen. Film is, then, quite literally a medium of light: it moves and has its being by throwing light up on a screen. We the viewers enjoy that enormously, because stories are made visible before us, full of words and action and pictures (and music, too). From the vivid wonders of Pixar to the gauzy lights of romances, most people deeply and mysteriously enjoy the simple (and sensual) play of light and images on the screen.

When done well, cinema dazzles and wows. Add to the mix that simple, deep-fun pleasure we get from good stories and stirring music, and movies can become an extremely potent medium. They can become so potent, in fact, that they may become another kind of light altogether, and many folks, youthful to elderly, find that other kind of light the one worth looking hard for, light that illumines the darkness in their own lives by supplying meaning and significance — if only for a little while. Unfortunately, film stories usually provide little, if any, light of any kind. The vast majority of movies are forgettable, providing at best a couple of hours of distraction. Some few films, though, do tell stories that display light itself in amounts that range from a faint warm glimmer to, in very rare and priceless instances, a burst of flame that sears the soul. Sometimes in those rare instances we can even experience transcendent Light.

What films typically depict is people on all kinds of pilgrimages who are longing for and moving toward some kind of illumination: they may be solving a mystery or finding romance or, in some dazzling cases, encountering Light. Among the thousands of films made in just over a hundred years of production history, only a handful have sought to show Light, either as an event that happens or an actual perceivable presence, whether the brilliant light in the sky in *Close Encounters of a Third Kind* (1977) or the still small voice inside us in *A Man for All Seasons* (1966). In other words, the effort to dramatize the coming of Light is a pretty rare cinematic occurrence.

Finding Light in the Movies

As for this discussion guide, first and foremost it considers movies about pilgrims looking for Light. The settings and *dramatis personae* range all over history and the globe, from a pair of spinster sisters in a tiny village on the shores of Jutland in the nineteenth century, to American soldiers in combat on the islands of Melanesia in the middle of the twentieth, to a small blind boy in a rural village in the mountains of Iran. Or it could be in Texas, Turin, Manhattan, Metropolis, or on death row that we find these worlds of widows, lost boys, bewildered and lonely grownups, murderers, priests, mercenaries, and so on — anytime, anywhere, anybody. A good imagination, a gifted filmmaker, and a searching story can move viewers into the heart of cosmic mysteries and, as these films do, a long way into the heart of Light, clarifying the hardest of all questions: When and how does the pilgrim find some measure of that Light? Indeed, if the film is really good, we become pilgrims, too, which is perhaps the toughest thing for a filmmaker to pull off.

The significant films I explore here are very much offbeat in their angles of approach in that they do not meet the usual criteria for what we think of as overtly religious pictures, meaning pious, preachy, churchy, sanctimonious, and (usually) bad. Within the history of Hollywood and still today, "religious" has meant films with straightforward biblical and/or religious subject matter, usually a historical subject of some kind, often involving one of the great narratives in the Bible, or one with an overtly religious and heroic character or theme. The 1950s and 1960s saw waves of such films, all meant to enhance religious feeling in predictable ways, films such as *The Robe* (1953), *The Ten Commandments* (1956), *Ben-Hur* (1959), and *A Man for All Seasons* (1966). That genre still periodically cycles around in the twenty-first century, most recently with Mel Gibson's *The Passion of the Christ* (2004) and the reemergence of evangelical/dispensationalist filmmaking in *Left Behind* (2000), *Facing the Giants* (2006), and *Fireproof* (2008). Though sometimes very popular, these movies usually do not fare well critically (though I hasten to add that critics can often be dead wrong), and very few have survived their initial popularity.

By contrast, the surprisingly religious films I explore here tend to surprise viewers in a host of ways. First, all have an ample dose of experiential realism that is focused on ordinary people, and most of that is situated in a quite recognizable or plausible world or, in the case of science-fiction films, in a calamitous future. Instead of focusing on "heroes of the faith," these narratives fasten on the struggles of quite ordinary people as they try to find some measure of light that will make sense of the world and themselves. Here we find ordinary people plopped down in a real — and often very messy — world, in which they seek and sometimes find, as pilgrims do, a sacred place that promises a measure of wholeness. Second, the light they shine dramatizes without necessarily solving the mystery of the divine, who usually shows up in unexpected, even astonishing, ways and places and hardly ever in the same way twice. What's more, viewers will encounter unforeseeable renditions of what God might look like.

Best of all, these are really wonderful films, full of surprises and unique angles on the character of the divine. None of them seems formulaic or predictable, due in large part to inventive storytelling that makes full and fresh use of the capacities of cinema as a medium. Not only do they tell different kinds of stories, but they do so in fresh, compelling, and even startling ways. The effect is one of surprise at the ingeniousness of filmmaking, how very good it can be, and especially when it is applied to a tale worth telling, namely, a story of pilgrims trying to find their way in a tangled and often very dark world. Thus, no matter how diverse they are in subject matter and content, these films deliver loads of meaning and also, along the way, quiet but dense joy in their masterful artistry and often in the surprising revelations of their endings, after which we experience wonder and then gladness. In these twenty films, old songs find a new tune, and old wine a fresh wineskin.

Domains of Light

This guide offers one set of organizational goggles for making some sense of the considerable variety of films that we might label in some way "religious." The first section, "The Gift of Splendor," gathers four films that in different ways meditate (and that is the right word) on the unfathomable, irreplaceable gift of being alive in a beautiful and sensually luminous world. These film stories range in setting from a contemporary American suburb to a large apartment complex in Communist Warsaw to contemporary Iran to the World War II battle for the Pacific island of Guadalcanal. All dwell on what used to be called the beauty of creation. Indeed, they are strangely resonant with the Genesis account of the natural world's goodness, the wonder of simply being alive in this world.

The second section, "Wrestling with Angels (and Demons)," emphasizes the connections between religious belief and conduct: specifically, what it is like to try to find light and what difference it makes, if any, when found. None of these films provides the kind of glib — and profoundly unbiblical — notion that belief is some sort of good-luck charm ensuring that all will go well forever for those who believe. Rather, these films combat the notion that belief is finally about the self at all, though the self is, needless to say, where it all starts. In Woody Allen's *Crimes and Misdemeanors,* we follow an eminently respectable central character, a revered ophthalmologist, who finds himself tortured by guilt in a sophisticated world that essentially scoffs at such passé notions. Similarly, *The Godfather: Part III* focuses on the guilt of the immensely successful mobster Michael Corleone and his search for some measure of redemption for his many crimes, both legal and personal. Last, on a happier note, we follow the story of a ten-year-old's search for religious assurance after the death of his loving grandfather. Along the way, as he learns a great deal, he comes to be "wide awake," and so do we.

The five films in section three, "The New Life: The Surprise of Love," show several registers of what used to be called "redemption," its connotation markedly different from what the term "salvation" usually suggests. In all of these instances, blind and benighted central characters come to know the unfathomable, and wholly unexpected, surprise that at the center of all things, at their beginning and end, is Love: a radiant, exultant, and all-consuming fire that transfigures the world and themselves. Some of the people in these stories should have known better all along, for example, the preacher Euliss "Sonny" Dewey in Robert Duvall's *The Apostle.* But then come surprises that encompass everyone, including those who do not have a clue about much of anything, such as Matthew Poncelot in *Dead Man Walking,* Rodrigo Mendoza in *The Mission,* and Mac Sledge (Duvall again) in *Tender Mercies.* Even those who know a lot do not necessarily know all they should, a condition that describes the sophisticated Andy Dufresne in *The Shawshank Redemption.* All of them stumble on an unexpected gift that shakes them to their very core and supplants the blindness of self with the Light that is love.

Section four explores "Facsimiles of God," specifically the different narrative guises that can convey what an incarnation might look and feel like. Steven Spielberg's classic *E.T.: The Extra-Terrestrial* contains the full clout of surprise that comes when we find the divine where the divine is least expected. The same is true in the superhero tale of Superman, a savior figure in a cape who eschews violence when he can and would save the world if he could (he's just not that super). Meanwhile, in *Millions*, Danny Boyle spins a witty and beguiling tale of a ten-year-old who keeps running into saints after he and his family are forced to relocate following the death of his mother.

The section where all of this comes together, reaching a kind of crescendo, is section five, "The Feast of Love," which here instigates the reconciliation of the human community, bringing to full flourish the delight and intimacy for which the world was made in the first place. And this happens in wildly different locales — historically, geographically, and culturally. Depression-era Texas is a long way from contemporary Los Angeles, or is it? The stories in *Places in the Heart* and *Grand Canyon* display the bridges that cross chasms of profound social brokenness and alienation. Both portray the new harmony that proceeds from the unlikely coming of divine love. Pretty much from the beginning, humanity has searched for some apt symbol for what relational wholeness might look like, something that might reveal a path toward the repair of the pervasive wreckage within the human community. In Gabriel Axel's luminous *Babette's Feast*, the tale of two maiden sisters and a refugee cook set in the late nineteenth century on the remote shores of Denmark, we have the most direct rendition of the feast of love, the eucharistic table that brings together and heals a community.

The last section contains two films that leap beyond themselves, so to speak: that is, *Magnolia* and *Heaven* are not examples of realism as it is usually defined. They are narratively wild and full of unexpected — if not miraculous — intrusions of the divine. Yet they are fully plausible, at least within the cinematic worlds their directors construct. Taken together, they remind viewers that the divine is not necessarily all that tame — and certainly not predictable.

How to Use This Book

In this book I seek to increase pleasure and understanding in film viewing. Like the films I have selected for inclusion, I try to avoid the preachy or didactic and strive to make the viewing and reflecting experience enjoyable and provocative. I try to demonstrate the enormous variety and depth of what we might call "religious film."

In each chapter, first comes the information about the film under discussion, the basic stuff of what is called a filmography: writer, direc- tor, cinematographer, production designer, composer, actors, and so on. This opening section also notes the awards, if any, a film has won. And it gives rating scores (in percentiles) from the two major search- engine Web sites for movie reviews, Rotten Tomatoes and Metacritic. For each film, I provide a general introduction that describes the who, the what, and the how of the making of the film, in addition to its narra- tive premise. This section introduces the central narrative and the- matic stakes in the film without describing pivotal events or resolu- tions that could ruin the suspense of the viewing experience. The bullet-pointed "Things to Look For" section suggests important cine- matic strategies that the filmmaker uses to make a point within his or her own style, given the storehouse of cinematic choices.

The "Post-viewing Comment" tries to make brief sense of viewer response to the viewing and of what the filmmaker seems to convey in the film, focusing on what the filmmaker's conclusions might say to the religious and theological community. Storytelling has an enormous ca- pacity to clarify, vivify, and explore shopworn truisms that religious com- munities seem to pass over, or, if they have ever known them, to forget at the earliest convenience. Indeed, with their enormous visual power, movies can display elusive realities with pungent, even iconic insight.

One useful discussion question for all the films here might ask what image in the film best articulates its meaning. The still photos that accompany the text offer some possibilities, but there are clearly a host of others.

The last element of each chapter/film is a series of questions that are meant to guide personal reflection and/or group discussion. These questions focus on cinematic elements that work to enhance both sto- rytelling and thematic depth. They can be read and discussed before another viewing of the film, though I would avoid reading them if the reader has not previously seen the movie. And, in any viewing of a film, whether for the first or tenth time, too much concentration on film style and meaning can divert attention from holistic engagement with the story.

To whet the reader's appetite, I conclude each chapter with some quotes by prominent reviewers of the film in question, plus a short list of other worthy films by the director and/or screenwriter of the film under discussion, or a brief list of films related to the style or subject matter of the film.

A Dozen Tips for Smart Film Viewing

Suppositions

1. Savor them. Movies are for enjoyment, so — first and foremost — enjoy their many varied pleasures. There's the eye-candy wonder and dazzle of *WALL-E, Avatar,* and *District 9,* and the spectacle and majesty (and tragedy) of *The Mission, The Thin Red Line,* and *E.T.: The Extra-Terrestrial.*

2. Always, at front and center, is the chief pleasure of the story, full of mystery and surprise, whether in the wit and fun of *Star Wars* or, for that matter, in the dark and sorrowful ones, such as *The Godfather.* The big story question is threefold: Where does it start? How does it end? And how does it get there (what happens)? We love stories and can't seem to get enough of them. Stories structure our world, show us good people and bad, via comedy and tragedy, farce and triumph. And movies give us — literally — some kind of *picture* of the world, visually and narratively, that inherently tests our own individual assumptions of how the world works. We sometimes wonder if pure fiction might in fact be more "true" in its depiction of the world than reams of statistical analysis about everything under the sun.

Pre-viewing

3. While you're watching a movie, avoid the temptation that guides such as this one put before you: thinking too much and overana-

lyzing. Too cerebral an approach to viewing deflates the film and actually gets in the way of your responding to how the film works to convey its pleasures and meanings. Films appeal to a whole range of human response, especially what we can call the emotional, affective, visceral, imaginative, intellectual, and — as this guide explores — religious. In any case, what is important is "the film experience." Save the analysis for later.

4. Likewise, the time to examine story and style is afterward, though sometimes viewers can't help but notice some unique uses of lighting or camera angles. Needless to say, cinematic elements such as lighting, palette, casting, acting, and production design are all terribly important; usually, however, if you notice them while you are in the theater, it means that they're not being used very well. These often disrupt the suspension of disbelief that makes watching films so enjoyable. And while we always know that we are only watching a film, we do not like to be reminded of that fact while watching. That is true, no matter what the genre — self-conscious art-house films, romantic melodramas, or cheesy sci-fi movies.

5. Don't read reviews before seeing a film. Do enough background investigating to determine whether a film is to your taste and worth seeing. You can take a look at ratings and Internet scores at review search engines such as Rotten Tomatoes or Metacritic. If you are still uncertain, perhaps consult a critic or a friend. But if you learn too much about a film, the likely result will be that you will see the film through some critic's eyes instead of your own.

6. Remember that not every film has to be "serious." Movies, like sports, are meant to be fun, and escapism is okay — at times downright necessary, given the pressures of life in the modern world. Most movies out there are meant to divert and nothing more than that; they are a convenient and pleasing minivacation. *Transformers* is intentionally mindless and, like most action-adventure flicks, is a live-action cartoon for underdeveloped males. Every taste culture — whether composed of snooty culture elites or Oprah fans — has its guilty escapist pleasures. Try, for example, a mystery and crime series from British television, such as *Prime Suspect* or *Foyle's War.* Though stoics and prudes often argue otherwise, entertainment is generally a good thing — psychologically, socially, and even religiously. It is as central to every culture

as food and procreation. And entertainment takes innumerable forms, ranging from music, sports, and fireworks to pageants, circuses, and museums, from the elaborate art of classical opera to the entertainment of "ordinary folks" in country-western music, to a simple recorder playing in a park. And "pleasurable" does not preclude revelatory, unless the pleasure itself be the revelation.

7. A caution. The above does not mean that movies, especially very likable ones, cannot be corrosive. That is true, for example, of slasher, slice-and-dice horror movies, especially those featuring gratuitous sexual violence. Movies about the pleasures of violent retribution are also in that categoy — from Clint Eastwood's early "Dirty Harry" period to the Mel Gibson of *Lethal Weapon II, Braveheart,* and *The Edge of Darkness.* And I suspect that Judd Apatow's immensely popular comedies, such as *Knocked Up* and *The Hangover,* with their exaltation of pubescent male sexuality and overall stupidity, do more harm than good, even though they all supposedly have conservative "traditional values" featured in their conclusions. Some of that is taste, to be sure, and some of it is serious business. Given the artistry of motion pictures and the medium's persuasive aesthetic power, movies can be potent advertisements for whatever their producers want them to be.

8. It is very beneficial to see and hear films with the best possible equipment, and thanks to recent technology, this means large (and sharp) video displays and good sonic reach (both for musical score and sound design). Most people cannot build their own private video theater, but each step toward a more complete presentation of the film helps with the experience (and understanding) of the story it tells. Academic critics can often make terrible mistakes in their judgments of films because they don't hear the whole soundtrack well or watch a poor print of the film — or on the screen of a laptop computer. Film is perhaps our most sensual medium, combining as it does the visual arts, music and sound, and age-old drama — the actual acting-out of stories.

Post-viewing

9. Trust your gut. Films are first and foremost affective in their impact: they make us *feel* particular ways. We feel certain emotions,

whether joy or dread, because of things we've seen in the film, and subsequently those emotions, if they are strong and memorable, prod us to think. With most films, understanding or interpretation simply seeks to identify what in the story occasioned the feelings that we take away from the theater. That's a good place to start personal reflection or group discussion. Did I like it (or not) and why? Filmmakers do what they do to make viewers feel and think in particular ways. If this is mystifying, remember that for a number of millennia now, philosophers have been — and still are — disputing the power and effect of art.

10. Film is a construct. That term simply means that movies, at least fictional ones, are made-up things, constructed out of cinematic materials — much like a high-rise apartment building of various ingredients — to serve a purpose. A good part of understanding film is simply recognizing all the elements the filmmaker manipulates to evoke feelings and thoughts in viewers. If a film is done well, viewers don't notice all that cinematic inner construction, just as they don't see the steel superstructure, the wiring, or the plumbing of that residential high-rise.

11. Today viewers have the luxury of enormous and convenient aids to understanding films. The Internet has provided "review search engines," which provide abundant commentary on films. Rotten Tomatoes and Metacritic are the best, offering percentiles of favorable reviews, as well as taglines that show the reviewers' judgments of a given film. Those taglines are then linked to full reviews in their home locations, whether Peter Travers in *Rolling Stone* or Roger Ebert in the *Chicago Sun-Times*. The fun here is not in "getting the answers," but in noting and understanding how very good critics can arrive at very different opinions about the same film. All of that helps in understanding how films work and why we think the way we do. Unfortunately, those reviews do not stay available forever, though Ebert's reviews are archived at www.RogerEbert.com. *The New York Times* (registration required) also has an archive of its reviews. For reviews and scads of additional film information, such as the entire cast and crew and locations, go to the Internet Movie Database (us.imdb.com).

12. An entertaining and usually informative source to spur understanding in film lies in the "extras" that come on many DVDs. These range from commentaries by the director and actors on the

film to the "making of" featurettes. On occasion, deluxe DVD editions, such as those that come with *The Lord of the Rings* or the *Narnia* cycle, come so fully supplied with featurettes on varying aspects of production that together they amount to a small course on filmmaking. The marvelous Criterion Company puts out classic films with unique features, including documentaries and commentaries by leading film scholars. If you are getting hungry, these can make a wonderful buffet.

I. The Gift of Splendor: "All Things Shining"

First there was Light, and that Light infused all that was. In the Jewish-Christian account of the origins of this world, humankind begins in a garden, a paradise of beauty, harmony, intimacy, and delight, a place of no want and no death (Adam and Eve were the first vegans, as were all the other creatures). There the lamb could lie down with the lion, and the first couple reckoned that trees were "pleasant to look at" and walked each day with the Creator "at the time of the evening breeze" (NEB). That harmony, intimacy, and beauty amongst all things — this is what made paradise paradise. Indeed, it was a time, as both Jewish *(Amidah)* and Christian *(Sanctus)* liturgies proclaim, in which "heaven and earth are full of the glory of God." And such glory is a good part of why God is God, a palpable loveliness that materially demonstrates the Love that made the world.

Later comes the cosmic breakage known as the Fall. Then and now, everything preys on everything else, and nature, of which humankind is a part, is "red in tooth and claw." Whether in jungles, in the cities and deserts of war zones, or on Wall Street, survival of the fittest seems to be how the show is run. Of the original glory, only shreds and tatters remain — or so it often seems. It is no wonder, then, that humans hunger for a return to the original Light, the beginnings of primal elegance and felicity.

Some recollection of at least traces of paradise seems to kick around deep in the very structures of what makes up humanness. Call it a great cosmic dream, the restoration of the world, the New Jerusalem, or other hoped-for outcomes. Whatever it is composed of, it is the

17

place of no tears where all things are joyous and dance in the relish of "the pure feeling of being alive," as a Mennonite woman puts it in Carlos Reygadas's *Silent Light* (2007). It is the great hope that, in the words of Saint Julian of Norwich (1342-1416), later adapted by twentieth-century poet T. S. Eliot: "All shall be well, and all shall be well, and all manner of things shall be well." Most of the time we catch only glimpses of the elegant, loving majesty of the world as it was first made, and sometimes — as the films in this section show — we find it only after tragedy clears our vision.

Surely, the one domain that seems to be a token, or a precursor, of paradisiacal perfection is beauty, the power of sheer gorgeousness to transfix and gladden the deepest parts of our humanness. Indeed, at times aesthetic pleasure leaps to a sort of religious awe, an intense delight and gratitude that wells up from wonder and awe. Those moments erupt from anywhere: music, stories, nature, people, and self-awareness, to name but a few, all endless signals of the glories of a carnal creation.

The films in this section all explore the fact that, at times at least, some folks chase down the hints of a magnificence that seems to "shine through" the material dross of daily life. That is just about the hardest thing any film could attempt. The stakes are pretty high: first, to clarify (i.e., to make clear), to ignite in viewers the recognition that this world is somehow "charged" with nothing less than what Gerard Manley Hopkins called the "grandeur" of the divine. We begin with two outstanding American films: the Oscar-winning *American Beauty* (1999) and the much-celebrated war movie *The Thin Red Line* (1998). The former tells of a middle-aged suburban everyman sleepwalking his way through a humdrum life as an ad agent, an uninterested father, and an inept husband. Part satire and part religious quest, *American Beauty* features Lester Burnham (Kevin Spacey in an Oscar-winning performance), who does awaken; but it will take him a full year to locate genuine beauty amid all the distortions of contemporary American culture.

Much the same sort of thing transpires in a very different kind of film and a very different setting. Terrence Malick's unconventional film of the World War II South Pacific battle for Guadalcanal tracks a solitary soldier's wrestling with the "big questions" of the relationship of beauty to hints of immortality. Aware of the horrors of war and of life in general, Private Witt (James Caviezel) moves toward a posture of all-encompassing wonder wherein, finally and lastingly, he sees "all things shining."

Iranian filmmaker Majid Majidi's luminous film about a small blind boy, *The Color of Paradise* (1999), contrasts the boy's own "vision" of the world with the blindness of his hard-pressed father. The boy's own search for religious certainty parallels his widowed father's search for a new wife. Another father and son lie at the center of the first installment of Krzysztof Kieslowski's *Decalogue,* the remarkable ten-part series on the Ten Commandments he directed for Polish television in 1988-89. A professor of computer science who largely trusts science in everything discovers, tragically, that the wonder of some things far exceeds the kind of knowledge to which computers are devoted.

All startling and all very different, these films together provide a haunting provocation to embrace the world in all of its complex and haunting beauty, beauty that emerges from the most ordinary and yet miraculous regions of human experience. Perhaps the world is not opaque, after all, for morning and light do break.

American Beauty

Director	Sam Mendes (Academy Award winner)
Original Screenplay	Alan Ball (Academy Award winner)
Cinematography	Conrad Hall (Academy Award winner)
Music	Thomas Newman (Academy Award nomination)

CAST	
Kevin Spacey	Lester Burnham (Academy Award winner)
Annette Bening	Carolyn Burnham (Academy Award nomination)
Mena Suvari	Angela Hayes
Chris Cooper	Colonel Fitts
Wes Bentley	Ricky Fitts
Thora Birch	Jane Burnham

Rotten Tomatoes	89
Metacritic	86

- -

General Comments

Poor Lester Burnham: he never really gets it until, of course, it's too late, which for him is about as late as one can get. Indeed, too late to do anything at all about his heretofore "stupid little life," as he himself calls it when it's already too late to fix it. We learn this right off in a voice-over in the first words of the film, a postmortem rumination that Lester provides to viewers — from wherever he is. And as Lester himself tells it, boy, did he get it all wrong, even though in terms of the "American dream," he's gotten it plenty right: a good job, a lovely house in the suburbs, a gorgeous and energetic wife, and an intelligent teenage daughter, though a bit on the sulky side. That is much of the point of *American Beauty:* How can it all be so wrong when it appears to be so right?

One part of writer Alan Ball's screenplay is a scathing satire of upper-middle-class American life, and middle-aged maleness in particular, and this shows up visually from the beginning in everything from production design and imagery to shot composition. The effect of all this is to subvert the attractiveness of the American suburban dream, the one that Lester has achieved only to find it hollow as he slogs his way into middle age. Bourgeois emptiness is an old and easy target to skewer, and films periodically undertake the task, as well they should. Satire is, after all, a humorous form of prophetic insight. And in many ways *American Beauty* simply repeats the themes of Mike Nichols's classic *The Graduate* (1967), a hilarious and masterful 1960s exploration of the ills of American success. In fact, Lester is a humorous male version of the bereft and sad Mrs. Robinson. In the end, American beauty is not necessarily so, but neither is the one Lester puts in its place, though it will take him the rest of his life to figure that out.

The satire is the easy part, and it is searching, accurate, and funny (and very adult in content, sometimes uncomfortably so). It is not difficult to mock American life, especially from a religious perspective, in its idolatry of wealth, bourgeois glamour, business success, romance, sex, status, and so on. It is not giving away the plot to say that this

Sad-sack Lester leaving for work

Lester's problematic angel

middle-aged milquetoast Lester certainly does rebel, and for that the audience is glad, insofar as he at last and at least shows sense and gumption in dumping the deadening routine of his daily life, especially his deadening job in — what else? — an ad agency.

Phase two of Ball's satire comes with what rebellious Lester chooses, problematically, to supplant what he has discarded. What compelling something might take the place of his lethargic life? It is in not offering an alternative to bankrupt American mores that a film like *The Graduate,* for example, fails. If this isn't "it," then what exactly is? From Lester's point of view, of course, his choice seems exhilarating and heroic, and his is the perspective that governs the long middle part of the film. Lester does awaken from his stupor as though touched by an angel, and we experience that along with him, thanks to wonderfully smooth and inventive filmmaking. Unfortunately, the catalyst for Lester's revival is not necessarily an ideal choice, to say the least: just when viewers rejoice that Lester is finally showing signs of life, they have to wrestle with the wisdom of his pursuit of another form of American beauty.

The full toll of these choices becomes clear near the end of the film, when screenwriter Alan Ball and director Sam Mendes lay out the costs in huge, graphic, and very uncomfortable terms. *American Beauty* is not for the faint of heart, for Lester can indeed have what he wishes, though he should, as the old saying goes, be careful what he wishes for, for he just might get it. That's where it gets dicey, because Mendes handles the sexual content with blunt candor and realism, so much so that the truth hurts, and it gets downright uncomfortable for both Lester and those in the seats watching. In short, this is not a movie for children or the timid, for the language is ripe and much of the content forthrightly sexual. Part of the discomfort in the film, a discomfort Mendes wishes to create, derives from the fact that what Lester wants is sensible and appealing, at least from a male point of view. In any case, that proves to be something for Lester and the audience to wrestle with.

The film resolves in an unexpected way in both the events and in what Lester, at long last, learns. And the same is what viewers have to learn over and over, and in that lies the religious worth of *American Beauty*. What Lester and we must learn is something that a "weird" young neighbor, a friend of Lester's plain-Jane daughter, already knows. Fortunately, he schools us, just as he schools Jane. The lessons glisten, quietly but persistently, thanks largely to the remarkable cinematography of the late Conrad Hall. And the acting from start to finish is simply wonderful, simultaneously very funny and believable, which is the thin wire satire has to walk. Kevin Spacey won the Oscar for best actor for his portrayal of Lester; Annette Bening plays his success-driven wife; and Chris Cooper dazzles as the retired marine colonel, Fitts, who lives next door. And there is, of course, Lester's own very dubious angel, the marvelous Mena Suvari.

In the title and throughout the movie, there looms the hard question of what makes beauty and where we might find it, at least beauty of the kind worth dying for. That is a good place to start, inside one's self, before turning on the DVD player to discover what Lester belatedly comes to know.

Things to Look For

- Red roses abound in this film — ones named American Beauty at that — at Lester's home, in his relationship with Angela, and in the title itself. This motif is both visually arresting and very symbolic, and Mendes seems to get double duty in his use of so many roses.
- Production design, much of it meticulously laid out by Mendes, also functions tellingly, especially in terms of settings. Some locations seem to convey a particular kind of meaningfulness, bringing to visual life something about the character's own experience or perception of the world. The same also applies to strategies

23

such as camera angles. Lester, for example, seems hedged in and diminished.

- The names in the film, though not all of them, seem to suggest something about the characters themselves or their roles. Some leap out as particularly telling about the characters in the story, such Lester, Jane, Fitts, and, of course, Angela.
- One point of controversy about the film, particularly among conservative Christians, was its portrayal of the next-door gay couple, Jim and Jim, who seem to be far and away the happiest of the three couples in the film. They seem to offer the only instance of a happy relationship (this debate was heightened by the depiction of the villain as a homophobe who is secretly gay). How do Jim and Jim function in the film?
- Ricky Fitts, of course, is a thematic all by himself, the one who lays out the substance of the recognition that Lester will arrive at in the last minutes of his life. We wonder what it is that Ricky has stumbled upon, and whether it might be induced by the product he sells.

Post-viewing Comments

The heart of the film, the real beauty in *American Beauty,* lies there in teenager Ricky Fitts's adoration of the very ordinary everyday reality. For him, this is the enormous gift of being alive: human consciousness glorying in the wonder of self-awareness and the perpetually stunning fact that anything at all exists, the stupendous first and fundamental miracle that is impossible to ever appreciate sufficiently. Such a small real thing as a white plastic supermarket bag tossing in the wind against a red brick wall occasions his rapture:

> That's the day I realized that there was this entire life behind things, and this incredible benevolent force that wanted me to know there was no reason to be afraid. Ever. . . . Sometimes there's so much beauty in the world I feel like I can't take it . . . and my heart is going to cave in.

On the other hand, while Ricky sees the deep-down truth of things, the adults, such as they are, are blind as bats. Carolyn (played by the marvelous Annette Bening, four months pregnant at the time of shooting) buys whole hog the entrepreneurial dream of success: budding real estate agent that she is, she thrashes herself to make that success happen. Power, glamour, and pleasure seem to be the lure. The fact of her blindness is nowhere more apparent than in, first, her treatment of her daughter, and second, her silly relationship with Buddy Kane (Peter Gallagher), the real-estate king.

Colonel Fitts has lost his dream of a "pure" America, certainly morally and maybe even racially, given his fascination with Hitler. His monomania — or is it self-loathing? — smothers all that's real and valuable in his world, particularly his virtually comatose wife. Needless to say, his son, Ricky, the boy who seeks beauty with his camera, rebels. And Jane's friend, Angela Hayes (Mena Suvari) — or "haze," for that matter — Lester's own seductive angel, has bought into the whole teenage sex hookup culture, a Paris Hilton-Britney Spears wannabe before they actually showed up on the national scene. And a rancid pose it is, as Lester belatedly finds out. The last scenes between them show that she is but a scared girl desperately trying to conjure some self-worth for herself. She's as deceived about herself as Lester is about her and about himself. In the end, she's just a kid, a lonely and scared little girl who covers her fragility with sex vamp bravado.

Most of all though, there's Lester. He knows readily enough the bogus dreams of suburbia and their soul-killing demands. The imagery early in the film, from the vast room of office cubicles to the fences and window grids at his home, makes clear the extent to which Lester is contained — indeed, imprisoned — by his world, though he is a pris-

Ricky's white paper bag

oner of his own making. His "liberation," when he comes upon it, is no less bogus and compromised, though it does not feel that way for him or even for the audience. As wrong-headed as his sexual pursuit of his teenage daughter's best friend is, Lester at the very least shows signs of life, however regressive those are. The film's great genius is its scathing satire of Lester's choice: it is, in effect, to continue in his suburban meaninglessness or to become an adolescent male again, the last time he was really happy — or so he thinks. So Lester undertakes full-blown adolescent rebellion: he quits his job to work at a burger joint, plays macho-man with his family (to the extent of throwing plates in the dining room), smokes pot, and buys a red Pontiac Firebird (he even buys a remote-control toy model of the same). Most of all, though, Lester lusts and lusts some more, as if he's still in the adolescent hormonal buzz of newfound sexuality. Lester does not quite infantilize himself, but he comes awfully close.

Surely Lester is alive again, but alive in behalf of what? This is the question of what idols people give themselves over to in a tawdry, glitzy, and hypersexed culture. Like most folks, Lester goes for the first thing that comes along that gives him a "rush," makes him feel fully alive, no matter how momentary and delusional that proves to be. He discovers how delusional he's become when he is on the very cusp of fulfilling his libidinal dream of bedding his angel. In a scene that is downright uncomfortable to watch, Lester proceeds with his "seduction" (legally, this would be statutory rape) until Angela mentions that this, despite what she has projected as her knowledge and experience of all things sexual, is her "very first time." Like a bucket of ice water, this confession jolts Lester to a sudden, stark reckoning, and he begins to "see" reality for what it is, especially that this Angela is not the queen of sex but a mere girl, a waif much like his own daughter has come to be — with absentee parents who are less mature than she is.

Finally — and it has been a long detour of false hopes — Lester finds his heart's desire, which lies in what has been there all the time in the radiant glory of the very ordinary: his wife and daughter (whom he now recalls and names "Janey"). In the last seconds of his life, he chants to himself in quiet awe, "Man, oh man . . . oh man, oh man." And the still-living soul that persists after he is murdered goes on to explain that luminous mystery in terms that Ricky Fitts would well understand. It seems that beauty, albeit commonplace and ordinary and all around us, is so dazzling and abundant that Lester confesses, "Sometimes it's

26

"Man, oh man . . . oh man, oh man."

too much, [my] heart fills up like a balloon that's about to burst." In this new life wherein he sees and feels all, fully and deeply, joy "flows through me like rain, and I can't feel anything but gratitude for every single moment of my stupid little life," something he assures the audience that they will come to know "someday."

Lester comes now upon the fullest moments of his earthly existence, which are also literally his last. He finally comprehends the irreplaceable glory that was there all around him all along, but that he never had the wit or soul to recognize. The bogus has been replaced by the real, the phenomena all around us that are worthy of love because they seem infused with divine love. For Ricky Fitts, as it comes to be for Lester, all the stunning uncompromised glory of the created and ordinary world consists of a beauty so intense and rapturous that no one can take it all in, lest their heart "cave in" from the joy it incites deep in the soul. Indeed, if we are lucky, we see the world in the very radiance that God sees.

Post-viewing Questions

1. How might one describe Lester's malady, and how symptomatic of American culture is it, both during his pre-Angela and Angela phases? What antidotes does American culture provide?
2. The music, by Thomas Newman, one of Hollywood's most successful composers, plays a vital role. How might you describe its unusual but haunting power?

3. Annette Bening's performance is a comic masterpiece, especially in those sequences where she "chats" with herself, whether in the house she's trying to sell or when listening to her motivational tapes. And what is it with the "gun," anyway? If Lester is deluded in his own way, what are Carolyn's delusions, and how typically American are they?

4. Both parents neglect their daughter, and both are remarkably immature, especially as parents. Marriage and family simply do not seem enough to satisfy either one. How does something like this go so wrong? As Lester's closing monologue suggests, they were once marvelous together, relishing each other and all of them together as family.

5. Are there better ways to describe what Lester stumbles on in the moments before his death? He suddenly realizes, for one, what it is to be a father, and he suddenly seems to see and embrace all the luminous small things that have made up his life but that he has overlooked. Is this conversion? If so, then to what exactly? Or is this part of a larger story?

6. The theological name for what Lester has stumbled on is *creation,* and in a way his primal error, grabbing for the apple, has been to want more. Wanting that — whatever it is — promptly obscures the value of what he has had, which is, ironically, infinitely richer than what he now craves. The ironies come out of the woodwork. Or is this trying to make something religious out of a roundly secular piece? And what about the film's motto, "Pay attention"?

Critical Comments

Critics of all kinds loved *American Beauty,* and they did so for many different reasons, not the least of which was the acting and also the film's adroit mixture of satire and its treatment of the metaphysical. They all emphasized the dark satire of suburban malaise, which is, after all, pretty hard to miss. Indeed, Peter Travers announced that *American Beauty* displayed "jolting comedy that makes you laugh till it hurts" (*Rolling Stone,* Sept. 30, 1999). Few critics — even really good ones — ventured very far into the religious core of the film. Usually the commentary focused on the insertion of metaphysical wonderment within the core of the tale. In this regard, Owen Gleiberman praised a pervasive "sense of entrancement" that derives from the "velvety, saturated richness" of Conrad Hall's cinematography (*Entertainment Weekly*, Sept. 10, 1999). David Denby went so far as to claim that the film had within it a "beatific" mood of blessing that culminates in "a burst of metaphysics" (*The New Yorker*, Sept. 20, 1999).

Other Notable Films by Sam Mendes

Revolutionary Road (2008)
Jarhead (2005)
The Road to Perdition (2002)

Forthcoming Films from Mendes

Butcher's Crossing (2011)
Middlemarch (2011)
Netherland (2013)

The Thin Red Line

Writer and Director	Terrence Malick
Cinematographer	John Toll
Original Music	Hans Zimmer

CAST	
James Caviezel	Private Witt
Sean Penn	1st Sergeant Welsh
Nick Nolte	Lieutenant Colonel Tall
John Travolta	Brigadier General Quintard
Adrian Brody	Corporal Fife
Elias Coteas	Captain Staros
George Clooney	Captain Bosche

Rotten Tomatoes	78
Metacritic	78

- -

General Comments

The Thin Red Line (1998) certainly ranks as one of the strangest war films ever, and it was directed by one of the film world's most unusual writer-directors. In the 1970s, the young writer-director Terrence Malick, with advanced degrees in philosophy (itself unusual for a film-maker), made two films that were critical sensations, *Badlands* (1973), based on the brief career of the young North Dakota serial killer Willie Starkweather, and *Days of Heaven* (1978), a tragic tale of itinerant farm workers in Texas at the turn of the twentieth century (the film was shot in Alberta, Canada). Both movies were beautifully filmed and haunting and remain very much so today. And then Malick just disappeared — for the next two decades. By then he was a kind of cinematic legend, and he resurfaced to make *The Thin Red Line* (1998) and later *A New World* (2005), both of which are unique and searching films — cinematically, philosophically, and religiously — which clearly indicated that his hiatus was worth the wait. Such was Malick's reputation that the best actors were eager to work with him. Another Malick film will appear (much delayed) in 2010, *The Tree of Life,* a family drama starring two of Hollywood's biggest male stars, Sean Penn and Brad Pitt.

In most of Malick's films, especially in *The Thin Red Line,* there is a full-blown religious riddle right down the middle, which is not a usual feature of a starkly realistic war movie (think of another 1998 war film, Steven Spielberg's *Saving Private Ryan*). The central story here, the battle for Guadalcanal Island in the Pacific theater of World War II, based on the autographical novel by James Jones, forms the crucible that evokes many of the perplexities of the central character and those around him. For young Pfc. Witt, the war on this tropical island presents an unceasing fundamental and cosmic puzzle. There is nothing here like the simple dichotomies of the *Star Wars*' Force or the tyrannical Matrix. Think rather of Job, Jacob, or Moses contesting and wrestling, begging God to appear and dispel the exasperating riddles that hound people, especially in places like war zones. Here are life's ambiguities swirling around in the shadow of rampant and agonizing death. Just look at that first shot of a large crocodile sliding into the green, algae-covered waters of a swamp.

The answer to those questions about the absence of the divine would seem obvious enough in a place like Guadalcanal, one of the hardest battles in a war full of infernal combat. And Malick drives the point home with graphic terror and ugly and violent death, hell above ground, not glory and bravery. Probably nowhere else, other than in this globe's natural calamities of famine, earthquake, or hurricane, is the slightest glimpse of divine light so necessary, so vital and redemptive. War is the absence of God, if not in itself the anti-God. As the die-hard skeptic 1st Sergeant Welsh (Sean Penn) puts it, acknowledging the possibility of God, praying, and finally challenging God himself: "A glance from your eyes, and my life will be yours."

31

An ominous opening shot

The substance of that glance — or what Welsh (or Malick) thinks of as a glance — comes in the perception of Private Witt (James Caviezel, who would later play the part of Jesus Christ for Mel Gibson), who apparently is in the habit of going AWOL to live with the mild and peaceful indigenous people, all of whom are conspicuous Christian converts. Of all the soldiers, it is Witt who senses the divine all around him, especially in the rapturous beauty of nature, something Malick strives to capture with both his camera and Witt's voice-over ponderings. Making sure that viewers both feel and understand Witt's sense of the world is perhaps the great challenge Malick takes up in *The Thin Red Line*. Witt will return repeatedly to the gnawing question of the possibility of God and the nature of God as he works progressively through the riddles, religious and moral, attached to those urgently pressing questions that surround the imminent possibility of great personal pain and sudden, gruesome death.

There's a hell's amount of woe that gets in the way, however, and by no means does all of it come from the enemy. Vain and ambitious commanders, in order to advance their careers, brutally ignore the costs to their soldiers. For these roles, Malick has cast actors who usually play Hollywood heroes — John Travolta, Nick Nolte, George Clooney — to play against type as villains of sorts. On the other hand, some officers sacrifice their careers to aid their men. And some who profess not to care about anything, such as Welsh, nonetheless risk life itself to help those in need. Always, though, the great enemy engulfing everything, suffering and death, brutalizes the expendable dogface

Nick Nolte as the dubious Colonel Tall

doughboy. In this regard, war is perhaps no more than ordinary life writ large and intense, the powerful roaring roughshod over the insignificant and powerless.

Things to Look For

- Private Witt seems to brood about a series of interrelated questions from the very first words of the film. They have to do with death, beauty, social concord, and acceptance — a whole range of life's urgent questions — and they do recur and *perhaps* reach some resolution.
- There's very little music in the film, and what little there is, is of a very unusual kind. In one sense it is emphatically non-Western, and in another it comes from the heart of Western culture. And it plays a significant role in the beginning and in the conclusion.
- Malick uses a tricky camera strategy in allowing for Witt (and others) to give us a first-person, or "subjective," camera, meaning that viewers see the world through the eyes of a particular character. In this movie the first-person point of view is usually Witt's, and ordinarily these shots try to capture the beauty that Witt sees, a beauty so resplendent, even in this war zone, that it suggests a kind of divine presence or at least some measure of divine intention that has been cloaked by humankind's depredations, namely war. And war and beauty tangle and cycle throughout the film to the very end.

- For this first-person view to be effective, James Caviezel must display a very specific kind of "look" at various moments during the film. Like the subjective camera, this look becomes another non-verbal, pictorial way of conveying information: it can certainly be less definite than words, and the reader is invited to interpret and wonder. It is clear, given the repetition, that Malick is directing Caviezel toward a certain demeanor in his look and his posture throughout the whole latter part of the film.
- And what about the "bad guys" — Tall, Quintard, and Bosche — all leaders in the American war effort? The novelist Jones and the director Malick seem to be trying to convey with their portrayal of the nature of evil the notion that "we've met the devil, and he is us," nowhere more true than in those self-absorbed people responsible for leading.

Post-viewing Comments

So Witt dies in the end — willingly, it seems, and "calm," as he puts it — accomplishing exactly what he worried about from the beginning of the film in his reflections on his mother's death. Indeed, he seems to have reached some conclusions, though Welsh persistently mocks Witt's "answers" — at least most of them.

The questions loom large for Witt, for he seems to have, even in a war zone, a considerable capacity for thought and reflection, which is in marked contrast to the plain old stark fear that predominates among combat soldiers waiting to go ashore and into battle. And well it should, given the horror of the combat that Malick takes great pains to display — even though this is ostensibly not an antiwar film. If anything, all that graphic violence plays as a memorial and a warning of the incalculable toll exacted by modern warfare.

Witt's ruminating voice-over, though, puzzles us in the film's very first lines, as the camera looks up — ironically — at what seems beatific light pouring through trees: "What's this war in the heart of nature? Why does nature vie with itself, the land contend with the sea? Is there an avenging power in nature, not one power, [but] two?" Darwin and the biblical Fall seem preeminent in this rendition of what the world is like, a place of ceaseless conflict between good and evil, life and death, beauty and destruction — all those binary opposites that plague human life. Don't forget that huge crocodile slithering under the water, as good an image of lurking evil as we have.

A good deal of Witt's meditations result from the proximity of his own death as a combat soldier, and we wonder how much his AWOL choice results from that fear. If the war lies before him, his mother's death and his recollection of it hounds his unquiet soul. For him, death is what it is, obscene and ugly: "I remember my mother when she was dying, all shrunk up and gray. I asked her if she was afraid. She shook her head. I was afraid to touch the death I seen in her. Couldn't find anything beautiful or uplifting about her going back to God. I heard people talk about immortality, but I ain't seen it." Yet, on the other hand, there was the "calm" with which his mother met her death, and finding that tranquility in the face of death becomes Witt's goal: "I wondered how it would be when I died. . . . This breath was the last one I was ever gonna draw. . . . I just hope I can meet it the way she did, with the same . . . calm because that is where it's hidden, the immortality I haven't seen. . . ."

The question of just what Witt "sees" looms large, indeed centrally, in this story, and it goes to the perennial question of how we can be sure we "know" what we claim we do. That is an especially hard question when it comes to intangibles that are not verifiable by empirical science, propositions such as the existence of God, or beauty, or immortality. Before long, AWOL Witt and his buddy are picked up by a patrol ship, and the pair are then brought to military justice. Court martial awaits them, but Witt's immediate superior, Sergeant Welsh (Penn), intervenes to place him instead in a disciplinary unit of stretcher-bearers. And somehow, as happens seemingly whenever these two talk, the conversation becomes metaphysical. Welsh claims that "in this world, a man, himself, is nothing, and there ain't no world but this one." Witt counters Welsh's nihilism with his own assertion: "You're wrong there, Top. I seen another world. Sometimes I think it was just my imagination." With a smirk by way of response, Welsh declares: "Well, then you're seeing things I never will."

Just what has Witt seen? That question hangs in the air throughout the whole course of the film, especially as the ravages of the battle emerge, and such sequences insistently ask what exactly Witt has seen that gives him such certainty, or at least hopefulness. Just what kind of knowledge has he acquired — and by what means — that allows for the assertion that counters the mounting darkness of war's obscenity for

Americans and Japanese alike? That is, what kind of knowledge can one trust, especially if it is not scientifically verifiable? All those domains that go under the label of personal experience — intuition, hunches, hints, guesses, clues, visions — all are pieced together sufficiently well, at least for the soul, if not for reason, to constitute that thing called knowledge or faith.

The opening sequence suggests four realities that seem to collaborate to provide Witt with new insight and knowledge. Clearly, the first one is composed of the multitudinous displays of beauty in the natural world: trees, light, water, people. We often see Witt amazed and glad at what he sees, a wondrous domain of natural dazzle and beauty such as he never anticipated or dreamed — and despite the crocodile under the water. Second, Witt comes to know the pacific and gentle ways of these indigenous people, at once physically beautiful and gentle and kind, despite the fact that he comes as a purveyor of the war that has disrupted their lives. That gentleness comes in the way kids play and their easy exchange with the physical world in which they live. And then, third, comes their obvious Christianity, an element that is not emphasized but neither is concealed, as they walk in process, singing behind a leader who carries a book crooked in his arm. We see and hear them singing hymns, and Witt himself seems to absorb the texture of joy in the music, for we hear those musical themes reprised in full orchestration. Something sufficiently mysterious and loving coalesces in these multiple displays to make Witt think that he has indeed seen a beatific world that is an embodiment — or at least an emblem — of a world beyond.

The fourth element, very peculiar in its own right, is his vision of

Light pouring through the darkness of the jungle canopy

his mother's death, wherein a very human-looking and handsome angel seems to embrace her heart and body as she dies. It is a strange sequence, and it seems very much a product of Witt's own imagination; nonetheless, it suggests that this mere dream provides some kind of "evidence" for its plausibility. This poses one of the hardest questions for all those who sense or believe in some kind of transcendent, meta-empirical reality: How much credibility should be granted these imaginings, if imaginings they are? And whatever it is that Witt "sees" — in his soul or his imagination — it seems enough to prompt his actions throughout the film, all the way to his death. Look again at the sequence of Witt's death and that curious expression on his face. Does he die with the "calm" his mother displayed?

Whatever Witt takes away from that vision, it seems to carry him throughout the film, and it seems that it is a frequent topic of conversation between Welsh and him, not all of which are included in the film. Late in the film, when the soldiers are taking their week of rest, Welsh jokingly asks Witt how he's doing with his "beautiful light." He wonders, though, at Witt's posture and hope: "How do you do that? You're a magician to me." And after Witt's burial, the only one of its kind that we see in the film — perhaps because of Witt's sacrificial death, risking himself so others can escape — Welsh squats by his grave, half weeping and half believing, wondering aloud to Witt, "Where's your spark now?"

By the very end, Witt does seem to have imparted a new openness and hope to Welsh, who wonders in a voice-over, speaking clearly to the God that embraced Witt, if indeed that God is there: "If I never meet you in this life, let me feel the lack. A glance from your eyes, and my life

Private Witt's look before his death

will be yours." Whatever it is that Witt seems to see, Welsh also — for all of his despair — seems to come to want it badly as well.

As for Witt, he has indeed embraced — or has been embraced by — the "glory," the glory amid the horror that Malick has labored to display throughout the film. "One man looks at a dying bird and thinks there's nothing but unanswered pain, that death's got the final word; it's laughing at him. Another man sees that same bird and feels the glory, feels something smiling through it." That kind of statement seems rather unambiguous, though interpreters of Malick have argued, at times heatedly, about Witt's final words in this film. And rightly so, for they are cryptic and contorted and do not make clear syntactical sense no matter how they are read — unless, of course, Malick intends to capitalize all those *y*'s in "you." "Darkness or light, strife or love, are they the workings of one mind, the features of the same face? O, my soul, let me be in you now. Look out through my eyes, look out at the things you made, all things shining." There is no printed text of the screenplay, so viewers are left to make their own best guess. A lowercase *y* makes the "shining" an imaginative construct, and thoroughly human; the capitalized *Y* makes all a divine display, "all things shining." The latter reading fits best with Witt's earlier ruminations, including his reference to a "You," and also with Welsh's read of what Witt has talked to him about. Let the viewers choose.

Post-viewing Questions

1. Witt's many interior voice-overs aid the work of the camera, and in these he meditates and questions the "big imponderables" about life and the possibility of God. How common and accurate are these questions for one trying to make sense of the world?

2. One of the big questions the film wrestles with — and very much central to the God question — is the status of beauty. Is it something each person conjures up for herself ("beauty is in the eye of the beholder") — that is, a matter of taste? Or are there some beautiful things that strike everyone, an objective reality or presence quite independent of the human mind? And what does the very existence of beauty suggest about the nature of creation and God?

3. Evil is in nature, to be sure, but where does evil of an even more bothersome kind erupt? If animals operate by instinct and sur-

vival, not really blameworthy for the violence they do, for what may we hold people responsible in their evildoing? And who are the chief candidates in *The Thin Red Line*?

4. What does Witt's final gesture in the film suggest about the resolution of his persistent questions?

5. Malick uses light, usually light pouring down through the treetops, to suggest the presence of some kind of numinous reality in human affairs. How effective is this crucial device in the film in inducting the viewer to the possibility of, in Witt's words, "all things shining"?

Critical Comments

In the Siskel and Ebert television review of *The Thin Red Line*, Roger Ebert did not much like the film, finding it directionless; his movie-reviewing partner, the late Gene Siskel, thought it a "masterpiece" (YouTube). And thus went the reviews of the picture: some found it moving and brilliant; others found it confused, pretentious, and bloated. And some who liked it were perplexed by the contrary impulses in the film. J. Hoberman, a critic who is usually tough but full of insight, found it as "mystical as it is gritty," a mix of "19th-century transcendentalism" and the horrors of war (*Village Voice*, Dec. 29, 1998). Janet Maslin praised Malick's "visual genius" in conveying his "intoxication with natural beauty." For her, the film followed very much in the footsteps of Malick's early films, which "were the most beautiful and elusive films of their time." Still, Maslin found Malick's goal in the film, as with the earlier films, "elusive" (*The New York Times*, Dec. 23, 1998). The same judgment came from the *Los Angeles Times* critic Kenneth Turan, who observed that the film's "moments to cherish" were lost in its lack of narrative focus (Dec. 23, 1998).

Other Notable Films by Terrence Malick

The Tree of Life (2010)
The New World (2005)
Days of Heaven (1978)
Badlands (1973)

The Color of Paradise

Writer and Director	Majid Majidi
Original Music	Alireza Kohandairy
Cinematography	Mohammad Davudi
Film Editing	Hassan Hassandoost

CAST	
Hossein Mahjoub	Father
Mohsen Ramezani	Mohammad
Salameh Feyzi	Grandmother
Farahnaz Safari	Big Sister
Elham Sharifi	Little Sister

Rotten Tomatoes	87
Metacritic	80

- -

General Comments

The story of a small blind boy in Iran, *The Color of Paradise* (1999) could hardly be further from Western stereotypes of Islam and Iran. That can be said of all of writer-director Majid Majidi's remarkable films about children and, more recently, about adults in modern Iran. Majidi, in fact, is but one part of a broad cinematic movement, generally known as the Iranian New Wave, that has flourished since the 1970s, making

Iran currently one of the world's most esteemed national cinemas. The Iranians have achieved this despite frequent internal censorship in Iran, first by the Shah and, since his overthrow, by the fundamentalist Muslim government. Attempting to do their work within the tight strictures of political and religious acceptability, a few filmmakers have ended up in prison, and many films that have won international acclaim have yet to be released in Iran. Even with these strictures, Iranian filmmakers choose to remain in Iran, where they find inspiration and subjects aplenty on their own soil, among their own people and their own history.

The best known of all these filmmakers, even better known than the critically celebrated pathfinder Abbas Kiarostami, is Majid Majidi, a middle-aged son of the Iranian middle class, who crossed over from acting into moviemaking. Beginning with shorts and going on to feature fiction and documentary films, Majidi has tracked the family life of Iran through his films in order to comment, at least implicitly, on social conditions in Iran. So penetrating and moving are his portraits that it is difficult to imagine that he has fastened on this domestic world simply to avoid political censorship, though that has been a suggestion made by many critics. After three films on children of various kinds, his most recent, *The Willow Tree* (2005), focuses on the life of a blind professor (first shown in the United States at the 2007 New York City Film Festival, and finally released on DVD in the summer of 2008). That film has been followed by *The Song of Sparrows* (2008), a film that has made its way around various film festivals around the world. Majidi's much-loved story of a brother and a sister and one shared pair of shoes, *The Children of Paradise* (1997), was nominated for an Oscar for best foreign film but lost out, remarkably, to the hoopla over Roberto Benigni's *Life is Beautiful*. What stands out in Majidi's films about family are delicate, precise images and stories of relationship, hope, and caring — though all of these are hard-won.

The most harrowing of these stories is *The Color of Paradise*. On the last day before summer break at a boarding school for the blind in Tehran, a ten-year-old blind boy, Mohammad, waits for his father to arrive from their remote mountain village to take him home. For a long while, after all the other children have gone, the father does not appear. That allows viewers a lengthy close look at the desolate young boy (splendidly played by Mohsen Ramezani, a child actor who is blind in real life), whom we perceive to be at once forlorn and kindly, though

41

the sequence is not in the least overplayed. And quite the opposite of the son is the father (Hossein Mahjoub), a hard-pressed widower who must attend to not only Mohammad but also to his two sisters and his own aged mother. He wants very much to marry again but now sees his blind son as an obstacle to that goal. What bride would want to take on that burden, even though the boy is away at school most of the year and is himself exuberant and eager?

That is the grim premise of *The Color of Paradise*, and in many ways the film does not get brighter, especially in the relationship of the son and father, because the latter feels increasingly compelled to somehow discard his son. Mohammad does make it to his resplendent mountain home for the summer, where he is warmly welcomed by his sisters and grandmother, a vigorous and kindly old woman who still works the fields. As for Mohammad, he is haunted by questions that leap beyond his age, questions about his blindness and where in this world, so irretrievably blank for him, he might find evidence of divine care. And for answers he "looks" everywhere, especially in the landscape and radiant natural world in which he grew up — though, of course, he cannot see it. Indeed, few films so directly confront the complex host of questions about the nature of divine presence in this world. The end of the film gives something of an answer to that, though it is also not without ambiguity and controversy.

A forlorn Mohammad awaiting his father

Things to Look For

- Mohammad's touching and feeling of just about everything he can get his hands on seems more than natural for a young blind boy. However, he seems to be up to more than that here. What does he seem to be reaching for with all this fervent activity?
- He also does a lot of close listening — again a product of his blindness — but he seems particularly attracted to certain kinds of sounds for special reasons. To appreciate this, watch the film, if you can, on a video system with good sound component, and turn up the volume a bit.
- There's the oddity of the title, which is strange indeed for a main character who cannot see. Let that hang in the back of your mind as you watch the film.
- Majidi's portrait of Iran is surprising, both in terms of landscape and culture. We venture to the mountains and deep into the lives of those mountain people, from teachers to peasants, and in those lives lie many surprises.
- And be alert for the ending, a controversial one about which some reviewers complained. However, it is not an unusual one within the context of European and Middle East cinema, specifically when one thinks of Carl Theodor Dreyer's classic *Ordet* (1955), or, more recently, Carlos Reygadas's magnificent *Silent Light* (2007).

Post-viewing Commentary

In the end, *The Color of Paradise* seems as much about the father as about Mohammad, his forsaken and forlorn boy, and in the end they both seem to find, though in unforeseeable ways, what they are looking for. Whatever that something is that they find, it is the color of paradise — what it looks and feels like. And perhaps the moviegoers, too, find what they are looking for. The "color of paradise" makes for a profound theological statement about the character ("color") of God. That this remarkable tale should come from Islam — and Iran at that — surely draws us up short regarding many assumptions about the religious complexity and depths of that culture.

First, though, comes loss and struggle. For Mohammad, it is the loss of the whole family he loves passionately when his father hands him off to become an apprentice with a blind carpenter. Though the man is patient and kind and loves his craft, Mohammad profoundly feels the gnawing bite of loss, both the separation from his sisters and granny and the betrayal by his father, whose grudging tolerance has for long been clear. There with his new mentor, he weeps and questions why God has treated him so poorly, pleading that while he has looked for answers, God has not answered. To these questions, his new guide has no answers, either because he has not asked them himself or, more likely, because there are no answers to these imponderables, as the histories of both Job and Jesus demonstrate. This is a mere boy who has long struggled and searched, and his wisdom is beyond his years; but no matter how lively, smart, curious, and eager he is, maybe there are no answers for some questions. Throughout the story, he has searched the landscape, from gurgling streams to birdsongs to thunder, to discern some kind of divine token that might deliver knowledge of the why of his afflictions, from his blindness to his luck in dying mothers and uncaring fathers.

Oddly, for all their distance from one another, though it is initiated by the father (he is never named in the film), the very same questions that afflict Mohammad hound his father as well. The man has lost his wife (the film never says how or why), and he is lonely and overburdened, though his mother lives with him and seems to fill some of the maternal void for his children. There is also the question

Sightless Mohammad in the landscape he loves

of what to do with the blind son. For the school year he boards at a school for the blind in distant Tehran, but he comes home when that is over, though the girls' school year continues. The father also fears that the scourge of a blind son will deter the interest of any prospective brides, of whom there are a quickly shrinking number, especially for an impoverished father as old as he is. His life has not been easy, having lost his own father as a youth and then his wife as an adult. Sullen and uncertain, he delivers Mohammad to his apprenticeship. When his mother protests this action, his response parallels Mohammad's protests. Nonetheless, the grandmother protests by leaving her son's protection. Repentant and fearful, he moves too late to rescue her. Soaked and chilled in a rainstorm, she falls ill and dies, a circumstance that judges him further and leads his fiancée to break off the engagement. Apparently chastened by the disapproval of so many, he travels to bring Mohammad home, though he vacillates until the very last minute. His grudging retrieval of Mohammad leads to that fateful ride in the mountain forest.

There comes the moment of real decision, such as no one could possibly foresee. The creaky wooden bridge collapses, and into the rain-swollen torrent Mohammad plunges and swirls along amid the tumult of the cascades. His father stands on the bank, again indecisive about what to do about his son, for this is his chance to be free of him. Only belatedly, after conspicuous fluctuation, does he himself plunge in, risking his own life in what turns out to be a futile attempt to save Mohammad's life and — in a strange way — his own life. Or is it futile after all?

The last sequence of the film features some grim realism. The father awakens from the exhaustion of survival on the shore of the sea into which that mountain stream flows. Fifty yards down the shore lies his son's body. That sorrowful discovery melts the father's rocky heart once and for all, and he dashes down the shore to cradle Mohammad's lifeless body in his arms. There the camera dwells, as birds call in the distance, a recurrent motif of image and sound. And the gray sky breaks as a golden light falls on Mohammad's hand, just as it did on his grandmother's in her death, and behold, his hand moves. The boy lives, either because he was not yet dead or, given the shining of that warming light, he has been given life back, not only by Allah but by his father's now unhesitating love, love for the son that he himself has foolishly ignored, as his losses mount, amid his own rank self-pursuit.

45

Father and son together: too late?

The debate among critics has been whether Majidi could possibly be serious about Mohammad's return to life, be it natural or miraculous — but especially the latter. The suggestion is that Majidi must have tacked on the ending to avoid the wrath of Iran's censors. God does not exist, Majidi's critics would say, and even if he did, life never ends that happily. But that would seem to ignore everything that precedes the event. In fact, Majidi carefully prepares us for this very event. Two elements stand out. First, Majidi continually emphasizes hands and touch, the primary conduit for young Mohammad's experience of the world, and it is only fitting and expected, then, that those should be the boy's route to knowledge and life itself. Second, there is also that telling play of golden light on the hands of Mohammad's grandmother as she dies, a clear indication of the filmmaker's esteem for her loving soul. With the light that falls on his hand, an emblem of his father's belated love, and also of Allah's care, Mohammad has been touched by the love for which his hands have so eagerly hungered and searched, and in that lies life itself.

Post-viewing Questions

1. Majidi sets his film in a gorgeous natural landscape, the radiantly beautiful world that Mohammad cannot see. The odd thing is

that perhaps Mohammad "sees" it better than anyone else. That is conveyed in the numerous shots of the boy relishing through hearing, touch, and warmth the congenial embrace of the natural world, from the bird he rescues at school to the water in streams and sunlight soaking the fields. What is Majidi suggesting about paradise, God, and the "color" of the two combined?

2. Mohammad's tearful inquiry of God parallels well-known ones within Judaeo-Christianity. How cogent and revealing is this? It rather goes to the heart of the matter, just as Jesus' words on the cross about being forsaken haunt human history. Differences, similarities? And is Mohammad's questioning answered? How close is Mohammad's complaint with respect to his father's?

3. Streams, flowers, thunder, and birdsongs — Mohammad searches all apparently for some clue about the "color" of the world: hostile or friendly, transparent or opaque. What kind of "knowledge" can people derive from such investigations?

4. Mohammad's grandmother seems to be a fount of wisdom and kindness, and she eventually decides to leave her son's house after the latter has sent Mohammad away. That will have multiple dreadful consequences for the father. What are they? And how much has he brought destruction on himself?

5. How compelling and/or convincing is the ending of the film? It is subtle — and is probably all the better for being subtle. Mohammad doesn't exactly come running down the beach. The sun warms and changes the color of his hand, as if life is returning, and then the hand moves. When what is happening finally dawns on audiences, they tend to gasp a bit. Indeed, what is the plausibility of miracle? The Mexican filmmaker Carlos Reygadas has said: "In reality, I do not believe in miracles, but reality is a miracle." How well does that apply to this circumstance?

Critical Comments

Critics in general praise Majidi's capacity, in the "profound" *Color of Paradise,* to render Mohammad's "moments of rapture" amid an "intensely colored natural beauty" (Lisa Schwarzbaum, *Entertainment Weekly,* Apr. 14, 2000). In the end, she says, the film feels much like "a prayer." Stephen Holden marvels at the surprise of an "explicitly religious movie [that] offers a visionary experience of the natural world" (*The New York Times*, Sept. 25, 1999). Marc Savlov joins the chorus in singling out "the rapturous gaze and exquisite camerawork that glimpses . . . the inner pinwheel workings of the human heart" (*Austin Chronicle*, June 9, 2000). Roger Ebert, recalling his days as a Catholic schoolboy, proclaims the film "truly intended for God's glory, unlike so much 'religious art' that is intended merely to propagandize for one view of God over another. His film looks up, not sideways" (*Chicago Sun-Times*, June 2, 2000).

Recommended Majidi Films

The Song of Sparrows (2008)
The Willow Tree (2005)
Baran (2001)
The Children of Heaven (1997)

Decalogue I

Director	Krzysztof Kieslowski
Writers	Krzysztof Kieslowski and Kryszstof Piesiewicz
Cinematographer	Wieslaw Zdort
Music	Zbigniew Preisner

CAST	
Henryk Baranowski	Krzysztof
Wojciech Klata	Pavel
Maja Komorowska	Irena
Artur Barcis	Young Man

Rotten Tomatoes	100

General Comments

This first of the ten one-hour films on the Ten Commandments is quite enough to make viewers question whether they really wish to see any of the nine additional installments in the series. The tale of a Polish scientist and his precocious and sensitive ten-year-old son is not easy to forget; indeed, it is harrowing. The story begins what is perhaps the most remarkable *series* of films ever, *Decalogue* (1989-90), directed and co-written by the late Polish *auteur* Krzysztof Kieslowski. *Decalogue* consists of one film on each of the Ten Commandments, though it is some-

49

times difficult to tell exactly what commandment a particular film tracks. The films are not set in ancient Israel, as was Cecil B. DeMille's epic film (1956) about Moses and the Ten Commandments, but in urban Poland in the late 1980s, the grim last days of the Soviet oppression behind what was then known as the Iron Curtain. The setting throughout is a large high-rise apartment complex, and while a few characters do cycle through the films, each film dramatizes the life crises of just two or three people. Two of the films, those on adultery and murder, were expanded into feature films, *A Short Film About Love* (1988) and *A Short Film About Killing* (1988). Nor are the tales in any way moralistic, which one might expect because they have to do with those original Judaeo-Christian laws.

Kieslowski and his co-writer, Krzysztof Piesiewicz, a lawyer for Solidarity, the militant anti-Communist labor union, and later a post-Communism senator in Poland, started the project as a kind of act of defiance. After their film *No End* (1987) was panned by all their major constituencies — the Roman Catholic Church, the Communist Party, and Solidarity — Piesiewicz joked that they should make a film on a nice safe topic, such as the Ten Commandments, just so no one could possibly object. Before long the taunt turned into a project. The two were going to write the screenplays, and they would assign each to a different director. But Kieslowski, who liked all of the screenplays, retreated from that plan. Instead, he chose to direct all of them, but he used a different cinematographer for each, so that every one would have a different visual imprint.

All ten films focus on how very different people in a common but difficult setting conduct their lives amid the usual kinds of misfortune that befall just about everyone, the good and the bad alike. None of these characters is, it seems, particularly bad or good or smart or unintelligent. They come from all different economic strata — some professionals such as doctors, musicians, and professors, and some delivery boys and street thugs — which perhaps accounts for some of what they do. However, most seem educated moderately well, though that does not endow them with any particular wisdom or virtue. Education might, in fact, prove to be a peril. One of the elements that makes these films so remarkable is that on first glimpse, and sometimes after several glimpses, many of the films do not — at least on the surface — seem to be about any particular commandment; for that matter, they seem to engage several at once. A frequent sensation one has while watching one or the other of these ten films is to wonder which of the commandments this particular film might be about, though in some cases it is obvious. This uncertainty is heightened by the fact that the writer/filmmakers chose not to put titles other than a number on any of the films. That number does no more perhaps than indicate the order in which they were produced.

The matter is further complicated by the fact that Jews, Protestants, and Catholics all have different orders for the commandments in the Decalogue. Nor are these films consistent in approach and tone. Some are dead-serious, even mordant, dramas, such as the one about killing; a few others, including the last chronologically, are satirical farces. In fact, one of the chief intentions of the writers is to update or contemporize the old laws for the present and pressing "now." And they do that with an extraordinary richness that reveals both the complexity and profundity of their imaginations and the complexity of contemporary moral choice.

Decalogue I is not a mild tale, though it is entirely lacking in sex, violence, or blasphemy, all those things that trouble many viewers — and rightly so — given the immense and gratuitous crassness that characterizes so many Hollywood films. Not so here, though the subject matter is definitely harrowing. And it is made more so by the film's precise and delicate sensitivity, both emotional and religious, on what is perhaps the most difficult subject of all.

The central concern is here unambiguous, the beginning not only of the series but of the Ten Commandments: "Thou shalt have no other gods before me." That seems fitting because, first, it sets the tone for the rest of the series; second, it poses the really big first question about any kind of legitimacy to belief in God (and the God here is clearly the Judaeo-Christian one); third, it poses the most wrenching of all tough questions about what kind of God this might be. The story focuses on a single father, Krzysztof (Henryk Baranowski), a professor whose wife is working abroad, and his brilliant and delightful ten-year-old son, Pavel (Wojciech Klata), whom he treasures and adores. The father is an eager and proud man of science and its new technologies as they expand humankind's ability to learn all we have to know to improve human welfare. We see him patiently and enthusiastically teaching classes and teaching his son.

The religious questions emerge — and this first one is the most theologically overt of all ten films — when young Pavel starts to ask his father about death, for Pavel has seen up close a dead dog that used to

What can be lost . . .

roam the neighborhood. The father does not disparage traditional Christian religious belief, something his sister Irena (Maja Komorowska) warmly embraces, but it is clear where his sympathies lie. When we die, the machines that we are simply stop running; the heart stops pumping blood, and we shut down, after which there is, for the dead personally, nothing at all.

Krzysztof's sister, Irena, on the other hand, believes in God and divine love, something that human love intimates as experience and proof, and she wants to open young Pavel to that possibility, which the latter makes easier for her when he simply asks her about the "meaning" of life. That a ten-year-old would ask such questions seems rather implausible, but this is a precocious and thoughtful little boy, who takes seriously what he sees, such as the dead animal, and what his father tells him, especially the father's take on the finality of this existence. In a patient, well-constructed scene, Irena explains to Pavel that in the love of one for another, amid and through the material, we know what God is like and we sense divine presence. She wants Pavel to undergo religious instruction, and his father does not object to that, thinking his son should make up his own mind.

All of this Kieslowski sets in a Warsaw housing complex during a

The mysterious stranger, who simply watches — and watches

gray and wintry pre-Christmas season. It is a very mundane and ordinary place, inhabited by unexpected — though they may not be strange — sights. There is in its midst, for example, a striking contemporary Roman Catholic church, an enormous cross cut into the brickwork above its entry. We also repeatedly see a mysterious, unspeaking young man who simply hangs around the housing complex, sitting by a fire trying to keep warm. The camera watches him and he watches back, and he appears in eight of the ten films in *Decalogue*. In fact, he seems to loom over the events, providing a frame for the action — or at least a silent interpreter or presence of some kind. These appearances may be providing atmospherics, but it is likely that something more than incidental mood-making is afoot.

Things to Look For

- The young man watching by the fire appears a number of times, especially at the very beginning, and he recurs throughout *Deca-*

logue. The question is: Where does he come from and why is he there?

- The exact field of knowledge Pavel's father teaches is not altogether clear, though it seems to have something to do with computer logic and theory. His lectures are interesting but perhaps also problematic in some ways, especially for what will follow.
- One of the computers in Pavel's apartment seems to perform strangely, which presents a puzzle to the father. It is an oddity, for sure, and it seems to have implications for the outcome of the story.
- Pavel's aunt, Irena, his father's sister, is a photographer and part-time caretaker for the boy, and she cares deeply for him (she seems to be unmarried and with no children of her own). We see her at the beginning of the film watching Pavel on a television in the front window of an electronics store, and the image recurs later.
- In the last phase of the film, as its crisis heightens, Krzysztof's first instinct is to rely on the measures of science for understanding and reassurance. It is a hard instinct to dislodge, requiring a lot of counterevidence. Unfortunately, he now is, as Kieslowski suggests, no longer a scientist but very much everyman. Of course, all of this stands in contrast to Irena's vision of faith.

Post-viewing Commentary

The worst thing that can happen does — to both Pavel and his family. What was not supposed to happen, according to advanced scientific prognostication, does happen. The father of the boy, Krzysztof (whose name may be ironic, given that it is the first name of both the film's writers), trusts his math and his computer to predict the thickness of the ice. Good man and loving father that he is, he goes out himself, while Pavel is asleep, to walk the ice to make sure of its strength. And still bad things happen to the innocent and the good and the loving, no matter how much care people take. Blasphemous evil strikes whom it will, and the toll simply devastates those left behind — something that *Decalogue I* certainly does not mince words about. That somber truth, in Poland before the fall of the Iron Curtain, was quite clear. The apparent certitudes of science perhaps only dull human awareness of the suppleness and strength of metaphysical evil.

Krzysztof seems to entertain the hope that, with computers, we can find a world immune to human error and flaw, though he seems also to acknowledge, as his lecture reveals, that computers might someday assume their own kind of autonomy. And perhaps he presumes their goodness, or at least their neutrality and impartiality. The movie precedent here is clearly Stanley Kubrick's daunting film *2001: A Space Odyssey* (1968), in which a spacecraft computer nicknamed Hal becomes self-conscious and self-willed (the same transpires in Danny Boyle's interesting but badly flawed *Sunshine*). In this film, Krzysztof twice returns to the apartment to find his computer mysteriously on and asking "Are you ready?" And if it can act on its own, might it deliver false information on the ice thickness? This question about the autonomy of cybertechnology parallels the larger question of how evil happens in human affairs, and the death of young Pavel ranks among the worst of evils, a hideous and unfathomable loss that utterly devastates his father and his aunt.

When Krzysztof first hears the distant wail of sirens, he pays little heed, occupied as he is with an ink spill from a cracked bottle on his desk — an ominous foreshadowing that some things do crack and break. When a neighbor child asks for Pavel, Krzysztof begins to check on his whereabouts, though he is not yet alarmed, for he still trusts the certainty of his calculations. Only when he learns that Pavel's English lesson has been cancelled does he begin to panic, and then he still tries to exert rational control over his increasing terror. He is uncomprehending when a neighbor tells him that the ice has broken. And he cannot reach Pavel by the usually reliable technical means, namely, the walkie-talkies that they share. Finally, at the edge of the pond, a dog ominously yaps, recalling the dead dog Pavel had earlier mentioned to his father, and the smoke lifts off the fire of the silent observer. Only when a neighbor boy tells him that Pavel had gone skating does Kryszstof finally crumple, knowing the inevitability of what divers will find at the bottom of the pond. And when a small body does emerge, father and aunt stand together — one of unfaith and the other of faith. The entire crowd of onlookers, except for Krzysztof, sink to their knees.

The remainder of the film is without words. The next scene shows Krzysztof sitting alone in the dark in his apartment, his face soaked in sweat and tears, when he notices the computer, again turned on, and inviting human trust with the simple words "I am ready." The question now becomes, "Ready for what?" The scene then switches to the interior of a large, unfinished, and dimly lit open-air cathedral, which we have already seen in daylight from a distance. Krzysztof enters from the rear, with the faint light from the exterior barely silhouetting his distant form. The camera shifts to his point of view to see a makeshift, candle-lit altar (a long, thick board resting on piled blocks); above and behind him, on the scaffolding, hangs a large color portrait of the Virgin and Child, candles burning below and above the portrait. Krzysztof proceeds to overturn the altar, toppling boards, bricks, and candles. The camera then cuts to the simple, iconic Virgin, and it appears that tear after tear are dripping down her face. These, of course, could be coincidental drips of wax from the candles arrayed along the length of the plank above. Or they could be something else, though still wholly natural — a wordless assurance of the miraculous presence of divine compassion in life, an image we have been prepared for by Aunt Irena's explanation of God to Pavel.

Aunt Irena deems divine reality palpable in two inescapable realms. The first is life itself: "One is alive, and it's a present. A gift." And the second is the current of love that courses through human experi-

An aunt tries to explain the reality of divine presence

ence, something that lies beyond explanation and measurement. This second manifestation of God comes in the subjective apprehension of what cannot be measured, and this she explains to Pavel by asking him what he feels as she hugs and holds him. The simple faith consists of the improbability but ever-pressing reality of love: "Exactly: that's where he is," she tells Pavel.

Krzysztof's last actions seem to support this as he reaches his hand in the baptismal font from which he removes a curved chunk of ice that he then holds on his fevered brow, and this suggests a different kind of holding, one akin to what Krzysztof's sister says about the nature of divine presence. Moreover, perhaps this is the kind of ice — which is, after all, frozen holy water — that one can indeed trust, though it bespeaks a reality whose presence and gifts are not subject to scientific measure. Kneeling there before the weeping, compassionate Virgin and Child, sacred water on his brow, the distraught Krzysztof seems to sense the very kind of holding his sister speaks about, and by which and through which one senses the very present reality of divine love. And there lies a hope of which measurement, mathematics, and computers can offer no account.

The striking open-air church where the story ends

Post-viewing Questions

1. What other ways might there be to interpret the closing wordless sequences? They are brief and worth replaying to observe and appreciate Kieslowski's precise and economical construction of the sequences, especially the taut and deft evocations of deep emotion.

2. Piesiewicz and Kieslowski construct the film along the well-established lines of conflict between religion and science, especially the difficult matter of how one knows truth or, in the case of religious belief, constructs faith. Krzysztof clearly embraces scientific materialism — physical matter is the only and final reality — whereas Irena allows for the soul's subjective apprehension of a spiritual reality impenetrable to scientific measurement or detection. For her, there abides a mysterious, unfathomable portion of the self that detects a transcendent reality of all-encompassing love. Kieslowski dramatizes the question with great poignancy and urgency. So, which is it?

3. Kieslowski cuts abruptly from Irena and Pavel's moving conversation about God to a shot of that silent stranger sitting by an open fire in the wind by the edge of the pond that will later that day claim Pavel's life. Does that shot undercut the cogency of Irena's words on the nature of God, for with him we have a picture of detachment, if not indifference?

4. Kieslowski poignantly begins and ends *Decalogue I* with pictures (shot by a film crew that had visited his school) of a running Pavel, an indisputably beautiful and exuberant child, a sensitive and smart kid we come to know and marvel at in the course of the story. What is Kieslowski going after with this frame device? Is it a bit excessive, pushing the sentimental?

5. Kieslowski soaks his film in the dingy gray of a sunless and snowy winter. And lighting throughout seems to accentuate that cold and drab world, one that from the look of it seems absolutely devoid of beauty or hope. Indeed, from the look and feel of it, this would be a hard place for the divine to break into. Can Aunt Irena's view of divine presence possibly counter this?

Critical Comments

The thoughtful and good critics seem to run out of words when they talk about Kieslowski, and especially *The Decalogue*. Stephen Holden says that, "as powerfully as his films portray human pain and longing, they also convey the preciousness of life with a conviction that few other filmmakers have succeeded in bringing to the screen" (*The New York Times,* June 9, 2000). Another very good critic, Lisa Schwarzbaum, finds the "10 profound human dramas" of *The Decalogue* "riveting," consistently "shocking, tender, sometimes funny" examinations of "ordinary people . . . with the ordinary mysteries of being human" (*Entertainment Weekly,* Aug. 4, 2000). Concerning the impact of *The Decalogue,* Roger Ebert again struck the right note: "If you are lucky and have someone to talk with, you discuss them, and learn about yourself. Or if you are alone, you discuss them with yourself, as so many of Kieslowski's characters do" (*Chicago Sun-Times,* Apr. 2, 2000).

The Early, Pre-*Decalogue* Feature Films of Krzysztof Kieslowski

> *A Short Film About Love* (1988)
> *A Short Film About Killing* (1988)
> *Blind Chance* (1987)
> *No End* (1985)
> *Camera Buff* (1979)
> *The Scar* (1976)

A Documentary on Kieslowski

> *Krzysztof Kieslowski: I'm So-So . . .* (1995)

II. Wrestling with Angels (and Demons): The Collision of Morality and Belief

The darkness will come, sad to say. Looking at the misfortune abounding all around him, inside and out, a character in Alan Paton's luminous novel of South Africa, *Cry, the Beloved Country,* laments the way things are with simple, penetrating eloquence: "The world is full of trouble."

There are wars and rumors of wars (and bombs and bombers, both small and fearsome); cancer comes, even to children; drunks drive and kill; addictions wither and blight people; bubbles burst (both personal and economic); and in the end everyone journeys to that "undiscovered country from whose bourn no traveler returns" *(Hamlet).* The strangely chirpy narrator of *Magnolia* (1999) repeats over and over again, Ecclesiastes-style, "And so it goes, and so it goes."

In other words, evil sooner or later encompasses all and visits everyone, coming from "out there" and also from the inside-out. Saint Paul knew the scale of it, invoking the notion of vast "principalities and powers" that eagerly shred every good thing and creature (Rom. 8:38). This we know in our own time, not only from all manner of fundamentalist terrorism, but even more in the monstrous social movements of fascism and communism, which have flourished in the very heart of Christendom. All of which says that this is a broken place that we inhabit, and that life within it sooner or later looks and feels like an open wound, at least in the suffering of others and sometimes also deep within ourselves. No amount of time in a self-help book or sweat lodge can begin to fix the woe of the world.

How difficult it is to break free from assorted forms of darkness and/or blindness toward something like moral and religious light becomes painfully clear in the central characters of the following three films. All of them are in various ways sorely broken, either by their own choices or by what life has done to them. And they wrestle with their brokenness wrenchingly, as well two of them should, given their cruelty and crimes. Two of these three are actually fortunate that conscience and guilt have at last caught up with them, for these often become catalysts for change — or at least a searching of some kind. What they look for is, in traditional language, some kind of grace, though that term by itself hardly proves sufficient to describe what falls on them. The third protagonist, a ten-year-old boy who sorely misses his recently deceased grandfather, suffers loss and limited vision; but time and events work to bring him from sorrow to a joyful vision of hope and charity, to a place where he is, in the words of the film title, "wide awake." And angels help, at least a little.

The fates of the villains prove to be not nearly as hopeful. In Coppola's *The Godfather Part III: The Death of Michael Corleone* (1990), the aging and ill protagonist of the *Godfather* trilogy, finally — and much too belatedly — comes to rue his life of crime and stone-cold cruelty. All of Michael's brainy calculation and shrewdness cannot liberate him from the illegal means by which he has made his enormous fortune — a vast and intricate murderous darkness. Freedom from crime has been his lifelong goal, but he ultimately confronts the inescapability of the old maxim that "evil begets evil." Or, to put it in homely terms, "You can't ever outfox the devil at his own game." After decades of trying to move the "family business" to legality, Michael comes to confront, much to his great surprise and against his will, his own deep evil. Plainly and amazingly enough, he comes to repent. However, the fierce tenacity of evil will not let him go, and he pays what is perhaps the ultimate price for having one more go in the game.

That is not the case, however, with Woody Allen's protagonist in his masterpiece *Crimes and Misdemeanors* (1989). The wealthy and eminently respectable ophthalmologist runs into an avalanche of torturous guilt after doing the unforgivable. The difference is that, if Michael Corleone pays in enormous personal woe for his crimes, Judah Rosenthal seems ultimately — in Allen's excruciating formulation — to flourish. Perhaps, in the end, as is suggested in one biblical formulation, evildoers do indeed prosper (Jeremiah 12:1). Go figure.

Crimes and Misdemeanors (1989)

Director	Woody Allen
Writer	Woody Allen
Cinematographer	Sven Nykvist

CAST	
Martin Landau	Judah Rosenthal (Academy Award nomination)
Anjelica Houston	Delores Paley
Woody Allen	Cliff Stern
Mia Farrow	Halley Reed
Sam Waterston	Rabbi Ben
Alan Alda	Lester
Claire Bloom	Miriam Rosenthal
Joanna Gleason	Wendy Stern
Jerry Orbach	Jack Rosenthal

Rotten Tomatoes	92
Metacritic	77

- -

General Comments

The tendency of just about everyone is to confuse Woody Allen, the writer-director, with the inept, self-involved nebbish he usually plays. The result is the notion that Allen could never rise to writing a screenplay that transcends those expectations, meaning stories that show the limitations and humor of being, well, a nebbish. However, they are not the same at all, even though Allen's personal life at times — including his pairing up with his grownup adopted stepdaughter — would suggest it might be. The fact is that Allen satirizes the kinds of people many people take him to be, and insofar as he resembles those folks, the humor is at his own expense. Messy personal lives do not automatically keep anyone from self-insight or, in the case of Allen, from the great moviemaking art of which he is capable but has achieved only rarely in recent years.

Now seventy-five, Allen is still going strong and, in some ways, getting better again (his career has gone through cycles). He has had a long and remarkably productive life of writing, acting, and directing over a forty-year career in films. His recent *Vicky Christina Barcelona* (2008), a biting but sympathetic look at the strangeness of romance, is the best romantic comedy he's done since *Hannah and Her Sisters* (1986) more than two decades ago. His *Matchpoint* (2005) explores self-absorption, murder, and guilt, and if done by any other filmmaker the film would have been seen as a remarkable accomplishment. Unfortunately, many saw it as Allen simply repeating himself — specifically his one unquestionably great film, *Crimes and Misdemeanors* (1989). We should all be so lucky as to have masterpieces to repeat, especially when the redo plausibly — and hauntingly — reverses the outcome of the original. And Allen does not seem to give up on this subject, for his most recent film bears the morally tantalizing title of *Whatever Works* (2009), though the film came and went without much notice.

Crimes and Misdemeanors is a masterpiece of bitter humor and moral suspense that probes both human desire and the flimsiness of conscience and guilt. At the center of this multiplotted tale, which is full of interconnected secondary characters, is prominent Manhattan ophthalmologist Judah Rosenthal, played masterfully by Martin Landau, who received an Oscar nomination for best acting. Judah's profession is appropriate, because eyes and what they see and cannot see — Judah's as well as others' — play a central role in the story. What a character sees, or imagines he or she sees, determines behavior — in romance as in morality.

The large formal banquet that opens the film honors Judah Rosenthal for his philanthropic work, and it is in his acceptance speech that the urbane Judah recalls the words of his devout Jewish father, "The eyes of God are upon you." These always watchful eyes are something that we can never escape. From the external look of it, Judah should not mind God's gaze: his life seems virtuous, even blessed with the approval of an all-seeing God. His beautiful and elegant wife Miriam (Claire Bloom) reveres him, as does their daughter, and he commutes to Manhattan from a luxurious oceanside home. All seems to be going well in his life. But there is a dark, hidden place that Judah is mortally loath to have exposed. Her name is Delores (Anjelica Huston), and she is not a happy camper.

Running parallel to Judah's story are the travails of an opposite sort, the professionally and personally inept Cliff Stern (Woody Allen), a bespectacled, mostly failed documentary filmmaker whose intrusive camera is yet another kind of "eye" that sees where it perhaps should not. And Cliff's own eyes should maybe have better vision than they do in both romance and film subject matter. He is in the last days of a sour marriage to Wendy (Joanna Gleason), whose fabulously successful brother, Lester (Alan Alda), a pompous, self-deluding television producer, only aggravates Cliff's raging insecurities. And in the midst of these circumstances, Cliff starts chasing Halley Reed (Mia Farrow), a public television producer, a waif of a woman who has about her a kind of ambiguous innocence. Exactly how ambiguous, Cliff will find out.

Helping Judah in his search for meaning and a way out of his

Delores and Judah in a tender parting

Cliff and Halley, a perfect pair?

adulterous moral muddle is one of his patients, a kindly rabbi known simply as Ben (Sam Waterston), who has quite literal vision problems: he is rapidly going blind. How much Ben, or anyone, can really help Judah remains to be seen. On the other hand, Cliff Stern has his own counsel, Louis Levy (Martin S. Bergmann), a philosopher who is the subject of Cliff's adoring documentary. Both men, the religious Ben and the secular philosopher Levy, are full of wisdom and thoughtful, penetrating insights into life, love, and human meaning. The extent to which either one of them can impose any kind of restraint on either of their advisees, either Judah or Cliff — in short, on the omnivorous human heart — poses one of the deeper riddles that runs through the story.

And finally, though their worlds have intertwined throughout the movie — unbeknownst to them — Judah and Cliff will finally meet at a wedding reception for Rabbi Ben's daughter. There they share a piano bench for a long ruminative talk. And so ends a stunning film of intrigue, guilt, and the pursuit of redemption. There's hardly a more surprising, and haunting, conclusion in any film, one that simultaneously chills the soul and provokes gratitude for searching, masterful storytelling. So ready yourself for a world of mistakes and messy moral choices and hopes for redemption.

Things to Look For

- As the commentary above suggests, eyes and vision — the notion of seeing — lie at the center of the story, especially as an "index to the soul," as one character puts it. Track these references through the film, but please don't get obsessive about it.

- With the notion of seeing comes the unique lighting and palette of the film, shot by Ingmar Bergman's renowned cinematographer, Sven Nykvist. Though shot in color, its "feel" is more akin to black and white, a format Allen has used very successfully over the years. Indeed, palette does have marked effect in how the director — and the viewers — feel about the film.

- Cliff Stern's sister, Jenny (Jenny Nichols), enters the narrative from time to time, and it is particularly from her experience that Allen seems to suggest certain realities of "the human condition." Her stories are memorable, and Allen seems to put them there just in case viewers don't get the plight of humanity.

- Allen uses flashbacks to portions of Judah's life as he tries to figure out the significance of his actions, including a conversation about God and guilt with his orthodox father. Track this and other religious markers throughout the film that perhaps explain how Judah ends up as he does.

- As inescapably moral creatures, how blind are we even when we know better, or at least should know better? How much, too, might a crystal ball help us to know the eventual fruit of what might seem casual or incidental moral choices at the time — both for good or evil? And worse still, how often do deeds done in apparent goodwill yield various kinds of calamity? Allen seems to wrestle insistently with these kinds of questions in the film.

- Judah's fate in the movie is controversial, so controversial that Allen, in his recent *Match Point* (2005), the story of a middling British tennis pro on the make, seems to go out of his way to offer an alternative conclusion to that of *Crimes and Misdemeanors*. That raises the question of what Judah should have done, or at least of how his story should have ended to make this a properly "moral" film.

Post-viewing Commentary

Judah Rosenthal, fancy ophthalmologist and benefactor, gets away with murder, both legally and morally. For just a few thousand dollars, Judah's brother, Jack (the late Jerry Orbach), the hard-edged, clear-eyed, and morally pragmatic gangster, arranges the "hit" on Delores, and the murder ends up as just another crime on the rap sheet of a drifter. Thus the police are not even bothering to look any longer.

And morally, for Judah, the guilt and anxiety just go away: one fine day, after a long slog through a swamp of anguish, Judah feels those twinges no longer, and life again proves inviting and full of enjoyment. This comes to Judah as a great surprise, for he had seemed ready to implode immediately after the crime. And it is no wonder. Guilt roars and stomps all over him; for a time at least, Judah *sees* all too well. After the crime he makes a surreptitious visit to Delores's apartment to retrieve anything that might incriminate him at the scene. He sees her dead on the floor, her eyes wide open. Allen's camera work and musical scoring here are breathtaking, Schubert playing urgently and loudly as the camera tracks down the length of Judah's well-attired self to Delores's open eyes. Those eyes bring to mind Delores's own words to Judah, that one can perhaps, as her mother told her, look through the eyes to see the soul. But she seems just plain dead, and what soul was ever there is plainly gone, though the body retains its beauty and "humanness," for lack of a better term. Judah has done what both Rabbi Ben and his visions of his father have warned against. Ben has told him that he can't just toy with this person and then throw her away; Judah's father, in the imaginary dinner-table conversation when Judah was a boy, admonishes his son with what the biblical law says about murder. And now, of course, the inescapable eyes of God — through Delores's eyes — are gazing on Judah.

In short, Judah finds himself in one huge mess, and its resolution will be wholly determined by his self-interest and the survival of his cushy life. Delores had wanted "satisfaction," something Judah, she contended, had promised her: specifically, a long life together. But Judah could not remember what he had said to her, or when, or how she might have construed it. If he had made promises to her — or even implied them — he is indeed culpable and really does owe her. If not, well, then she's insane, just another irrational woman, a little less than human, who deserves to be gotten rid of by any means necessary. And Ju-

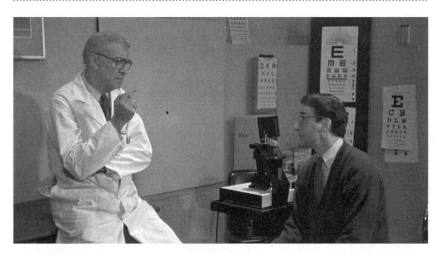

Doctor Judah and Rabbi Ben in conversation

dah also factors in a calculus of self-interest: he's got more to lose than she does, namely his reputation, his wife and family, his good works, and his honored and affluent world.

The logic here seems to be that Delores is a "nothing," an obscure, self-deluded stewardess whose disappearance from the world almost no one will note. That is, within the framework of "palpable significance," she won't be missed in the least. That is a long way from Rabbi Ben's transcendent vision of the incalculable worth of every human life, in its own right, especially because it is esteemed by God. For Judah, as refined and thoughtful as he seems to be in his profession and life, a crude Darwinian survival prevails. The weak — or the bothersome — perish for the benefit of the strong.

Apparently, at least for a time after the murder, those eyes, both God's and Delores's, will not remove their insistent glare, and Judah begins drinking, his marriage suffers, and others seem concerned for his mental health. Wracked by guilt, he revisits his childhood home only to imagine a debate among his kin about God and morality. Though his aunt dismisses everything religious, Judah's father insists on the persistence and finality of God and God's law. Judah's ravening guilt even brings him to contemplating turning himself in to the police, an option that could prove fatal when he informs his gangster brother of his temptation to confess.

And then, suddenly, in the last sequence, we discover that the hounding and lingering pangs of guilt have simply disappeared, and Judah is again "whole and healthy." As Judah himself puts it, his life has gone "back to normal, back to [his] protected world of wealth and privilege."

This is in contrast to Cliff, Judah's woebegone conversation partner at the wedding. Cliff has lost it all: his marriage has fallen apart; his life-affirming philosopher, his ticket to having his documentary broadcast as a special on PBS, has jumped to his death from a window; and now the woman he really desires has gone off, unbeknownst to Cliff, to marry his nemesis, the genuinely odious Lester, an amoral egomaniac who wraps himself in a mantle of "creativity" clichés and liberal pieties. Knowing Cliff's low opinion of Lester, Halley tries to console him by saying that Cliff does not know the "real" Lester. She has apparently not seen him at his worst, as has Cliff and his prying camera (somewhat like the eye of God), which catches Lester hitting on every attractive female in sight. Or, worse still, maybe Halley knows full well what Lester is but marries him anyway for his power and influence, the easy way to win interest in her own flagging film career. Allen does not tell viewers which is true; but he does show us Cliff, multiply defeated and morose, sulking in his booze alongside the triumphant Judah, a fellow whose sins (crimes) dwarf Cliff's middling appetites (misdemeanors), however noxious they might be. Think on that one.

That is just what the last sequence in the film invites viewers to

Rabbi Ben and daughter dancing in the dark, or is it the light?

do, or at least to make the best sense we can of a perplexing array of events. The camera patiently watches the now blind rabbi, Ben, dance with his daughter, whose wedding has occasioned this reception (for which Lester has paid). A voice-over comes from philosopher-suicide Louis Levy, saying that we are what we choose, the sum of all our decisions, and that meaning comes from acting morally and enjoying simple pleasures such as family. Only love gives meaning to an otherwise indifferent universe. While the audience hears Levy's mini-lecture, the camera replays critical shots from the film, such as Delores striding toward her apartment, Judah conspiring with his brother, and so on. All of this suggests that life is indeed a desperate business, so desperate, in fact, that Levy himself chooses to go "out the window," as Cliff puts it.

However, Woody Allen does not leave it at that. For all the time that this long argument plays out, there is a kind of silent counterevidence before our eyes: simply, it is the image of Ben dancing happily with his daughter, though he is blind and seemingly the character with the most cause for complaint. It is Ben who seems to embrace life and fathom it most deeply, holding out, contra Levy, that there is a transcendent Being who cares about human welfare, one token of which is the law, a document that restrains the predatory so that life itself may flourish within an ethos of respect and reverence. Perhaps Ben fits within the long literary tradition in the West of blind prophets whose blindness allows them to see far better than the sighted.

Post-viewing Questions

1. Allen uses music marvelously in the film, and all of it has resonance for the story, intensifying the emotional clout of the film and also, at times, clarifying meaning. No music in the diverse score is more powerful than Schubert's, whose violin seems to distill all the fevered madness that descends on people from time to time. How effective is this, and what does this music seem to evoke or "tell" about the nature of human life?

2. Another technical aspect of the film that delivers considerable storytelling force comes in the production design, the creation of settings that are just right and can infuse the drama itself with additional meaning. Delores's walk to her death is along a long wrought-iron fence that stands between her and the camera, and

that seems, along with the Schubert, to be a forewarning of what awaits her. Are there others that seem to work particularly well?

3. Allen uses a lot of visual and aural imagery to aid his plot. For example, Judah leaves a party to meet Delores in the middle of a thunderstorm, and his insomnia finds an echo in well-placed thunderstorms. And he sits by a fire as he contemplates his evil, as if that itself were the entry to hell. And the same goes for his fireplace, whose fires seem to hint at approaching evil and hell. Somehow these work to add intensity to the storytelling, though different viewers may gloss over them (the story hardly depends on any of these "extra touches"), and others may differ on how these images strike them. Are there others that seem memorable as particularly effective in distilling the mood or gist of the film?

4. How effective is that central metaphor of seeing? For all of her limitations, Delores does see, and she does have a soul whose heart cries for acceptance and trust. Her eyes at least see far enough to recognize her own soul; on the other hand, Judah hasn't seen through her eyes to the soul (person) inside. Where else does the enigma of seeing resonate in the tale?

5. At the very end, how much does blind Ben's dance with his radiant daughter counter the cynicism and despair we witness on the piano bench? Or see in Levy's suicidal departure? Indeed, the only one who seems to have an honest, healthy, and happy relationship with anyone is Ben. How much of a token is that for the truth Ben reveres, namely a transcendent love that means well by humanity? Does the image perhaps speak more loudly than the argument?

Critical Comments

The unique character of *Crimes and Misdemeanors* — part comedy, part murder mystery, and part religious inquiry — posed a challenge for critics. Roger Ebert thought the film "bleak and hopeless" because "the evil are rewarded, the blameless are punished, and the rabbi goes blind." His comments on the villain note the dreadful irony of Judah's sight insofar as he "sees what he does, and does nothing to stop it. In his own world, he is the eyes of God" (*Chicago Sun-Times*, Sept. 11, 2005). Yet, years after its release, Ebert would include *Crimes and Mis-*

demeanors on his list of all-time great films. Prominent Catholic writer Peter Steinfels saw some hopefulness in the otherwise bleak film in Allen's portraiture of Rabbi Ben: "That second climactic shot, at the end, shows the now blind rabbi dancing with his daughter at her wedding. Again the camera is loath to let them go, showing a man of faith haltingly but firmly embracing not just his daughter and his destiny, but his God." Allen makes it clear, says Steinfels, that this is not his own belief, but Allen at least has the sense not to mock another's clear-eyed belief, though he be blind (*The New York Times,* Oct. 15, 1989). Indeed, Allen seems to reflect on the question, perhaps with some envy, of whether the blind rabbi is the only one with enough insight to be genuinely happy.

Other Notable Films by Woody Allen

Match Point (2005)
Husbands and Wives (1992)
Hannah and Her Sisters (1986)
Annie Hall (1977)
Play It Again, Sam (1972)

The Godfather: Part III

Writers	Mario Puzo and Francis Ford Coppola
Director	Francis Ford Coppola (Academy Award nomination)
Cinematographer	Gordon Willis (Academy Award nomination)
Editor	Walter Murch (Academy Award nomination)
Original Music	Carmine Coppola
Production Designer	Dean Tavoularis

CAST

Al Pacino	Michael Corleone
Talia Shire	Connie Corleone
Andy Garcia	Vincent Mancini (Academy Award nomination, Best Supporting Actor)
Diane Keaton	Kay Adams Corleone
Sofia Coppola	Mary Corleone
Eli Wallach	Don Altabello
Joe Mantegna	Joey Zasa

Rotten Tomatoes	66
Metacritic	60

- -

General Comments

Francis Ford Coppola's *The Godfather* (1972) is probably the greatest American film ever, and almost everyone has seen it — or plans to sooner or later. Fewer have seen *The Godfather: Part II* (1974); and many fewer still, perhaps only a handful, have seen *The Godfather: Part III* (1990), the final chapter in the saga of mobster Michael Corleone (Al Pacino), a film that was released nearly twenty years after the first two.

To some extent, that decline in interest is understandable. The last film did not fare well with the critics and, especially, at the box office — and for good reason. Supposedly, Coppola and his writing partner, Mario Puzo, whose best-selling novel had inspired the series, agreed to do it simply for the money, since the studio had made them "an offer they couldn't refuse." Another big problem was Coppola's disastrous decision, when Winona Ryder fell seriously ill a week before shooting was to begin, to cast his own nineteen-year-old daughter Sofia (now a distinguished film director in her own right) as Michael Corleone's daughter, Mary, the female lead role at the film's emotional center as much as was Al Pacino's role as the aging Michael. The young Mary struggles between her love for her father and a romance with a dubious family pariah, young Vincent Mancini (Andy Garcia), the hotheaded illegitimate son of the hotheaded Sonny Corleone (James Caan) from the first *Godfather.* Despite a game effort, young Sofia's performance lacks the dramatic fire needed to ignite the whole tale. Even more than the critics, audiences had little tolerance for the blandness of Sophia Coppola's screen presence or the ineptness of her acting. One can only wonder, in hindsight, what the result would have been had Ryder not fallen ill.

However, despite the struggles of a miscast young actress, *The Godfather: Part III* remains a fascinating and wrenching film that depicts one of the most poignant moral-spiritual wrestlings ever put on film. In that regard, the film retroactively clarifies what the first two *Godfather* movies were really about: for Coppola sets out in the third installment to do nothing less than chart the ultimate damnation of Michael Corleone. It was rumored that Coppola wanted to dump the "Part III" of the *Godfather* brand and instead entitle the film "The Death of Michael Corleone," a choice that would have emphasized, especially in the way Michael dies, what the *Godfather* trilogy was really about from the beginning. It was not a question of who was going to whack whom to become boss of the New York mob; rather, it was about the spiritual seduction of Michael Corleone. The brilliant "hit" montage near the end of *The Godfather,* in which Michael wipes out his enemies, shows that he is not only smart enough to win the mob war but corrupt enough to lose his soul — not to mention even the mob version of integrity — and, tragically, his wife. In *The Godfather*, Michael does win the mob boss wars. But in truth he loses everything of value. That is something that he finally comes to realize in *The Godfather: Part III*.

Worrying that his audiences did not get his point, Coppola set out in *The Godfather: Part II* to make the "lostness" of Michael all the more evident, especially as a counterpoint to the history of his father, Vito (played by Robert De Niro in Part II and Marlon Brando in Part I), whose early days are shown in counterpoint to Michael's career as the leader of the Corleone crime family. In an extended feat of elegant construction, the second installment interweaves the early history of father Vito with Michael's history after the original *Godfather*, as the latter moves to consolidate his power, legitimate the family business, and move everything and everybody from New Jersey to Lake Tahoe. If Vito's rise displays complex moral ambiguity, Michael's "progress" rests on enough unmitigated moral treachery to make a mobster wince. Again Michael wins, defeating his formidable enemies, from gangster Meyer Lansky to Attorney General Robert Kennedy. But he loses more than ever, including his brother and his wife and family, and ends up a lonely, brooding fratricide, a man who has become Cain himself. The closing images of *The Godfather: Part II* show Michael sitting alone in the dark at his Lake Tahoe estate, and it is as terrifying as anything in American film history. Michael has become his own deepest enemy and chief horror. As for audiences, those who have always rooted for a beleaguered Michael, there comes a deep and nagging moral chill.

And that is where, decades later, *The Godfather: Part III* begins. Now fabulously wealthy and living in a large New York City mansion, Michael receives, in an elaborate ceremony, an honor from the Vatican for his generous gift of a hundred million dollars for the restoration of Sicily (and even that is a scam, one in which a corrupt Vatican bank knowingly cooperates). As Michael kneels at the front of the church (all three *Godfather* films begin with a religious ceremony), he guiltily remembers the pointless murder of his inept brother Fredo (John Cazale) — because he "offended me," as he will confess later in the film.

What happens, then, is Michael's pursuit of redemption, in spite of himself, and the film excels in chronicling that tortured history. And Pacino's acting is superb throughout, in scenes ranging from his confrontation with his ex-wife, Kay (Diane Keaton), and his diabetic collapse early in the film, to his meeting in the latter half with a future

Michael Corleone brooding on his own darkness

pope, a subsequent encounter with Kay, and his opera-house scream at the very end. Soon after that performance, the Academy gave Pacino the Oscar for his scenery-chewing performance in *Scent of a Woman* (1992). More than likely, that award represented a belated recognition of his repeated brilliant performances for Coppola in the *Godfather* trilogy, but especially in the third one. (This is the kind of thing that often happens with Oscars, where sentiment and politics of various kinds trump judgment.)

So follow Michael's story as he, in multiple ways, tries to escape the very person he has become to find forgiveness, healing, and new life. His life has hitherto amounted to a series of losses: his father, his brother, his brother-in-law, his wife, his other brother, and now maybe even his children — and this in a family where the value of family has counted above all — at least according to Vito, the first godfather.

Things to Look For

- Coppola has always soaked his plots in the life of the Roman Catholic Church. All three *Godfather* films begin with religious ceremonies, and Michael's murders at the end of the first installment happen as he stands in the church, pledging to renounce

Satan, as godfather to the new nephew being christened. This was a stunning alibi, and it was all done in one of the most remarkable montages in cinema history. The same flaunting of the core of the church's teachings, the supremacy of love, human and divine, recur in this last film, and as usual, they have considerable emotional and spiritual clout.

- Coppola has always used the play of light and dark and the brightness of the film's palette marvelously and subtly, especially with the help of cinematographer Gordon Willis, who shot all three films. These add power to the story and clarify its thematic thrusts, and in Part III these work especially well.

- The same can be said for Coppola's use of sound, especially in accentuating human viciousness (e.g., Sonny's assassination and the horse's head incident in the first film). Here Coppola uses these same strategies to good effect, especially the crushing last sequences.

- Michael's relationship with his ex-wife, Kay, remains an emotional focal point of this last film, though that is to some extent displaced by his relationship with his daughter, Mary (Michael also tries to control her life, for that matter). Indeed, some of the best scenes in the film feature the two acting pros together, Keaton and Pacino. Kay consoles Michael after his diabetic stroke, and they converse as old friends (or enemies) when they meet in Sicily for Tony's operatic debut ("I've always loved you, Michael"). One wonders what it is that these two see in each other, she of old New England WASP stock and he the son of an immigrant mobster.

- Was there anything at all that young Sofia Coppola might have done to save her performance? She was and is a superbly talented and successful young woman and movie person, but not as an actor; rather, like her father, she is a writer and director who has at least two excellent films, *The Virgin Suicides* (1999) and *Lost in Translation* (2003), to her credit. In any case, it is interesting to think about who else might have played the role and what difference that might have made in the romance that supplies much of the dramatic tension in the film.

Post-viewing Commentary

In the end Michael loses it all — including his soul. The human toll alone is simply incalculable, and we see him at his death, blind and frail, physically a mirror of his insides, falling into dust, the victim yet again of his own notion that he's smarter and more savvy than all his foes. The ironic tragedy is that this happens when Michael is finally actually getting smart, wising up, realizing his own finitude, his grievous errors and crimes, and perceiving something of a wondrous redemptive reality beyond himself. Early on, barely alive after his diabetic implosion, he jokes to Kay that he'll be really smart when he's dead, and in a bit of foreshadowing, it seems that that is exactly what it will take.

What Michael comes to sense is a great surprise, as much for himself as for viewers, especially for those who've seen him for what he was. With his back against the wall in his encounter with a crime syndicate that includes a cardinal who is director of the Vatican Bank, he turns for counsel to the reputedly trustworthy Cardinal Lamberto (Raf Vallone), a character modeled on the future Pope John Paul I (who died suddenly after only thirty-three days in office). Michael wants "business" advice, but the wily cardinal goes for his soul, prodding him to confess, which Michael hasn't done in decades. In that confession he weeps for his crimes (especially the wrenching admission, "I killed my mother's son"). It is a rending sequence, and despite Michael's obvious remorse, Cardinal Lamberto is not optimistic that Michael can renew his soul if he stays in his business. After all, as the cardinal observes, "Christ has not penetrated it," referring to the soul of Europe, even though Christianity has surrounded it for two millennia.

The evidence of Michael's turn to something beyond himself shows up right away. He mentions his confession to his sister, Connie (Talia Shire, the director's sister), who is the princess of darkness in the film (consider the way she's dressed and lit in the film). Connie scoffs at the very idea of Michael confessing, asserting that he has nothing to confess and certainly not any responsibility over the "accident" that killed poor Fredo. From there, remarkably, Michael goes on to apologize to Kay, confessing that "things" did not turn out the way he'd planned and that "every night in Sicily I dream of how I lost my family." But he continues to plead that he had no choice, for he had to protect his family (in *The Godfather: Part II,* he wondered to his mother if it was

Michael, at last, in the agony of confession

possible to lose one's family while trying to save it). It is a wonderfully tender scene played extraordinarily well by two masterful actors.

And finally, in his vigil by the casket of his murdered patron, Don Tommasino, Michael prays, simply and wholeheartedly, wondering aloud why he himself as a godfather was "so feared and you [his patron] so loved," and he vows that given another chance he "will sin no more." Tragically, his resolve does not last long, for once again Michael endorses, albeit reluctantly, the preemptive slaughter of his enemies, and he almost wins, save for one errant shot that kills the daughter he cherishes, Mary (named, not coincidentally, for the mother of Jesus). With her death, as that long silent scream indicates, Michael also dies, losing his faith as he loses her. There are some crimes for which guilt runs so deep that they preclude even asking for forgiveness: for choosing as he did, Michael in effect murdered his daughter, just as surely as he murdered Fredo. In the end, Michael kept his empire and his wealth, again by rampage, something his father would never have done, and his "winning" has surely damned him and everyone around him.

In this last film in this very American saga of the lure of success, Coppola and Puzo make clear what its "hero," Michael, has missed all along. That is, plainly put, the supremacy of love in all things, including in the business of the mob. The two earlier films make this clear insofar as Michael's way of "doing business" constantly contrasts with his fa-

The reconciliation, however momentary, of Michael and Kay

ther's mores. Don Vito was careful — that is, full of care — never to instigate violence or to use more than was necessary. In fact, Vito ran his crime family as a fabric of mutuality, interdependence, and respect, which becomes clear in the first *Godfather* in the "favors" he grants on the day of his daughter's wedding. For Vito, someone has to do the work that he does simply because the world is full of bad guys, and the American justice system is itself horribly corrupt, especially for penniless immigrants, such as he was.

Vito lives well with ambiguity and insecurity; Michael does not. For Michael, everything boils down to controlling his world, especially after the assassination attempt on his father. And it is Michael who goes back on his father's promise in *The Godfather* not to be the one "to break the peace" between the contending families. He does that with a cold, ruthless totality that is simply appalling. For all the dark tangles of his deeply flawed world, Vito assumed "responsibility" for moderating that world as best he could, taking care of his extended family of undertakers, bakers, and orphans (even the Irish street kid Tom Hagen). In other words, Vito has taken responsibility for "being a man," as he admonishes the singer Johnny Fontaine. The medieval social code of mutual obligation persisted for Vito. For his brilliant son, American individualist to the core, winning came first and last — and cost absolutely everything. The cardinal was, sad to say, right on target.

Post-viewing Questions

1. Coppola has commented that he wrote *The Godfather: Part III* after reading a good deal of Greek tragedy, noting in particular the Greek emphasis on fate and cycles of vengeance. Where does this play out in this last segment of the trilogy? Or is Part III more like Ecclesiastes?

2. Do the three *Godfather* films make Coppola a serious moral philosopher, especially when it comes to depicting the paths by which well-intentioned people do enormous harm to the people they most love?

3. All of Coppola's *Godfather* films feature unexpected eruptions of violence. A distinctive mark of Coppola's use of violence is that it is not cartoonish, though he delivers it with enormous skill. It is generally unexpected — and it is genuinely horrible — startling viewers into recognizing its immorality, something most Hollywood films disparage in their persistent glorification of carnage. How successful is *Godfather III* in sustaining this pattern from the first two?

4. Michael's physical health is brittle, and it is obviously subject to emotional upset, as in the aftermath of the helicopter attack. Something more than emotional stress is going on, however, as the future pope quickly diagnoses in Michael's furtive desperation as he approaches him. Coppola seems to ride this hard, especially in the last scenes, where we see the devastation of the man following the death of Mary and what is probably the loss of his newfound repentance and trust in God. How well does this work in the film, or does Coppola overdo it?

5. As Michael struggles his way toward redemption, he passes through a number of recognitions and confessions, followed by petitions for forgiveness. That begins in his talk with the future pope, in his conversation with Kay, and in his prayerful vigil by the casket of his assassinated protector, an event that immediately precedes his decision to kill preemptively, as he always has, all of his enemies. How sincere and lasting is all of this likely to be?

6. Michael's tearful confession of his crushing load of guilt for his innumerable crimes makes clear exactly how burdened and guilty he feels. And it is clear that he senses that the pope-to-be is a dif-

ferent kind of priest. What in particular does he find in the man, and by implication, the God whom the cardinal serves? To what extent is that made clear in his subsequent words, both in conversation with Don Tommasino and in his soliloquy at the latter's casket?

Critical Comments

"Flawed" but "spell-binding" in its "operatic realism," *The Godfather: Part III* "has attained a deep-grained emotional grandeur that can hold its own with that of the other two films," says Owen Gleiberman (*Entertainment Weekly,* Jan. 11, 1991). Janet Maslin found the film a "valid and deeply moving continuation of the Corleone family saga," which "daringly holds forth the possibility of redemption" (*The New York Times,* Dec. 25, 1990). Ebert caught the way Part III accomplishes what it does: "It is, I suspect, not even possible to understand this film without knowing the first two, and yet, knowing them, Part III works better than it should, evokes the same sense of wasted greatness, of misdirected genius" (*Chicago Sun-Times,* Dec. 25, 1990). Still, as one might expect concerning this last installment of the trilogy, not all critics liked it; in fact, some loathed it, wishing it had never been made. Hal Hinson, in the *Washington Post,* moaned that the film "isn't just a disappointment, it's a failure of heartbreaking proportions" (Dec. 25, 1990).

Other Notable Films Starring Al Pacino

The Merchant of Venice (2004)
City Hall (1996)
Glengarry Glen Ross (1992)
Scarface (1986)
Dog Day Afternoon (1975)
Serpico (1973)

Wide Awake

Writer and Director	M. Night Shyamalan
Cinematographer	Adam Holender
Editor	Andrew Mondshein

CAST

Joseph Cross	Joshua Beal
Robert Loggia	Grandpa Beal
Dana Delaney	Mrs. Beal
Dennis Leary	Mr. Beal
Julia Stiles	Neena Beal
Rosie O'Donnell	Sister Terry

Rotten Tomatoes	41

General Comments

It is not a likely premise: a really cute ten-year-old boy, especially one growing up on Philadelphia's tony Mainline, has a crisis of faith. This we might understand for spurned blind boys in Iran, as in *The Color of Paradise* (discussed in Part I above), but here among fancy Catholic prep schools with sports-loving nuns (Rosie O'Donnell) for teachers and physicians for parents — well, that's a stretch. Or is it? After all, writer-director M. Night Shyamalan grew up there with physician parents and attended the very school that provides the set for the film. In fact, *Wide Awake* was the first film Shyamalan made after finishing New York University film school, though it was not released until much later because of a somewhat tangled dispute with the Weinstein brothers, producers of the film. Alas, Shyamalan's parents wanted him to be, like them — and apparently like nearly all of his aunts and uncles — a doctor. Maybe life would have been simpler. In any case, Shyamalan's first venture into filmmaking was one of his best, though he was later to make such blockbusters as *The Sixth Sense* (1999), *Unbreakable* (2000), and *Signs* (2002). This film is funny, visually witty, and poignant as it ventures into a young boy's effort to validate God's existence so that he can know that his dead grandfather is "okay," even though, staunch Roman Catholic that Grandpa was, he, if anybody, certainly would be.

Young Joshua (Joseph Cross) runs into a crisis of belief — or is it really a crisis of experience? — after his beloved grandfather (Robert Loggia) dies of bone cancer. The vigorous and kindly old gentleman lived with his daughter and her family in their sprawling, stately manse on the Mainline, those gracious old neighborhoods inhabited by Philadelphia's rich, old and new alike. This was particularly important for Josh because his parents, while attentive enough (especially his mother), were nonetheless busy with their medical careers. No less important is it that Josh is small for his age, though his charm, brains, and good looks seem to make up for this, except in such endeavors as football.

In Josh's memories, done in flashback, we get a glimpse of just who the old man was. And we see Josh in the first months after his grandfather's death, unable to awaken in the morning (a sequence that starts the film), periodically sad, retreating into his grandfather's room to don his shirt and put his pipe in his mouth, and mildly fretful too, if only with his skeptical good buddy Dave O'Hara (Timothy Reifsnyder), who has troubles of his own and will end up having still more.

So Josh will set out on a religious quest of his own, which is dead serious but nonetheless comically rendered, playing on the limits of how a ten-year-old, even a precocious one like Josh, understands the world and belief. When it comes down to it, Josh simply does a lot of things that grownups do, but more extremely and publicly. He'll shop around, for example, always looking for easy answers, sampling this or that possibility for religious certainty, and he will suffer some crushing defeats when those options play false. He will at one point, after long

A sleepy Josh's futile attempt to brush his teeth

searching, arrive at despair, even relinquish his quest, concluding that there is no God and that he cannot ever know for sure that his grandfather is "okay."

All of this takes place within the confines of a traditional Roman Catholic family of earnest but not complex belief. In some of the first words of the film, we hear Josh's grandfather's advice that one should always hold on tight to two things, "the football and faith." Josh also has serious talks with the school chaplain, a priest who himself seems rather dispirited in his dealings with pubescent boys. And on one occasion the local cardinal visits the neighboring girls' school, but the results are plainly disappointing. Josh is ensconced in an upscale prep school, blazers and all, and while the staff goes out of its way to care for Josh, not even enormously fun and enormously caring Sister Terry (O'Donnell), who meets with Josh regularly because of his parents' concern, seems able to make a dent in Josh's skepticism.

Caught as he is in a fog, trying hard to see through a dark glass, just like Job and Oedipus and televangelists, Josh is especially on the lookout for "signs," obvious tokens or signals of God's presence amid the struggles of humans. Shyamalan, as he breaks the film into chapters to mark aspects of Josh's passage, even entitles one of this film's chapters "Signs." (*Signs* is also the title of his later movie blockbuster of personal tragedy and alien invasion in which an Episcopal priest regains his belief and calling.) As this film seriously considers, signs can come from

All that Josh has lost

anywhere and be anything, even something so commonplace as an un-expected snowfall, an event his grandfather relished and praised.

So Josh sets out on a mission to discover the deepest truths about life and death. And there the fun begins, even though it remains dead-serious for Josh throughout the movie, a venture that comes close to ending in despair. And though sensitive and smart beyond his years, Josh goes about that quest just as any ten-year-old would. There is in his "research," however, continuity with the ways adults undertake the same, especially in the vast smorgasbord of religions now kicking around, sampling and testing this or that.

As a means of loving his grandfather still, keeping him close, he'll attempt just about anything, try any route, worry his parents and ex-haust his concerned teachers, grasp at straws — some conspicuously magical — hungry for omens and portents, signs and wonders, and dis-appointed over and over when a promising lead proves empty or bo-gus. There are no easy answers for this destination; nor are there even clear paths to an answer. By the end, however, Josh does discover sure proof, of a kind, as much as anyone probably gets. Moreover, much to his surprise, this confirmation of his grandfather's lasting well-being emerges from a place he never thought to look, and it comes, not as the product of his efforts, but fully as a gift from nowhere. Only then is the rightness of his startling recognition plainly enough confirmed in signs and wonders. And this search he conducts while trying to contend with the usual challenges of the sixth grade, such as bullies, girls, parents, older sisters — and, in this school, nuns. But the result is a singular and fetching religious vision of what people and God are all about.

Indeed, insofar as Josh does get "answers," they come, finally, from places neither he nor we expect. And they are several in number, even more and better than Josh imagined. And they are, one after another, grand and jubilant. Shyamalan duly announces these "answers" with pleasure and, at least in one instance, cinematic fanfare. Find them if you can and, better yet, embrace them if you can.

In short, this is not the ordinary kids' flick. Hollywood usually waits until puberty to find children sufficiently interesting — or at least profitable. There are good kids' movies, of course, such as *Charlotte's Web* and *Harry Potter*. But those pictures are produced specifically for the young. While this film is about a young boy, it is pitched almost entirely at adults, and surprisingly it works because it is at once poignant, funny, and religiously searching. With Shyamalan refracting a religious search through the perception of a precocious ten-year-old, viewers of all kinds, religious and otherwise, engage in what amounts to a sophisticated wrestling with the question of how anyone can "know" some portion of the Holy One and, in so doing, know lots of others things as well.

Things to Look For

1. Shyamalan uses an unusual device in this story: chapter title inserts that mark segments of Josh's journey. Sometimes these are the seasons of the year; at other times they're more significant.
2. Does Shyamalan overdo the comedy within Josh's quest and end up mocking it too much? Or does his humor — since religious people can tend to be overserious — finally make the quest palatable?
3. Josh's world looks a little too perfect, very affluent and protected. What does Shyamalan put in here that makes him just a normal kid? What would make for normal today, anyway?
4. A good deal of the humor in the film is visual: Shyamalan simply shows us the unexpected, and as a filmmaker he is good at this (show, don't tell). What visual strategies does he bring out to conjure up the sense of the divine, to thin out some of the opaqueness of that dark glass?

5. Before watching the film, viewers may wish to think for a bit about the nature of their own religious knowledge, specifically the means and moments wherein they "know" God — or at least have some sense of the divine presence.

Post-viewing Comments

Through the course of *Wide Awake,* Josh's "mission" plays out. Shyamalan lays out the story in discrete units, helpfully supplying chapter headings to make sure that viewers "get it." The first, "September: The Questions," begins on the first day of the sixth grade (and is also the beginning of fall, that time of seasonal dying), and Josh is, as his mother says, "almost a man," though he certainly doesn't act like it. He sleeps with plenty of "comfort objects" (stuffed animals) and is deeply sleepy, showing no desire at all for the first day of school, even falling back asleep while brushing his teeth. Almost all the humor in the sequence derives from Shyamalan's visual smarts, a trait that works extremely well in critical parts of the story where the director again does more showing than telling. And the writing is good, showing a boy who, even before the personal tragedy of losing his grandfather, had an enormously quizzical mind. His father warns him on the way to school not to ask probing questions of his teachers. Josh ignores that advice on the very first day when he asks Sister Terry hard questions about baptism and who's bound for hell.

On that first day, having escaped class with his friend Dave, Josh comes up with his "mission" as the two are walking down a sun-flooded Waldron Academy hallway. Josh stands looking at the light in a posture of quiet amazement, asking Dave if he believes in God. Dave's negative response is followed by the explanation that "too many bad things happen to people for no reason," though he does not mind if Josh believes in God. As he explains, "I drink chocolate milk through my nose, what do I know?" Though a voice-over comments that the idea being born in his mind is maybe not such a good idea, after the two exit the camera lingers briefly on those shafts of light, and then the image fades to an entirely white screen — something that rarely happens in the film. But this is where, in this random meditation on light, Josh's quest emerges. That Josh's venture is perhaps in some way blessed is suggested by that closing shot. In any case, wondering about the light (or the Light, given the question it inspires), as Josh surely seems to do, indicates an unusual aesthetic and religious sensitivity in him that melds instances of exceptional beauty with the notion of God. That certainly is a fairly sophisticated conversation for a pair of ten-year-olds.

That evening Josh looks for hints of God's presence on the nightly news, and, as suggested by Dave's observation that too many bad things are happening, Josh quickly gives up. And the signs of frailty and mortality that his grandfather suffered subvert the trustworthiness of the Cardinal whom Josh seeks out, about whom he concludes: "I don't think God talks to him." In his hunger for conspicuous signs of God's presence, Josh is not that different from many grownups. It will take the whole film for Josh to move beyond that kind of reductionism in assessing how God shows up. The episode concludes with Josh recognizing, with a bit of dismay, that "this mission could take days."

As December and Christmas go by, Josh is still looking, but by this time disappointment has set in. He even asks the weary Fr. Peters if they can just talk instead of doing the whole confession ritual: "You ever feel like giving up? Since it's been so long and all [and] you haven't met him? You don't even know if he's made up or not." The priest soon takes Josh less lightly, conceding that he, too, has the boy's feelings at times. But he counsels that "doubt's a part of everyone's journey, no matter what they're looking for. . . ." He assures Josh that if he does find sure proof, Josh will be the first one he tells. And Josh, as we see, is willing to try anything — from Judaism to Buddhism, and beyond. In one happy instance he even tries, on Fr. Peters's suggestion, singing his way into the recognition of God.

And then there's the snow. One evening, sitting in his grandfather's room in what was the old man's favorite chair, Josh senses a mysterious, miraculous something afoot in the house. He runs around to others, asking them if they've sensed anything. All respond that they have not, and when he goes back to the room, he recalls a conversation with his grandfather about death, fear, and parting, in which the old man tells Josh about the intricate beauty of snow as a palpable example of divine love: ordinary beauty as sign and grace. Josh soon runs to the window to see the ground covered with snow. As with music, beauty here proves one telling factor in constructing, or confirming, belief, and this too Josh will find out. With this scene as a pivot point, the remainder of the film displays Josh learning to recognize an altogether

90

Josh sings to get God's attention.

different kind of revealing splendor that soaks the world all around him.

In May come "The Answers," which consist of hints and guesses, as T. S. Eliot put it, that together amount to a resounding "probably" to Josh's hopes. And just when Josh begins to give up, feeling all the more lost — even going so far as to bury his grandfather's sacred shirt in the backyard — these "answers" are full of blessed surprise. The first, strangely, is the wonder of compassion, shown to him by a young girl when she breaks ranks to greet and reassure Josh. And it is also Josh's own realization of compassion, first with the class bully, Freddie Waltman, the Jewish kid whose family's deteriorating finances have forced a painful departure from Waldron, and then also Frank, the lonely overweight kid Josh always says he will play with "tomorrow."

Then there's the very different matter of his friend Dave. When he is absent from a school exam, Josh checks on him on the way home from school, and finds him in the midst of an epileptic seizure. Later, much to Josh's surprise, the skeptic Dave interprets Josh's appearance as a mysterious — if not exactly miraculous — rescue, which suggests to Josh that he is on the right track in his quest. The world is stranger, and more wonder-filled, especially on beatific occasions, than Dave had thought, and while his survival, thanks to Josh's appearance, is not proof of God's reality, it raises big questions and validates Josh's line of inquiry. So keep looking, Dave advises.

Josh tells the social outcast Frank that "today is tomorrow."

And finally, in his year-end speech for the sixth grade, Josh confesses to having become "wide awake," putting behind childish things to become aware of exactly how alive the world is with wonder and beauty. Josh is seeing for the first time with the eyes of love, much like his grandfather saw the snow and saw and loved Josh, diving whole into the joyful, multifarious wonder of being. During the length of his speech Josh has a pensive, faraway look on his face. Yet the speech as a whole plays well, winning huge smiles from his new friend, Frank, and an approving warm smile from the stern Sr. Sophia (Camryn Manheim).

Those affirmations pale, however, compared to the sequence that closes the film. The mystery that surrounds Josh's rescue of Dave only seems to push Josh into a mystical magic land, inducting him into a further realm of "wide awakeness." In this last scene, he ventures out into the hall to look for an absent classmate (Sr. Terry has, in fact, miscounted; no one is absent). There Josh encounters the small blond boy who has shown up regularly on the periphery throughout the story, though this is the first time Josh actually talks to him. When he informs the boy that he's missing the class picture, the boy — even smaller than Josh — reports that he's not in Josh's class, news that surprises Josh and prompts him to ask the boy's name. The response that follows is strange indeed: "This is the first time you're seeing me, isn't it?" Not at all, insists Josh, for he sees him all the time. "You're always around, always smiling, and you're always watching me." Still, the small kid pushes the matter: "But this is the first time you've really seen me." And there the conversation would end if not for the boy's cryptic declaration, with dead-serious intensity in his face: "You don't have to worry, he's happy now."

Josh thinks the blond boy is talking about Dave, of course, to which the boy replies that he does not mean Dave. A little spooked, Josh turns to rejoin his class, and then the question dawns in a flash: "You mean Grandpa?" Alas, when he turns to the boy, he is no longer there. After a few seconds of stunned perplexity, Josh breaks into a broad smile as he gets some idea of what the small kid has told him and just who the small kid really is (whatever he is). The voice-over, echoing the film's "I believe in . . ." posture, informs viewers of the plain fact that "not all angels have wings."

The last shot retreats from Josh to take in the golden light pouring in through the windows, bathing the setting in quiet but arresting visual splendor, as befits revelatory appearances of the divine — mimicking, in effect, the kind of light and color that flood a Monet sunset of haystacks in a snowfield. This is the same place where Josh, earlier in the film, first noticed the beauty of the light from the window, which perhaps presented him for the first time with some thirst for a numinous reality, either in beauty or in the divine itself. It is this same light, in fact, that seems to have instigated his quest for certainty about his grandpa. And if there is any doubt about what Shyamalan is up to, at the far end of the long hallway, looming immediately above Josh,

Wonder and light pour in on Josh.

stands a statue of the shepherd Jesus with outstretched arms, seeming to bestow on Josh a dose of divine embrace and blessing. While it is certainly true that "not all angels have wings," it is also true that not all light is mundane and ordinary.

Post-viewing Questions

1. What is the best way to describe what it is that Josh finds? He seems to locate a kind of divine presence amid life, but where and how does it show up? How many different kinds of presence are there?
2. Does Shyamalan favor certain kinds of revelation over others? Or does he simply take what he can get?
3. What is the essence of Josh's relationship with his grandfather? What is it, in short, that Josh most misses about the old fellow?
4. On some occasions Shyamalan uses light and music together rather effectively. What is he trying to express with these? Should we see and hear the world as the director does, or as Josh does?
5. In his strange appearance at the very end, the "missing student" seems to link to different kinds of strangeness that Shyamalan puts front and center in the films that made him famous, such as *The Sixth Sense, Unbreakable,* and *Signs.* How do these varied "signs" relate to one another, and how serious is he about these? Or are they just "entertainments"?

Critical Comments

Most of the reviews of *Wide Awake* were not enthusiastic, though its stature has risen since. Roger Ebert, for example, thought the film fell between the cracks — too somber for small kids and too cute for older ones — and he instead recommended the French film *Ponette* for its "more intelligent treatment of a child asking hard questions about heaven" (*Chicago Sun-Times,* Mar. 27, 1998). On the other hand, while acknowledging an excess of cuteness, Peter Stack of the *San Francisco Chronicle* still liked the film because it had "its heart in the right place, and for many people that's all that really matters" (Mar. 27, 1998). So did another Californian, Kevin Thomas, who found *Wide Awake* to be "a wonderful family film that deals sensitively, and even with humor, with a fairly unusual situation for the screen: a 9-year-old's struggles with his faith in God" (*Los Angeles Times,* Mar. 20, 1998).

Other Notable Films by M. Night Shyamalan

Signs (2002)
Unbreakable (2000)
The Sixth Sense (1999)
Praying with Anger (1992)

III. The New Life:
The Surprise of Love

Against all odds, every once in a while it really does happen, usually quietly but sometimes spectacularly: people without an ounce of goodness or hope left in them do really come upon something new, something dazzling and shimmering, so that they are moved to embrace this something that they had never imagined or dreamt. And the whole process comes as a profound mystery and surprise — and from unlikely sources. Typically, at its core lies one word, a word spoken in whispers, though ever so emphatically: "Love," a gift so bright and ravishing that it changes the very self.

What we are talking about here, of course, is the old Judaeo-Christian notion of *conversion,* which these days has pretty much been associated with revivalist preaching, altar calls, and megachurches, where you can save your sorry soul from judgment, damnation, and eternal torment. The films in this section offer a very different kind of paradigm for what is meant by that old term, and a different means by which a conversion sort of thing happens. Here salvation does not mean saving yourself from something as bad as hellfire, but saving yourself *for* something else entirely, something akin to a new being that embraces and venerates the world in which we all live.

These films work to reinvigorate worn and hackneyed religious terms. For example, one prominent meaning for the term "redemption" is to exchange one thing for another: in this case, evil and darkness for goodness and light. And conversion means not just *seeing the light* but, as the term suggests, changing one thing into another, just as one converts currency when traveling from one country to another.

Something has fundamentally altered. In recent decades American revivalism, shaped by the threats of modernity and American hyper-individualism, has tragically shrunken all these meanings into trite certainties about personal security, wealth, and righteousness.

The assortment of films in this section detail what can happen to a person — the soul or self — when a character moves from the darkness of being lost to an embrace of the Light. Here we look at stories of convicts (twice), a broken-down music star, a mercenary, and even an ornery preacher. The characters chronicled here stumble upon — or are visited by — something quite beyond themselves, something that displays for them a radical love, despite all the momentous harm they have inflicted on others. Finding the palpable reality of a transcendent care, they themselves are pulled into the precincts of love, exchanging their despair and meanness for a realm of "love and delight," as the old Shaker hymn puts it. And having had the good done unto them, they themselves become instruments of love, though imperfect instruments they remain.

Most often this happens with few words: gestures and images are quite enough in these film portrayals to show the depths and fullness of what befalls these assorted villains. Insofar as they "preach," these movies do it by showing rather than telling: they distill the gist of the story by using images that, with the power of the narrative, become iconic and potent portraits of how and where God shows up in this tangled world. Thus do these filmmakers follow the advice of Saint Francis, who argued that instruments of love should preach continually, but use words only when necessary. In our word-bound culture, the poignant absence of words makes these stories all the more powerful.

In a film very few people saw when it was first released, *Tender Mercies* (1983), Robert Duvall plays Mac Sledge, a washed-up and boozed-out country-and-western singer who has the good fortune of landing in the middle of nowhere (west Texas) on the doorstep of a widow who has herself known a dose of sorrow, since she lost her husband in Vietnam and is now a single mother of a fatherless young son. To some extent, not much happens out there on the limitless, sun-baked plains; then again, everything happens — at least the most important stuff. The flow of trouble does not stop, for this life has no good-luck charms, and the real miracle comes in how these folks survive the storm.

The same is true in one of the most popular films ever made, Frank Darabont's *The Shawshank Redemption* (1994), though it did not have great success at the box office. Only when it hit video did word of mouth elevate it to near the top of filmdom's all-time most-popular list. This film, based on a novel by Stephen King and starring Tim Robbins and Morgan Freeman, recounts the story of young Andy Dufresne, a banker convicted of murdering his wife and her lover. The remarkable material comes in what happens to Andy during his many years in Shawshank Penitentiary, where he does ample penance for his crime. Within the prison walls we see some remarkable images — and hear some words, too — that potently define what redemption looks and feels like, though it is a long, dark journey getting there, for both Dufresne and the audience.

Another inmate, one closely modeled on an actual convict who died in the Louisiana electric chair, is Matthew Poncelot, brilliantly played by Sean Penn in Tim Robbins's *Dead Man Walking* (1995), adapted from Sister Helen Prejean's memoir of the same title. Poncelot faces execution for a double homicide when Sister Helen, played by Susan Sarandon in an Oscar-winning performance, signs on to serve as Poncelot's spiritual advisor as he prepares to meet his maker. And while he never leaves death row, the reluctant pilgrim Poncelot travels to a very amazing place, given the no-good, miserable thug he has been for virtually his entire life. Almost as bad is the fictional Rodrigo Mendoza (Robert De Niro), the central character in *The Mission* (1986), a mercenary and slave trader who, deep in guilt and remorse after killing his brother, retreats to a cell to waste away and die. He takes on the daunting penance laid on him by the Jesuit monk Gabriel (Jeremy Irons), an equally fierce warrior, albeit for a different kind of kingdom. Mendoza's penitential pilgrimage takes him to a domain he shares with Matthew Poncelot.

This section ends with another Robert Duvall project, this time one he wrote, directed, and funded — as well as starred in. *The Apostle* (1997) shows us Euliss "Sonny" Dewey, a lifelong Pentecostal preacher who falls into deep trouble that puts him on a path to who-knows-where. To the preacher's great surprise — and ours — he, too, becomes a pilgrim, so much so that he understands, perhaps for the first time, exactly what is at the core of what he has been preaching so sensationally and sincerely for so many decades (he was a child-preacher prodigy).

All these diverse characters, all reluctant pilgrims, go places they never dreamed necessary or possible, where — to their everlasting amazement — a supremely grace-filled and necessary dawning awaits them.

Tender Mercies

Director	Bruce Beresford (Academy Award nomination)
Original Screenplay	Horton Foote (Academy Award winner)
Cinematography	Russell Boyd
Production Design	Jeannine Claudia Oppewall

CAST

Robert Duvall	Mac Sledge (Academy Award winner)
Tess Harper	Rosa Lee
Allan Hubbard	Sonny
Wilfred Brimley	Harry Silver
Betty Buckley	Dixie Scott
Ellen Barkin	Sue Anne

The film itself was nominated for an Academy Award for Best Picture.

Rotten Tomatoes	86
Metacritic	85

- -

General Comments

The premise of this film is not very promising, and surely not very Hollywood. The first sequence gives us a picture of two drunks fighting at night in a motel cabin in the Texas outback. The credits roll as one of the combatants slowly picks himself up off the floor the next morning amid the rubble. For music, such as it is, a country song intones lament about disappointment amid life's hard times. We get the point. Outside, wincing in the bright sunlight on the Texas flatlands (landscape is a major player in this film), flat broke and abandoned by his buddy, Mac Sledge (Robert Duvall) promises the comely young widow who runs the place that he'll work off what he owes her for lodging.

These are not the usual makings of romance. But romance is what happens — that is, at least marriage happens. A scant fifteen minutes into the movie, *Tender Mercies* contains one of strangest marriage proposals ever put on celluloid. And the next scene finds them married. It's pretty clear, though, that whatever this film is about, it's not about romance — at least not of the usual kind. There's Sledge, his new wife, Rosa Lee (Tess Harper), and her eight-year-old son, Sonny (Allan Hubbard). And there's the past. Rosa Lee was first married as a teenager, but her husband has died, mysteriously, in Vietnam, and the son hungers for a father he never knew. And Sledge — well, he really has a past: he's a onetime country music star, both singer and songwriter, and is now the boozed-out former husband of country music's reigning diva, the not-so-nice Dixie Scott (Betty Buckley). The latter has kept Sledge — not without good reason — from contact with their eighteen-year-old daughter, Sue Anne (Ellen Barkin).

This world is as messy as the real one, with lives full of loss, grief, remorse, and plain old loneliness — and hauling around a lot of baggage. They are a little bruised and down-in-the-mouth, neither cheery nor bouncy, but nothing out of the ordinary: like just about everyone, they're creatures of what life has done to them and what they've done to themselves. The latter is particularly true of Sledge, the violent drunk who up till now has drowned his talent, wealth, and family obligations in a bottle.

This is exactly what the Oscar- and Pulitzer-winning screenwriter of *Tender Mercies,* Horton Foote, is so famously good at: displaying the tangled, very ambiguous weight of being alive, never diluting either sorrow or hurt. Very ordinary ragged souls try to find their way on a hard path to their heart's home, a place of contentment and wholeness, though most of the time they have little idea of what that might be — or that it even exists. Foote's screenplay for Steinbeck's *Of Mice and Men* (1992) makes the point well enough, as does *The Trip to Bountiful* (1985). We should not forget to mention Foote's first big success as a screenwriter, the film version of Harper Lee's best-selling novel *To Kill a*

Mac Sledge works off his unpaid bill.

Mockingbird (1962), which is where he first ran into a young actor named Robert Duvall.

The choice of the Australian director Bruce Beresford, who was making his first film in North America, proved marvelously fortuitous for the visual power of the film, something one would not expect from a flat and empty Texas farmscape, a site that film snoots scorned as an unlikely setting for significant lives. (No one scorned it more than *The New Yorker*'s celebrated critic Pauline Kael, who dismissed the film in two brief paragraphs, implying that no one west of the Hudson could actually have a rich, authentic life.) The film bombed at the box office, but when it won five Oscar nominations and two actual Oscars (acting for Duvall and original screenplay for Foote), it hit the marketplace again in the summer of 1984 and probably eventually made some money.

The narrative question, then, hangs on what these strangers will make of each other and the possibility of life together, and by what means they will achieve what they do. And in the Texas outback, of all places.

Things to Look For

- Part of the visual power of *Tender Mercies* comes in its many shots of roads and people traveling roads (spot the funny signs, placed by production designer Jeannine Oppewall, on the Coke machine at the Mariposa hotel and in the bar Sledge visits when he storms off in a huff). They all gather a kind of narrative heft that adds to the weight of the theme and shows the significance of production design.

- The same is true of the landscape on which Beresford shoots the film. His one requirement for the set, for example, was that the motel be located in an isolated place from which no other building could be seen, and this has a powerful effect on the characters and the viewers. One critic has suggested that Beresford was aiming for the same emptiness he had witnessed in his native Australian outback.

- A last part of the visual power lies in the very shape of the motel, which is unlike any other, at least according to Oppewall. There is the central building with the motel's two wings extending diagonally from that main cabin where Rosa Lee and her son live. This design makes a particular kind of visual suggestion that reinforces the story and themes of the film.

- The songs that Duvall sings (and apparently wrote, at least some of them) have a strong presence for both their mood and their lyrics, for they provide some revelation of his soul, as good songs do.

- Mac Sledge is a complex fellow. For example, he doesn't tell his grown daughter that he knows the song that she partly recalls. As soon as she leaves, he stands by the window watching her car drive off and sings it straight through with quiet but intense emotion.

Post-viewing Comments

Tender mercies do happen, and Sledge comes to learn how to accept them: he finds a home, at long last, with other exiles who have known, by no fault of their own, the hard and lasting toll of loss. And the angel who bestows these mercies is Rosa Lee, whose patience, affirmation, and wisdom provide a refuge for Sledge. (The little we see of Dixie Scott makes clear that, whatever problems Sledge brought into their marriage, she must have vastly aggravated them with her strident narcissism.) Or one might ask, given the recurrent imagery in the film, whether this improbable place on the Texas plains might actually be a garden close to Edenic, for the husband and wife seem to have all their most significant encounters while tending that small patch of dirt behind the motel. As they tend it, they tend to one another, even if it is only Rosa Lee listening to Sledge's anguish and doubt after he returns from his daughter's funeral. To his perplexities and questions, she wisely offers up no platitudes or religious sentimentality, since she has been down that same path herself in the wake of her young husband's death. She knows well enough that for some questions there simply are no answers. Indeed, the glass we see through is dim, and nowhere more so than in the midst of disaster and loss.

Perhaps Rosa Lee is the dove of Mac's song, the one his daughter remembers and he sings of quietly at the end of the film: God sends his "pure sweet love" on "the wings of a dove," lyrics that seem to sketch perfectly the gist of the story. In such loving mystery lies the answer to the riddle of the universe for Sledge, and somehow it suffices. After his tortured confession of despair to Rosa Lee in the garden after his daughter's funeral, Sledge's next scene (the film's penultimate one) finds him again by the side of the road — just as he was at the very beginning when he volunteered to work off his bill — this time picking up trash. This is the same road that has repeatedly tempted Sledge to get on and flee. But slowly, during the course of the film, it has become the road that he instead takes to town, to church, to the burial place of his stepson's father, and to the roadhouse where he sings of his debt to

Sledge and Rosa Lee talk over life's woes in their garden.

Rosa Lee, a far bigger one than the lodging bill ("If you'll just hold the ladder, baby, I'll climb right to the top").

Mac's picking up trash is an apt metaphor for how one handles the mess of living, though now he knows mostly gratitude and hope, even in the midst of his own earthquake in his daughter's death. And following that, in a wordless dance of celebration and connectedness, he and son Sonny play football. All the while the camera lovingly lingers on this scene — watching, adoring, embracing — like God's own self: the winter sun soaking the land, the expanse of plains, and the little white motel with its outstretched arms in the background (itself dove-shaped, wings flung out in welcome), holding both man and boy. In one cutaway, the dove-like Rosa Lee watches her two orphans, her son and his new father, revel in their play and one another, just as if they were now rejoicing in the original communion in that first garden.

One mark of a good film is that each repeat viewing rewards, and that is especially true with *Tender Mercies*. The film is full of the delicate orchestration of notes of tragedy, sorrow, hope, loss, and an agapic love. The makers of *Tender Mercies* wrestle with crushing personal tragedies and treat them with precision, tenderness, and honesty. A good deal of the film's considerable power derives from their refusal, first to last, to contrive sentiment or easy answers to the difficult riddles it poses. In fact, the filmmakers seem to go out of their way to respect

Mac and Sonny play football within the arms of the motel
(and the arms of Rosa Lee)

these characters, who have suffered their fair share of hard knocks. Sledge is especially beset by demons; but against all odds, against everything he has come to expect of life, against the emptiness of darkness, he comes upon the waters of tender mercy. On the vast empty plains of Texas, that small white motel of open arms, a pinpoint of light and warmth, shelters the wanderer. What Sledge does find, as much as this earth allows, is consummate Love itself, embraced as he is by the "wings of the dove." Sledge finds not only respite from the storm but a welcome of sufficient kindness that he again finds music in his weary, booze-sodden soul.

Just as the opening shots of Sledge alone under that blank sky almost perfectly convey his real circumstance and its metaphoric existential import, so the film as a whole — narratively, visually, and aurally — almost perfectly realizes his subsequent course. There is throughout the movie a lovely and potent consonance between image and theme, each perfectly representing and catching up the other. His effort — and ours — to know and understand drives the film from beginning to end and explains its starkly elliptical narrative. The storytelling leaves out many of the usual features of Hollywood stories in order to attend to more pressing matters, an approach that drove a number of critics to distraction. But in their own odd way, Foote's story and Beresford's direction make for a measure of visual clarity and expressiveness that is rare in cinema, even though film is, obviously enough, a visual medium in which the image itself provides the simplest and most basic element.

Post-viewing Questions

1. One of the more cryptic incidents in the film is Mac's denial that he knows the song that Sue Anne asks him about. After she leaves, he then watches her car drive away as he sings the song through, word for word. What might explain this strange turn of events?

2. The film takes place on the prairie, clearly enough. And out behind the motel is the garden where Sledge and Rosa Lee have almost all of their significant conversations. How appropriate are these settings, and what might Foote/Beresford be suggesting with them?

3. Foote offers a corrosive picture of Nashville celebrity in the back story of Sledge, with the self-concern of Harry Silver and the nar-

cissism of Dixie Scott. What does it take to correct that cumulative toll in Sledge?

4. Much to everyone's surprise, Duvall won the Academy Award for best actor for *Tender Mercies*. Is his performance that good? What stands out in different phases of his experience in the film? What kind of fellow does he make Mac Sledge into?

5. The religious content of the film is central, though it is not melodramatized or sentimentalized, as is often the case in treatments of religious anything in Hollywood. What language best describes the overall mood and "view" of the film with regard to religious belief?

6. Rosa Lee's religious belief is clearly sincere and deep, while not in the least showy. What is its substance, so far as you can tell, and what is its posture? How does it affect Mac?

Critical Comments

Janet Maslin thought *Tender Mercies* "a small, lovely and somewhat overloaded film about small-town life, loneliness, country music, marriage, divorce and parental love, and it deals with all of these things in equal measure" (*The New York Times*, Mar. 4, 1983). That echoed the favorable assessment of many critics. On the other hand, Pauline Kael, of *The New Yorker*, scorned it entirely in her presumption that only people east of the Hudson live significant lives. Writing about the re-release of the DVD in 2009, Roger Ebert praised the minimalism of writer Horton Foote and director Bruce Beresford. "When interesting people have little to say, we watch the body language, listen to the notes in their voices. Rarely does a movie elaborate less and explain more than *Tender Mercies*" (*Chicago Sun-Times*, June 11, 2009). No one has had higher praise for the film than the writer "DA" in *The Time Out Film Guide*, who notes that *Tender Mercies* "bears more resemblance to, say, the filmmaker Wenders (or even, at a stretch, Ozu) than to commercial Hollywood, though it grips from start to finish. Beautiful" (Timeout.com).

Notable Films About American Forms of Music

Crazy Heart (2009)
Cadillac Records (2008)
Walk the Line (2005)
Songcatcher (2000)
Honkytonk Man (1982)
The Buddy Holly Story (1978)
Bound for Glory (1976)

The Shawshank Redemption

Director	Frank Darabont
Writers	Stephen King ("Rita Hayworth and the Shawshank Redemption") and Frank Darabont (Academy Award nomination for Best Screen Adaptation)
Cinematography	Roger Deakins (Academy Award nomination)
Production Design	Terence Marsh

The film itself won an Academy Award nomination for Best Picture.

CAST

Tim Robbins	Andy Dufresne
Morgan Freeman	Ellis "Red" Redding (Academy Award nomination)
James Whitmore	Brooks Hatlen
Bob Gunton	Warden Norton

Rotten Tomatoes	88
Metacritic	80

- -

General Comments

He's a fancy young banker, dapper, calm, confident, and self-contained, and the state of Maine has sentenced him to life in prison for the murder of his lovely wife. So Andy Dufresne (Tim Robbins) goes to the Shawshank Penitentiary. From the opening sequences in the film, and from his own witness-stand testimony, it certainly looks like he did commit the murder — and that life in the hellhole of Shawshank is exactly what he deserves. And it is here that he will get an education — though he is already well educated — such as he never dreamed possible or necessary. And here he will also find redemption, as the title suggests, though of a kind he never imagined. Apparently reviewers couldn't imagine it either, because many of them expressed perplexity about the meaning of the title.

The back story of *The Shawshank Redemption* (1994) has some surprises. The screenplay came from a novella by best-selling horror writer Stephen King, "Rita Hayworth and the Shawshank Redemption," though the story first appeared under a pseudonym and had none of King's usual horror aspects. King and Frank Darabont became friends when King read a draft of the screenplay by the then largely unknown writer-director Darabont, though he knew of Darabont from correspondence and Darabont's work as director of an episode in the 1980s *Night Shift* television series. After *The Shawshank Redemption,* Darabont made another of King's novellas, "The Green Mile," into a movie, this one starring Tom Hanks (who reportedly turned down the role of Andy in *Shawshank* because of a schedule conflict).

Even more surprising, perhaps, was the odd public reception of *The Shawshank Redemption.* The reviews were generally not good,

The dapper young banker Andy Dufresne testifies at his murder trial

and the box office was worse. Then, oddly, the video release became the top rental of the year, partly by word of mouth and perhaps partly because it was nominated for seven Academy Awards, and it has remained a favorite of movie watchers ever since. The Internet Movie Database voters ranked it as their all-time favorite, even outdoing *The Godfather* juggernaut (second place). Among students it remains a passionate favorite, and many recite an array of favorite lines. Indeed, the film has some eminently quotable lines that for some seem to provide maxims for approaching life itself (e.g., "Get busy living, or get busy dying").

Some reviewers complained about the title, especially the reference to "redemption." First of all, they didn't understand the notion of redemption right from the get-go. And the secularity of many reviewers is so profound that the movies form a sort of substitute church, full of wisdom, happy endings, and dazzle. Second, many reviewers just could not see how redemption showed up in the film. The same can also be said of many viewers, even though they know and enjoy the film inside and out, and they both grieve and joy in the film's climactic sequences. In a way, that kind of tone-deafness amounts to missing the proverbial forest for the trees.

While *The Shawshank Redemption* is soaked in an uncomfortable realism — its language and violence graphic and abusive in the extreme — be forewarned! — the story is also deeply metaphorical. Andy Dufresne does not go so much to prison as to hell itself, or at best purgatory, where even the seeming good guys, such as the professedly Christian warden, are thoroughgoing sadists who take pleasure in their power and abuse. Warden Norton (Bob Gunton) tells new arrivals to "put your faith in God because I got your ass." And the bad guys are rapacious, evil, and devouring ("the sisters," for example, not to mention the guards). In short, the story of Andy Dufresne is steeped in a violence that is typical of prisons, all vividly depicted, and we at least see what he suffers and why anyone would want to escape from that world. Fortunately, Darabont does not dwell on its horror.

The question of redemption is further complicated by the fact that the one person who seems to need it least is Andy Dufresne, who in this harsh world is invariably polite, calm, and hopeful. Of all the different kinds of people in Shawshank, including the guards and the warden, Dufresne stands apart, detached and enigmatic, as above the fray, a faint smile always playing on his face. Dufresne possesses a rich inner

Shawshank Penitentiary: a few acres of hell

life and even an inner kind of freedom, taking joy in simple pleasures like his recollections of Mozart and the carving of chess figures.

But redemption is necessary and does happen, and the film is unambiguous — indeed, insistent — about this, especially in the way Darabont scripts and shoots crucial sequences. Fittingly, exultation follows, both for Dufresne and the audience, though viewers apparently never quite nail down exactly why. And it continues on in the history of Andy's bosom friend, Red (brilliantly played by Morgan Freeman) right on to the last frames of the film (which were added after a previewed final cut seemed to leave the story incomplete).

So the questions are: Who needs redemption? From what and why? And what does redemption look like and provide when it comes? And while Darabont is justifiably tough on the representatives of organized religion, such as Warden Norton, he seems to have a clear fix on the necessity for it and for what goes on within.

Things to Look For

- The actual prison, formerly the Ohio State Reformatory, now abandoned (though open for tours), is located in Mansfield, Ohio. The interiors were reconstructed at a remote location, and they play a huge role in the effectiveness even before the first events happen within its walls.

- Lighting and palette are closely controlled in the film to create particular kinds of effects, and here we have the cinematography of Roger Deakens, one of Hollywood's masters of the craft.
- Darabont's portrayal of Shawshank's warden, a self-proclaimed devout Christian, is not one of a pleasant or good person. Does this make the film a pronouncedly antireligious movie?
- A lot of critics liked neither the term "Shawshank" nor the notion of "redemption," which they did not see as a concept operating in the film. It's true that the word never shows up in the script. This means that, if it is there in the film, it must come about by other means.
- And narratively speaking, the pivotal event in the film follows what kind of recognition for Andy, something that is new for him?

Post-viewing Comments

In the midst of a tremendous thunder storm, Andy finally enters his pinup-covered tunnel exit (remember, the title of Stephen King's novella is "Rita Hayworth and the Shawshank Redemption"). He then crawls down the long, airless penitential sewer of feces, gagging and retching along the way, nearly passing out from it all. It surely makes for bold, unforgettable filmmaking, especially with the voice-over commentary of his friend Red. And what follows pretty much speaks for itself, words in this case being quite beside the point. At last Andy spills out the far end of the sewer amid flashing light and pouring rain, and there in that stream he is washed clean of filth and its moral symbolic counterpart, the evil he himself has done. Yes, despite his apparent virtuousness and calm, he is also evil, as he belatedly realizes. He has escaped and is free at last, to be sure, and things will be put right. Andy has very neatly arranged for that: the stinking foulness of life in Shawshank Penitentiary will be exposed and cleaned, and those responsible for that hell will be made accountable. However, that is hardly the whole of it, or even the heart of it.

Out there in plain sight, though usually glossed over by viewers who are mostly interested in what happens next, is the fact — as Andy comes to realize after his nearly two decades in Shawshank Prison —

Andy stands — exultant, clean, and free — in the waters of Shawshank Creek

that he is guilty, that he, in effect, killed his wife. In his long dark night alone in the depths of his soul, which is all one has left during months in the dark blankness of solitary confinement, Andy realizes that his own coldness, his aloofness, insulated as he was in his well-furnished mental world of Mozart and others, drove his young wife into the arms of another. While very much in love with his wife, he nonetheless understood her hardly at all, especially her emotional needs, which the young Andy had difficulty understanding. So self-contained, content, and sealed off was he that that he had difficulty understanding *need* in others. At least that is the gist of Darabont's portrayal, an accent that is much sharper in the film than in King's novella.

And it is only then, after this pivotal recognition of his own culpability, his own very real guilt, that Andy moves to escape. Now he has attained the inner freedom that comes only after self-knowledge, remorse, and finally confession (to Red). The success of the escape and the righting of wrong signifies absolution, a telling forgiveness from some transcosmic powers that be. Only after all of that is Andy suited for freedom, both physically and spiritually. Oddly, his lifelong insularity — what some might call self-reliance — is the very trait that has allowed him to survive life in Shawshank. He is certainly smart enough, and that has given him a certain guile and savvy that brings him friends, as in the roof-tarring incident.

There is also something else. When he emerges from his first stint in solitary confinement, he confesses that his time was not "hard" because he had with him "Mr. Mozart," a composer whose music not only diverts him but brings him, he implies, both joy and hope. That has made for a peculiar kind of inner freedom, so that the years in prison do not rob him of hope. That's the thing he tries to impart to others when he plays the soaring theme from Mozart's *Marriage of Figaro* over the prison public address system. Red finds it difficult to put into words, though his fumbling amounts to some of the finest writing in the film: "I have no idea to this day what those two Italian ladies were singing about. Truth is that I don't want to know. Some things are best left unsaid. I like to think they were singing about something so beautiful it can't be expressed in words and makes your heart ache because of it. I tell you those voices soared, higher and farther than anybody in a gray place dares to dream. It was like some beautiful bird flapped into our cage and made those walls dissolve away. And for the briefest of moments, every last man in Shawshank felt free." Beauty does indeed elate and transfigure, and art brings others into the world as the artist has experienced it.

Beauty alone, though, does not suffice, and that is what Andy Dufresne learns. In his former life he had, in effect, forsaken personal intimacy, something that goes far deeper than the rituals of romance. Now he has finally come to recognize the sacredness of human rela-

Red and others stand in wonder as they listen to Mozart.

115

tionship. The chief indication of that, fast on the heels of his confession to Red, is his extending to Red the choice of freedom, giving him the means to flee, not Shawshank Prison, for Red is out of there, but the withering of the self that Shawshank has accomplished. He tells Red that when he gets out of Shawshank, he should look under a tree at the end of a rock fence in a field near a particular Maine town. Of course, Red thinks he will never get out, and he cannot imagine — nor can the viewers — what might possibly lie in such an out-of-the-way spot. But there, after the great escape by Andy, comes the second great surprise in the film. Red will find a box full of money and an invitation to join Andy, his dear friend, in the faraway Mexican seaside village with that exotic name. It is no coincidence that that box is buried under the tree where Andy and his dead wife first made love, a fitting memorial of the human consideration Andy had so neglected throughout his life. That Andy would choose to bury the box there, and bother to do it amid the hurry of his escape, says much about the new lessons he has learned about what counts in life.

That last gesture constitutes the fullness of Andy Dufresne's redemption. It is not only the recognition and remorse for past coldness but the move to cultivate the fullness of relationship: as the story plainly suggests, that is not confined to romance and marriage but pervades the whole of human relationships. It suggests, in that remarkable closing sequence on the beach, that this kind of mutual trust and delight in one another constitutes the very end for which people were made in the first place, way back there in Eden, as the biblical account makes clear. The best thing to happen to Andy (and Red) is that one very big thing that redemption is for.

In the end, *The Shawshank Redemption* goes beyond narrative excitements and suspense — no small accomplishment — to a depth that earns it that enigmatic title. A remarkable man in just about every way — smart, brave, beauty-loving, resilient, hopeful, kindly, and yet stone-cold ignorant and self-contained — Dufresne has contentedly lived at a remove from deep connection with other humans, what Nathaniel Hawthorne called "the magnetic chain of humanity." Andy has attributed his long time in prison to a fearsome "storm" of bad luck that has blighted his life. That may be true, but there is also the sense that his time in prison is, given his coldness, a necessary penitential rite that takes him to an inner place where he can recognize his own transgression and at the same time see the depth of mature agapic love, which

The fullness of redemption displays as Andy and Red
reunite on the beach in Mexico.

he bestows on his friend Red. In the "making of" documentary that is
part of the DVD package, Morgan Freeman even suggests that prison
was the best thing that ever happened to Andy.

A few have suggested that Dufresne, being so good in many ways,
must be some kind of Christ figure. But that simply won't wash, because all along *he* is the one in need of redemption, and the suffering
and sacrifice that he undertakes seems mostly self-inflicted from his
own profound error. Furthermore, what hope he has is mostly for the
liberation of the self, and no matter how much he enjoys the beauty of
the earth, he has yet to learn to love people. That in itself bars him from
sainthood. What he is, though, is that most common of all types: the
pilgrim, the benighted soul thirsting and stumbling his way with hope
toward freedom and an embracing of life. The great surprise for him,
though he is religious and self-assured, is guilt, specifically guilt about
his failure to love and venerate other people, the lesson he belatedly
absorbs as it becomes manifest in his tender and trusting relationship
with the most unlikely of people, an ill-educated confessed murderer
and black man named Red.

Post-viewing Questions

1. Andy confesses his great love of beauty, especially when it comes to Mozart. The film treats that twice. Are there other instances in which viewers can observe Andy's rather unconventional love of different kinds of beauty?

2. The interior design of the prison, lighting, and palette all contribute to the darkness and fierceness of prison life (and even the souls of those who live there). Maybe a picture is worth ten thousand words. How significant are these different elements in creating the "experience" of the film?

3. On rare occasions the camera goes "airborne" for downward-looking shots. However, Darabont is stingy with those shots and saves them for special occasions. Where do they come, and what do those shots seem to signal?

4. Andy seems to be guilty of what the great American novelist and moralist Nathaniel Hawthorne called "the violation of the human heart." In what ways is that true? That certainly applies to what he belatedly recognizes about his marriage. But are there other instances where he overlooks obligations to others? And how does this relate to the fear prisoners have of being released? For all of its horrors, does life in prison also seem to have some benefits?

5. The relationship between Andy and Red becomes profound, though there is much they do not understand about each other. In a way, the narrative of the novel is Red's own way of trying to figure out that relationship. Perhaps that only becomes fully clear in the last sequence in the film, wordless and fittingly panoramic, as Red walks down the beach to discover Andy sanding his wreck of a boat. This sequence was shot and added after reactions to a sneak preview of the movie. What would it have lost without it?

Critical Comments

The mystery has always been what turned this relative box-office flop into one of the most popular films ever. Peter Travers has cited the "no-bull performances that hold back the flood of banalities," crediting Robbins and Freeman for connecting "with the bruised souls of Andy and Red to create something undeniably powerful and moving"

(*Rolling Stone,* Apr. 18, 2001). Noted online critic James Berardinelli pointed to *Shawshank's* uniqueness in going beyond "the violence and hopelessness of a life behind bars" to finally being a film "about hope and, because of that, watching it is both uplifting and cathartic" (*Reelviews.net,* Jan. 1, 2000). Janet Maslin perhaps comes closest to recognizing its great popular appeal when she locates the film's success in writer-director Darabont's restraint of "loving care" in the storytelling, one that forgoes the usual prison violence for "a slow, gentle story of camaraderie and growth, with an ending that abruptly finds poetic justice in what has come before" (*The New York Times,* Sept. 23, 1994).

Other Notable Films Starring Morgan Freeman

Invictus (2009)
Million Dollar Baby (2004)
Unforgiven (1992)
Driving Miss Daisy (1989)

Other Notable Films Starring Tim Robbins

Mystic River (2003)
The Player (1992)
Bull Durham (1988)

Dead Man Walking

Director	Tim Robbins
Screenplay	Tim Robbins
Book	Helen Prejean
Cinematography	Roger Deakins
Original Music	David Robbins

CAST

Susan Sarandon	Sister Helen Prejean (Academy Award winner)
Sean Penn	Matthew Poncelot
Raymond J. Berry	Earl Delacroix
R. Lee Ermey	Clyde Percy
Celia Weston	Mary Beth Percy
Robert Prosky	Hilton Barber

Metacritic	80
Rotten Tomatoes	94

- -

General Comments

Something big at the heart of the movie *Dead Man Walking* (1995) was certainly unexpected. Most everyone out there — conservatives and liberals alike, film buffs and film naifs — expected that a film by Tim Robbins on Helen Prejean's well-known memoir of the same name about her experience of the death penalty would turn out to be a maudlin lefty screed against capital punishment. But the film version most certainly is not that. Prejean herself was surprised by the route Robbins took in the film, and she tried hard — as the film's technical advisor, virtually sitting at Robbins's elbow as he wrote — to steer the film in a direction more akin to her own very pronounced opposition to the death penalty.

Writer-director Robbins (an Oscar-winning actor in Clint Eastwood's *Mystic River*) arrived at the movie version of *Dead Man Walking* via a strange path. Helen Prejean published the book *Dead Man Walking* in 1994, to admiring reviews; while the book fell short of being a bestseller, its readership grew by word of mouth. A friend of the celebrated actress Susan Sarandon gave her the book, and she was so enthusiastic about it that she pushed it on her domestic partner, Tim Robbins. Somewhere along the line, the idea of doing a film version came up. Robbins had written and directed only once before, the deft political satire *Bob Roberts* (1992), and he did so again in 1999 with *The Cradle Will Rock*.

Dead Man Walking, though, is the master work. Robbins writes and directs with surprising dead-serious passion, precision, ingenuity, and restraint, ending up with an emotionally and intellectually harrowing journey into the darkness of violent death, whether by homicide or state execution. And he does not diminish either one to fit a convenient political position. Fortunately, the film entirely lacks the formulaic melodrama of Hollywood's long-profitable death penalty genre, wherein innocent people die or are absolved in the last minutes before execution (for recent examples, see *The Green Mile* [1999], *True Crime* [1999], and *The Life of David Gale* [2003]). In stark contrast, *Dead Man Walking* offers an unsentimental, straight-on look at the grim realities of murder and execution, crime and jurisprudence, murderers and victims, and punishment and justice.

This is not a pulp movie. For one thing, Robbins looks hard and long at a murderer, at his crimes of torture, rape, and double homicide, and, not least, at the ravaged families of his two teenage victims. Indeed, the screenplay seems yanked from hearts and headlines, and the film yanks viewers from one side to another, pro and con, over and over. Regardless of where one stands on the death penalty, *Dead Man Walking* will at least for a time bring that opinion into serious consideration of what the other side contends about the death penalty. For efficiency, Robbins compacts the stories of the first two death-row inmates whom Prejean advised, combining the crime of Patrick Sonnier (and his brother) and the personality of Robert Lee Willie and folding them into the film's Matthew Poncelot (played magnificently by Sean Penn). In fact, quite apart from the acting, Penn is a dead ringer for Willie, with his rakish goatee, pompadour, and sideburns. (Robbins wrote the screenplay with Penn in mind for the role.)

And Robbins holds little back. Poncelot is repulsive, and guilty as sin: he is a predator, both sexual and racial, nasty and mean, not at all easy to like, pity, or sympathize with about his death sentence. As one of the victims' parents tells the novice spiritual advisor (Prejean), "This is a very evil man," and before very long viewers begin to share that opinion. And that same blunt honesty characterizes Robbins's portrayal of the parents of the dead: one father is hungry for revenge, and another is bewildered and adrift. Watching these people subverts the old pious notion that suffering softens and ennobles. As for Prejean herself, played quietly by Sarandon in her Oscar-winning role (and appearing on screen without makeup for the first time), she ventures into the alien land of death row, naïve but gutsy, far from the supports of the cloister and her affluent upbringing. Bringing a cross, so to speak, to a modern techno-Golgotha of bars and needles (the two inmates Prejean worked with were electrocuted, but filmmakers thought this too graphic to put on the screen) sets off all kinds of alarms — literal and existential.

The tough-guy prettiness of Matthew Poncelot

Helen Prejean's cross sets off the metal detector as she enters Angola Prison.

This was a destination that Prejean never thought she'd end up in, though she was indeed game for a life of sacrifice as demanded by her commitments to Christianity and the vision of the Roman Catholic religious order she joined as a teenager. At the beginning of the film she lives and works in the projects in Baton Rouge, Louisiana. One of her co-workers on her day job, which is teaching literacy to adults, asks her to become a pen pal to a death-row inmate, Matthew Poncelot. That correspondence leads to a visit to Poncelot, and from there Prejean becomes, as his execution approaches — and to her great surprise — his spiritual advisor. This means that she may, if she chooses, accompany him to his death. This is no easy route, for women do not typically serve in such roles, and in opting to do so she runs smack into the resistance of the very old-school Catholic chaplain at the prison. But that's the least of her problems, for an even more formidable problem is Poncelot himself, a very problematic human being indeed. First of all, there's never any doubt that Poncelot participated in the crimes for which he is incarcerated. This he readily admits; but he contends that he did not kill either of the victims, a pair of teenage sweethearts whom he and his buddy abducted, violated, and executed. Throughout the film, in very brief black-and-white interludes, Prejean will try to make his story jibe with the evidence of the graphic police reports to which she has access. And while Poncelot is amiable, even jaunty, it quickly becomes clear that the individual Prejean is to advise religiously is a natural-born liar, a very obnoxious egotist, and a monstrously malicious person — all of which is portrayed in the film in a bluntly honest way.

A bigger jolt for her — and for the audience — comes when she enters the worlds of the victims' parents, who are played with wrenching honesty. Again, Prejean has much to learn about them and about herself, and that journey is in many ways as arduous as the one she'll take down death row. If she travels with Poncelot to his death, she begins here with the agonizing deaths and at the graves of the teenagers who were horrifically brutalized and coldly murdered with a kind of psychopathic glee.

The story, then, is very much about crime and punishment. But perhaps in its biggest surprise, *Dead Man Walking* is about something more that far transcends the specific debates about adequate and just means of punishment. Almost all of the central characters — Prejean, Poncelot, and the parents — travel to unexpected places, and the film offers a heartfelt rendition of the most difficult and most necessary journey of all, one that first startles and then demands that all viewers, in their sympathy and sorrow, undertake it. If you can, find where the light shines in this labyrinth of suffering and grief, for Robbins wants everyone to wrestle with it.

Things to Look For

- Look for the "look" of the characters: Robbins uses a kind of shorthand to tell viewers a lot about who they are. Sean Penn bears a striking resemblance to the actual Robert Lee Willie, the character on whom his personality is based. Susan Sarandon goes on screen for the first time ever without makeup of any kind.
- The prison setting literally allows for very little space. Look for the ingenious means that Robbins and celebrated cinematographer Roger Deakins used to demonstrate the growing trust between Poncelot and Prejean. This involves both production design and where Robbins places the camera.
- Throughout the film Prejean tries to envision Poncelot's actual crime, as she tries to decipher the difference between the police reports and what Poncelot tells her. That motif carries through all the way into the execution sequence. Look for Robbins's exten-

sion of this strategy to ease viewers into some of the film's most surprising "revelations."

- A useful question throughout the film is what this film is really about, though it is, to be sure, set within the context of questions about capital punishment.
- Prejean's conflict with the official Roman Catholic chaplain at Angola Prison adds drama to the story; but it also dramatizes two starkly opposed views of what constitutes "salvation," an issue that replays in her discussions with Poncelot. Far from filler, these point to central disputes in the history of Christianity.

Post-viewing Comments

Like the thief on the cross, Poncelot both loses and wins, giving up his evil earthly life to find a greater life or, as Poncelot puts it in his last minutes, "die in order to find love." That is what he ultimately realizes when he arrives at his dire end. More than simply "home free" — escaping hellfire because he simply believes in Jesus, as Poncelot puts it at one point — he enters into a fullness of redemption, reckoning with his guilt and in his last words seeking forgiveness from the parents who witness his execution. As Prejean tells him in her words of absolution, he becomes "a child of God," though that term is indeed hard for us to swallow, given what we've learned about him. Theologically, though, it is as true as it was for the thief on the cross with Jesus: in such moments, illumination and change happen. "God is even here, Christ is even here," says Prejean — maybe especially here. Knowing what we do of Poncelot's cruelty and pretense, that's a hard proposition, for surely Poncelot seems very undeserving of deliverance. But that, after all, is a central point and purpose of the Christian gospel that Prejean has brought him. It is toward remorse and reconciliation that Prejean has pushed him, insistently challenging his expedient notions of what belief will do for him, namely, keep his pathetic self from hellfire. Running to Jesus, she tells him, is more than a get-out-of-hell-free card.

That destiny, though, has nothing to do with the death penalty, and if in the end Poncelot seems like a redeemable human being, he still must die, at least according to the state of Louisiana. And here, concerning the question of the morality of the death penalty, Robbins greatly complicates the matter, just as he regularly has throughout the film. For one thing, Robbins displays at length the multiple kinds of rottenness that Poncelot is: an arrogant, narcissistic racist and sexual predator. So it's simply very difficult, through most of the film, to muster much sympathy for this fellow. But even more than that, the portrayal of Poncelot seems intended to subvert liberal portraits of "oppressed" felons who are as much victims as those they maim and kill. A glimpse at the afterlives of the wrecked, grieving parents, whom Poncelot has taunted, only adds to viewer horror at what Poncelot did in pursuit of having some "fun." Indeed, as he awaits execution, he seems finally to be getting exactly what he has coming to him. As he is lying on the lethal-injection table, Robbins cuts between Poncelot and his crimes, graphically cast in their hideousness, suggesting by this visual means some just and proper sort of equivalency. This is especially true when the faces of the dead teens peer down on the corpse that was Poncelot. An eye for an eye — it seems only right.

At the same time, remarkably, Robbins manages by the end of the film to elicit a measure of sympathy for Poncelot. When the audience gets to know him, it becomes quite clear that in many ways he has never had much of a break. His old man took him drinking when he was twelve, which did not do much, needless to say, for his moral education. Furthermore, Poncelot belongs to a vast underclass of poor white people whose "advantages" — economically, culturally, or legally — are no greater than those of countless African-American inmates. As the activ-

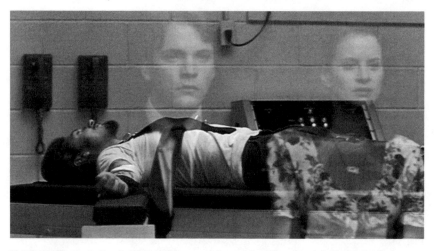

Matthew Poncelot's victims loom over him as he dies from lethal injection.

ist and historian Will D. Campbell has argued, the great irony of the American South has been the extent to which these two groups have been brought to see each other as the enemy. Tragically, that conflict has ensured the perpetuation of an exploitative economic power structure that is more than happy to let both groups see one another as the problem instead of seeing those who run the show as the problem.

In very affecting human terms, Matthew Poncelot is part of a family that loves him, and he clearly loves them. Except for his enormous trouble-making, he has been a decent enough brother and son. And how easily Poncelot might have been better appears in his relationship with Prejean, who steadily prods him to "take responsibility," as she puts it, for what he has done. This he evades for multiple reasons, and only as he finally sits in his death-row cell minutes from execution, does he confess, amid tears and fear, that he killed Walter Delacroix. And Prejean, in effect playing the role of priest, offers him absolution and welcome into God's enduring domain of penitence and love. This now seems genuine: it is certainly a step beyond the self-interested "save-me-from-hellfire" salvation Poncelot was angling for earlier in the film. This seems more like redemption, and everything that term means: it replaces Poncelot's vitriol and bitterness with a genuine remorse for the world of sorrow he has caused the victims' parents. At last Poncelot stumbles on care: Prejean's insistent care for him and his soul and his own care for someone beyond his own family. This constitutes a crucial step in the movement of redemption to full-fledged reconciliation.

Nor does Robbins stop there — at what seems to be the logical end of the story. Rather, he goes on chronicling the movement of reconciliation from graveside ritual to the film's wordless but eloquent last scene, in which we see Prejean and the father of one of the victims praying together in an empty country church. The task for the bereft father is to arrive at the same place of love that Poncelot found, a realm of reconciliation that is the fruition of redemption and love. The context for this story is, of course, the death penalty, and on that Robbins gives no answers. Who can give answers? he seems to ask. But what is clear is the stark reality that redemptive love goes to the damnedest places, a reality that seems to supersede thorny questions on the death penalty. In Poncelot's case that reality — the very hound of heaven — is compelling and bright, thanks to Prejean. Robbins finally seems less interested in resolving the irresolvable than he is in rendering an honest portrayal of woe, sorrow, hatred, and, finally, the territory of joy that lies beyond. Light does shine in the darkness.

Post-viewing Questions

1. With the last sequences in the film, the funeral and Delacroix and Prejean praying in that rural chapel, Robbins pushes the film far beyond the question of the rightness or wrongness of the death penalty. What is the point of these last shots?

2. Periodically throughout the film, Robbins supplies, in black-and-white inserts, Prejean's attempts to understand Poncelot's guilt as she reads crime files and tries to imagine the actual crime (with Poncelot asserting his innocence throughout). These prepare viewers for seeing the actual crime as it is intercut with the execution sequence. At the end of that, as Poncelot dies, close-ups of two other faces appear on the screen. Who are they, and what is the effect of their carefully timed appearance?

3. Poncelot seems to find God, as unlikely as it may seem. The bigger matter is: What is the nature of the God he finds? Prejean has been pushing on him a particular conception of God that is opposed to the one offered by the prison chaplain, Fr. Farley. Choose two or three words that would best describe these different concepts of divinity.

Critical Comments

Critics expected Robbins's film, given his political leanings, to be a blatant indictment of capital punishment. And some, like Janet Maslin (*The New York Times,* Dec. 29, 1995), found the film "at times too speechy in tackling these issues." But she also praised the acting and direction for being "graceful and finally devastating." Some notable critics did pick up — and celebrate — the film's religious seriousness. Maslin, for example, notes that "Poncelet undergoes some extraordinarily well-evoked changes, to the point at which the audience must ultimately adopt Sister Helen's view of him" that is informed by a "Christian generosity" that is evident "in practice as well as in principle." Roger Ebert loved the movie, calling particular attention to the fact that, while "critics have asked for more films that deal with the spiritual side of life," he doubts that *Dead Man Walking* was what they were thinking of, but that this "is exactly how such a movie looks, and feels" (*Chicago Sun-Times,* Jan. 12, 1996). Gary Kamiya of *Salon* comes perhaps closest to the film's core in seeing it as "a kind of ethical laboratory" wherein "Robbins refuses to load the dice." In the end, for Kamiya, "this is a story about redemption — a secularized version of Christ's passion. In its piercing spiritual simplicity, *Dead Man Walking* recalls Dickens, the great artist of spiritual regeneration" (Jan. 27, 1996).

Other Films About the Death Penalty

The Green Mile (1999), based on a Stephen King novel (and full of Kingesque elements), adapted and directed by Frank Darabont *(The Shawshank Redemption).*

The Life of David Gale (2003), a turgid melodrama of murder and death penalty gymnastics starring Kevin Spacey and Kate Winslett. Rarely does any film get so low a rating as this on Rotten Tomatoes, a mere 20 percent.

True Crime (1999), another melodrama, much like *David Gale,* in which a reporter tries to save the life of a wrongly convicted man.

I Want to Live (1958), directed by Robert Wise, a Susan Hayward vehicle about a woman framed for murder.

The Mission

Producer	David Puttnam
Screenplay	Robert Bolt
Director	Roland Joffé (Academy Award nomination)
Cinematographer	Chris Menges (Academy Award winner)
Music	Ennio Morricone (Academy Award nomination)

The film itself received an Academy Award nomination for Best Picture.

CAST

Robert De Niro	Rodrigo Mendoza
Jeremy Irons	Father Gabriel
Ray McAnally	Cardinal Altamirano
Ronald Pickup	Hontar
Chuck Low	Cabeza
Liam Neeson	Brother Fielding

Rotten Tomatoes	65

- -

General Comments

What a story! Geopolitical intrigue (eighteenth-century style), priests and indigenous peoples and slavers and mercenaries all mixed in a brew of fratricide, betrayal, martyrdom, and most of all, love — a profound and expansive love mediated by titanic but flawed souls. In the first shots

130

we see Cardinal Altamirano (Ray McAnally) absorbed in the delicate task of writing to inform his boss, the pope himself, of the fate of his diplomatic mission to South America to mediate a territorial dispute between Portugal, Spain, and a bunch of blessedly ornery Jesuits. Even though the stakes are high — economically as well as geopolitically and morally — especially in terms of a potential slave trade, this plot certainly does not sound like a hopeful premise. And it would not be if it were not for — much to the cardinal's (and our own) utter consternation — the many startling people he runs across on this relatively obscure diplomatic mission. There is even some question of whether the results of his mission have been precooked, the outcome predetermined, and the trip itself a sham to give everyone political cover.

The historical, geographical, and dramatic tours make for quite a ride. Much of the credit for the film's success — and courage — goes to British producer David Puttnam, who brought exceptionally powerful projects to the screen over the years, notably *Midnight Express* (1978), *Chariots of Fire* (1981), *Local Hero* (1983), and *The Killing Fields* (1984). But *The Mission* (1986) stands out among these in multiple ways, especially in its acting and in the depth and complexity of its story. One also needs to wonder whether Puttnam may have undertaken a good deal of the direction of *The Mission,* given the ham-handedness of director Roland Joffé in his later, not very successful, career — including such disasters as *City of Joy* (1992) and *The Scarlet Letter* (1995). That speculation is only further bolstered by Joffé's muddled audio commentary on the 2000 "collector's edition" of the film: the "making of" featurette in that two-disc set confirms the impression, because in it Puttnam seems as involved in the envisioning and actual shooting as was Joffé.

The film was shot deep in the jungles of Paraguay, Brazil, Argentina, and Colombia in a sublime landscape that matches the momentousness of its story. What stands out in that landscape, of course, is Iguazú Falls, a stupendous expanse of waterfalls on the border between Brazil and Argentina (it is rewarding to Google that site). The falls show up right away in the second sequence of the film, and thereafter regularly provide a haunting grandeur that fittingly envelops the story itself. Some people go over the falls, and some climb them, but always the falls are there as an almost insurmountable physical and spiritual reality. Both ascent and descent are perilous. Rarely has a natural setting of any kind been used to such powerful dramatic and thematic effect as it is here in *The Mission.* All of this is brilliantly filmed by British-born cinematographer Chris Menges in his Oscar-winning endeavor. It is stunning camera work that does full justice to its spectacular setting and its powerful display of the extremes of human emotion and fate.

Of equal power for the film is the arresting musical score of Ennio Morricone, one of cinema's great composers, first known for his haunting work on Sergio Leone's "spaghetti westerns," which starred Clint Eastwood in the 1960s. With nearly five hundred projects under his belt, and five nominations for best score from the Academy (though he never won), Morricone was given a lifetime achievement award in 2007, when he was seventy-nine. His score for *The Mission* stands out for its significant contribution to representing the thematic heart of the action, alternating between moments achingly delicate and lilting and others wildly percussive and driving. So apt and haunting is the music that it seems to become an individual presence all its own, another character with particular life and vitality. Most of all, it goes a long way toward furnishing an arresting moral and religious passion and clarity to an arduous tale.

All of this rests on the remarkable original screenplay by Robert Bolt, a two-time Oscar winner and the writer behind many of the eminent British film spectacles of the 1960s: *Lawrence of Arabia* in 1962, *Doctor Zhivago* in 1965, *A Man for All Seasons* in 1966, and culminating in *Ryan's Daughter* in 1970. Bolt's film-writing career went quiet for fifteen years, until he wrote the screenplay for *The Mission*. A troubled and enigmatic figure, Bolt made something of a mess of his own life; but he was able, perhaps because of that messiness, to distill in events and words the depths and the heights of moral and spiritual experience.

Father Gabriel climbs the perilous falls to risk martyrdom.

On the banks above the remote Iguazú Falls, then, transpires a kind of combat for land, power, and — ever so dauntingly — souls. And a fierce contest ensues, first, for one rapacious soul, and, second, over what that redemption means when it runs up against geopolitical might. The story is bathed in amazing light, internal and external, and in the deeply searching music, while viewers witness the collision of two fierce souls, loving brothers though they be. And then one slain brother is replaced by a brother of another kind. *The Mission* is by no means a tame picture: it demands almost as much of its viewers as it does of its characters, and it is as current as tomorrow's headlines.

Things to Look For

- Chris Menges's camera work in *The Misssion* is remarkable, and it is especially notable in wide-angle "spectacle shots" of the Iguazú Falls and all that transpires below — on and above its wet-rock surfaces. These elicit gasps readily enough, both for their scenic grandeur and for the grandeur of the moral and spiritual drama that transpires all around them. The camera goes many other places as well — low as well as high, inside and out — and it proves agile and fluid. In fact, some of the most powerful sequences are shot in gorgeously lit close-up and from below the action itself.
- While the film displays startling camera work, editing also contributes a great deal, adapting to the dramatic need of the story. Sometimes, of course, the takes are long and slow; at other times, though, the pace of edits speeds almost to the kind of rate that is used in music videos.
- Best of all perhaps is Morricone's score, which is stunning in its range and complexity of moods.
- The cross is an obvious symbol in the film, and look for one that gets passed along. What other Christian emblems and stories assume symbolic importance in this film?
- The final clincher, so to speak, comes after the film itself ends, so keep watching right on through the credits. That won't be difficult: many audiences simply remain in place — astonished — right through to the end of the credit sequence.

Post-viewing Comments

There on the top of the falls, after days of a perilous shoeless climb up the sides of water-slick rock and mud, comes Rodrigo Mendoza (Robert De Niro), guilt- and grief-stricken, a fratricide and a ravenous marauder of booty and people. He has taken on the penitential challenge pitched to him by the Jesuit priest Gabriel (Jeremy Irons). The volatile Mendoza has killed his own brother in a fight over a woman, the one Mendoza thought was his mistress. In the aftermath of that, he has been seeking his own slow death by starvation in a monk's cell in a monastery in São Paulo, Brazil. And there Mendoza wastes away until Fr. Gabriel, implored by the abbot, confronts Mendoza with a charge of cowardice, mocking Mendoza's spiritual timidity, a taunt that rouses the tough guy to action. Gabriel's challenge is for Mendoza to take on a penance whose magnitude promises to assuage the remorse that has engulfed him. Believing that his sin exceeds any penance, Mendoza defies Gabriel's dare; however, he embraces the challenge simply to prove the priest wrong.

That contested penance, of course, is climbing the falls straight up, a treacherous ascent, one that Gabriel himself made in the film's opening minutes. Only now, to up the stakes of the penance, so to speak, Mendoza will do it tethered to an enormous bag of his armor and weaponry, an appropriate symbol of his mountainous personal evil, the means by which he has lived his long predatory life of mayhem and murder — of which the killing of his brother was only the most conspicuous event, harking back to the original, post-Eden killing of

Mendoza's wager in mire and pain

134

Abel by Cain. It also raises the question that is pivotal to New Testament concerns, namely, the question of just who our brother (or neighbor) is. Mendoza has mightily trespassed against both Old Testament and New Testament commands. In fact, despite his looks and manliness, he is a really rotten individual, and De Niro has a history of playing no-good tough guys, such as Travis Bickle in *Taxi Driver* (1976), boxer Jake LaMotta in *Raging Bull* (1980), and gangster Jimmy Conway in *Goodfellas* (1990).

Mendoza does finally make it to the top of the falls after miserable days of mire and peril. It is not without a little help from the monks who accompany him, even though Gabriel has forbidden them to do so (he himself at one point keeps Mendoza from plummeting off the rock face). And then a strange and wild thing happens, one that is completely unforeseen by either Gabriel or Mendoza. On the top of a cliff, as the native Guarani gather to greet the returning monks, they are shocked to see the monks' new companion, whom they quickly recognize as the very person who has killed members of their community while hauling others off to slave markets. Now, however, he is soaked in mud, head to toe, and he is crawling, his armor still in tow. Now that they have him defenseless in their midst, most viewers would find it understandable for them to want to slit his throat. Then comes that wild surprise: instead of slicing him open, the Guarani leader chooses to remove the burden of Mendoza's armor from him and to dump it over the cliff into the river below. This is as apt a symbol as any for the remission of sin (the guilt of Mendoza's evil deeds), and here it is offered by those immediately and monstrously offended.

Mendoza himself is incredulous, first, at the act and then, second, as it sinks in, at the forgiveness and love that prompts it, the fruit of the gospel of love and mercy that the monks have been preaching to the Guarani. To his utter, soul-shaking astonishment, Mendoza has been mugged by a love he never imagined possible, and his response is a joyful mixture of laughter and tears. Throughout this long, virtually wordless sequence, the camera simply watches, allowing the action itself and Morricone's delicate score to do the talking. There are, after all, many mysterious realities that lie beyond words, no matter how we try to verbally express and contain the mysteries that encompass life and death.

This sequence is certainly the most dramatic, powerful, and profound conversion sequence ever put on screen. Divine love, pure and

Mendoza tries to comprehend the gift of the Guarani.

simple, mediated through these sorely oppressed people — the very least of these! — has penetrated the craggy barriers that have long encrusted Mendoza's heart and soul. He is blitzed by what has been shown and given him on that cliff by the most unlikely people, as he has witnessed a magnanimous turning of the other cheek.

It is an added magnificent irony that what happens to Mendoza proves that the predictions of both Gabriel and him about the effectiveness of the penance are dead wrong. While Mendoza has remained defiant and contemptuous through the whole journey, the trek ends in a way he never contemplated, and he recants his earlier claim ("for me there is no redemption") in tears and laughter. And Gabriel is wrong in his claim that the penance will prove sufficient to assuage Mendoza's sense of guilt. Instead, for both, some mysterious and unforeseeable Other does its fearsome, loving work. From there, having come upon such "wondrous love as this," Rodrigo Mendoza's future journey unfolds with a kind of inexorable grace. When he asks Gabriel how he can repay him and the Guarani, Gabriel gives him a New Testament, and we then hear Mendoza's voice-over reading from 1 Corinthians 13 as he becomes assimilated into the life and play of the village. That process culminates in his request to become a Jesuit, and Gabriel accepts him as a novice.

Before that, though, the film opens with the crucial back story that prepares us for Mendoza: Gabriel's own perilous journey to evangelize the Guarani, who have already killed one of his Jesuit brothers. The film opens in breathtaking wordless fashion as that monk is set adrift on a cross in the river that will plummet over the high falls, a sequence that is then followed by Gabriel's own climb up the arduous falls to the land of the Guarani. There, deep in the jungle, though he is terrified (he is, after all, an ordinary human monk), Gabriel woos the Guarani with the lovely, lilting music of his recorder, which seems to descend on the land like a sweet balm, a reflection of the gospel of love that he brings them. And from there the village grows into the forgiving community that will welcome the predatory Mendoza.

Tragically, the story does not end there, for geopolitics and greed fast invade the momentary equanimity. Here the church and the other powers that be resemble the early moral posture of Mendoza. The cardinal, who now narrates the story, has come simply to hand over the land of the Guarani, which is protected by the powerful Jesuit order of the Roman Catholic Church, to Spain or Portugal. And the Guarani become the proverbial lambs to be sacrificed on the altar to appease earthly greed and power. Like the defenseless biblical Lamb, they are annihilated, along with the priests who love them. With a long sequence of wordless majesty that repeats the beginning of the film, *The Mission* makes clear in image and music the full measure of the love and courage that resists the sacrifice of the Guarani. Some do resist, and Mendoza resorts to arms to lead them; but this time most do not, and the pacifist Gabriel leads them to greet their death before the insatiable appetites of the "Christian" empire. The Guarani martyred but one priest, but the church sanctions the genocidal martyrdom of the whole group and, with them, the church's own priests.

In the end, the Vatican emissary knows this all too well, and he assumes a measure of responsibility that cannot be expiated — for which, perhaps, there is no forgiveness. This proves immensely painful for him, for he has seen on his own the rare and precious light of love that is gently but intensely aflame in the remote jungles of an obscure part of the world. He himself sees all of this in uncomprehending wonder, for the Guarani testify to the reality of a gospel of love that the cardinal himself, prince of the church though he be, has come to disregard.

Post-viewing Questions

1. Once, very long ago, after I showed this film to a college class, a middle-aged woman, brought to class by an enrolled friend, came up to indignantly ask me how I could show *The Mission* on a Christian college campus. I was perplexed, wondering what there

The Guarani and their priests die with the permission of the pope.

was in the film that she could possibly object to. After all, she was a grownup, and while there is violence in the movie, none is of the gratuitous or guts-and-gore variety. And there is nudity, but it is decidedly nonerotic, very much of the *National Geographic* travelogue variety. So I asked what troubled her. Her answer was brief and unforgettable: "The Christians lose." What does that outcome suggest about the film?

2. What impact does the score by Ennio Morricone have on the experience of the story and how far does it go, in the delicate texture of Gabriel's playing, to display in music the character of God? Might there be, in the unique capacities of film as a medium, instances in which music and narrative mutually inform each other?

3. Obviously meaningful to the people who wear it, the crucifix in this story gets passed on from one person to another. What meaning does it begin to gather as the film moves to its climax? Is it uniform, or does each person (or giver) ascribe to it his own significance? And how effective is it as a plot or theological device? Or do you feel that in both cases it's just a gimmick?

4. Mendoza's life is full of symbolism, from the money he receives for selling his human booty, to the light that shines on him in his monk's cell, to the bag of armor he hauls up the mountain in penance, and finally, to his gaze on the cross as he dies. How effective is this, and how much is Mendoza really everyman?

5. In the long, wordless welcome given to Mendoza after his climb up the falls, viewers perhaps glimpse the furthest extremes of

what Christian love looks like. It is no small irony that it comes from these very new and very humble Christian people, and not from the masters of the church and government. What might we call this? What parallels might we find in our own time and place?

6. The ending of the film has all kinds of surprises. The first and biggest is that the village is utterly obliterated, the innocent simply slaughtered, and the physical remnants burned to the ground. It's all completely gone, and in the long silence that follows, we glimpse for a moment the stark voraciousness of evil. And there is also the choice the surviving children make when they scour the river below to find what might prove useful in their new life of survival in the jungle. They pass over the emblems of the church, but they retrieve the broken violin.

Critical Comments

The critics, especially American ones, were not kind to *The Mission* when it appeared, even though it won the grand prize at the Cannes Film Festival. Some, like the usually reliable Ebert, complained that the film was incoherent, wondering "why so many talented people went to such incredible lengths to make a difficult and beautiful movie — without any of them, on the basis of the available evidence, having the slightest notion of what the movie was about" (*Chicago Sun-Times,* Nov. 14, 1986). Vincent Canby called it "a singularly lumpy sort of movie," a distinctly "lesser variation on the kind of stately, 'important' movie" spectacle that was popular in the 1970s (*The New York Times,* Oct. 31, 1986). In a recent look back, James Berdanelli seems more generous than critics were at the time of the film's release: "Overall, it's an impressive motion picture," one that is "beautiful to look at, features impeccable period and setting detail, and offers a fascinating and tragic backstory," though it "lacks the epic greatness sometimes associated with it" (Reelviews.com, June 27, 2009). Another recent consideration, by Steven Greydanus of DecentFilms.com, concedes that while it "is not a perfect film," it is nonetheless "a rich, challenging one that explores the spiritual and the temporal, and the relationship between them, in a thought-provoking way." Its "images of despair, penance, and redemption . . . are among the most evocative ever filmed," rendering "a positive depiction of Catholic missionaries as selfless champions and defenders of indigenous peoples and their ways of life rather than as oppressors or imperialists."

Other Notable Films Produced by David Puttnam

Memphis Belle (1990)
The Killing Fields (1984)
Local Hero (1983)
Chariots of Fire (1981)
Midnight Express (1978)

The Apostle

Director	Robert Duvall
Writer	Robert Duvall
Cinematographer	Barry Markowitz

CAST

Robert Duvall	Euliss "Sonny" Dewey (Academy Award nomination)
Farrah Fawcett	Jessie Dewey
Billy Bob Thornton	Troublemaker
Miranda Richardson	Toosie
Norman Beasely	Brother C. Charles Blackwell
June Carter Cash	Mother Dewey

Rotten Tomatoes	90
Metacritic	83

- -

General Comments

America's best living actor (according to *Film Comment* magazine), nominated six times for Academy Awards (winning the Oscar for *Tender Mercies*), Robert Duvall is still going strong, directing and acting into his late seventies. No actor appears more often than Duvall does in the American Film Institute's top 100 films. He has given the word "versatile" an entirely new meaning, playing — in over ninety films — roles as different as the gentlemanly lawyer Tom Hagen in *The Godfather* (1972) and the rough-hewn cowboy Gus McCrae in the epic TV serial *Lonesome Dove* (1989). But nothing quite stands out like the project that was near and dear to Duvall's heart, the one he wrote, directed, starred in, and paid for, *The Apostle* (1997), the story of troubled Pentecostal preacher Euliss "Sonny" Dewey. And a magnificent thing it is, the performance for which Duvall clearly deserved his second Oscar for best actor (instead, it went to Jack Nicholson's scenery-chewing performance in *As Good As It Gets*).

Duvall first bumped up against his subject matter decades ago when he ventured into a small Texas town where he was getting ready to act in *Tender Mercies*. Arriving at a filming location early is apparently Duvall's habit: he wants to absorb the speech patterns and mores of the culture he's going to portray. On this occasion, bored and with nothing to do on a Sunday evening, he happened on a worship service in a local Pentecostal church. He was immediately hooked by the whole ethos of that service, but especially by its innovative and unconventional preaching, the like of which he had never seen. (Duvall grew up in a devout Christian Science family, and even attended the church's college, Principia, in southern Illinois.) Duvall subsequently turned his new curiosity into a passion, visiting Pentecostal congregations all around the country to absorb the preaching. He has since come to regard holiness preaching as one of America's few authentic art forms. To make his point about the vitality and freshness of this tradition, Duvall

A quartet of holiness preachers letting loose

142

Flashy Sonny

Plain Sonny

went so far as to put on display a number of noted Pentecostal preachers in the tag-team tent revival sequences in *The Apostle*.

At some point Duvall began making notes for a screenplay, one that went through numerous revisions and made stops at various studios, none of which showed any interest in the project. Sometime during the mid-1990s, Duvall's accountant told the actor that he had now saved enough money to make the movie that no one wanted. So Duvall made the film, and then he went all around on radio and television talk shows to promote it, knowing that the story of a hell-raising Pentecostal was not likely to draw huge audiences from either the religious or secular side. Given the story line, not even Pentecostals would necessarily like it all that much.

The Apostle is no extravaganza: the sets are minimal and in low-budget locales; nor are there any big-ticket actors. The biggest name other than Duvall is Billy Bob Thornton, with whom Duvall has had a long relationship (he even performed a small but important role in Thornton's breakthrough 1996 movie *Sling Blade,* which Thornton wrote, directed, and starred in himself, as Duvall did here). The other known actor was the late television veteran Farah Fawcett (of the *Charlie's Angels* TV show, 1976-80). Both Thornton and Fawcett have difficult roles: Thornton is the bulldozer-driving racist who doesn't like Sonny Dewey's interracial congregation; Fawcett is Dewey's frightened — and roving — wife. Another notable appearance — but by a singer rather than an actress — is by June Carter Cash, wife of the late Johnny Cash, who plays Sonny Dewey's mother, even though she was only two years older than Duvall. The rest of the notable performances belonged to largely unknown or first-time actors, though Norman Beasely, who plays Dewey's friend and sponsor when he lands in Louisiana, was a well-known stage actor in Chicago. British actress Miranda Richardson also makes an appearance as a radio-station secretary.

All do sterling work, but the power of the film really lies in the narrative and character of Sonny Dewey as performed by Duvall. Whatever his gifts as a preacher — and they are considerable — Dewey is very much a mixed bag as a human being. On the one hand, the portrait of Sonny Dewey is of a preacher who was called to be so from childhood: he is, in fact, a sincere "apostle" of God as mediated through the Pentecostal-Holiness tradition. There is nothing to suggest otherwise. He believes in deathbed salvation and in miracles, and he may even perform a few, as Duvall is careful to suggest concerning Sonny's earnest car-wreck intervention. On the other hand, he is carrying around some serious human baggage, which the story lays out piecemeal. Thus it takes a while for the audience to adjust to the fact that Sonny might not be exactly as illustriously blessed as we — and Sonny himself — like to think he is. What happens to Sonny as these two domains of the soul, the sincere and the nasty, collide is the core of this story. It's a tale as old as King David.

As you're watching Sonny's development, be attuned to his glories — one of his favorite exclamations is "glory" — and his foibles. Duvall simply inhabits Sonny Dewey in this sensational performance.

Things to Look For

- It is often as important, in viewing *The Apostle,* to watch the nonverbal acting of Duvall as to hear the words in the script, for he communicates a lot about his character by how he moves when by himself and also with others. That is what good actors can do, relying on words only when necessary.
- The role of Dewey's wife, played by the late Farah Fawcett, is one of the more difficult roles in the film: she, more than anyone, needs to show the dynamics of the marriage and the reasons she has strayed. Again, she communicates much of this nonverbally.
- Duvall esteems the kind of holiness preaching at the center of *The Apostle* as an authentic American art form that has been neglected by the artistic establishment. How true that is might be indicated by the fact that, when compared to others in the film (nonprofessional actors but professional preachers), Sonny Dewey is not all that good at it, though Duvall has apparently labored hard to develop a distinctive and compelling style. No matter how good an actor, there are some things that just can't be mimicked.
- The harsh realities of Sonny's painful exile teach him a few things that alter his understanding and his behavior. Duvall inserts these into the script without making a big deal of them; we most often see them in Sonny's deeds more than his words, though his words are also significant.
- Though much of the script is not particularly memorable for its eloquence, late in the film a few lines work well to distill much of what happens to Sonny. Keep your ears open.

Post-viewing Commentary

This time, for sure, especially in plain old moral terms, Sonny has really gone too far. It is not without some cause, unlike his earlier history of shenanigans (a polite way of saying his womanizing). However, no matter what the cause, murder is off limits; furthermore, it is ironic here that Sonny kills over the very kind of adulterous relationship that he himself has repeatedly undertaken. He seems to regard serial adultery as a kind of occupational hazard that cannot be avoided, an inescapable cost in his love of preaching. That much is clear in the "conversation" he has with his wife, Jessie, who is consorting with the youth minister of the couple's flourishing Pentecostal congregation in Fort Worth. Even though he concedes his history, Sonny simultaneously makes light of his "wicked, wicked ways."

Sonny's recourse to violence is worse still, though it is perilous to rank evil deeds. He is not by temperament or redemption a turn-the-other-cheek kind of fellow. When it dawns on Sonny that Jessie is having an affair, he arrives on the scene in the middle of the night and reaches for a handgun he keeps in his glove compartment. A verse from Scripture restrains him from doing what he'd like to do, so instead he contents himself with terrorizing the two by throwing a baseball through the upstairs bedroom window. Later Sonny begins the conversation with Jessie about reconciling by putting a loaded handgun on the table (Jessie is careful to unload it at the first opportunity). Throughout their talk, Jessie is skittish, keeping her distance from Sonny, ready to flee at his every twitch. Her behavior makes it clear that Sonny has regularly resorted to intimidation and physical violence in the past.

All of this goes to suggest that Sonny, though he is a preacher, is not very far along in becoming the "new creature" that the salvation he preaches is supposed to produce. While Sonny has clearly understood some of it, he has in many ways missed the moral work of the cross for the glamour and power of being "the preacher." In short, Sonny confuses his own satisfaction and glory with God's desires: that is, belief for Sonny is more about celebrating himself than about exalting God. The first glimpse is the vanity license plate on his fancy car, the thing he submerges when he's on the run. That also fits in with the fancy white suit, gold tie, sunglasses, and melodrama that is his preacherly self (contrast that hype with his attire and demeanor in his fugitive "new" life). At the beginning of the movie, after he ministers to the couple who have had the accident, he's very proud of himself. He proclaims to his adoring mother, "We made news in heaven today." Later, in his nighttime "argument" with God, he sees his life as a privileged drama in which he and God are the two central participants, and he is God's own fair-haired boy. In this regard he resembles the biblical David, who apparently thought God wouldn't mind his adultery with Bathsheba and then his killing off of her husband.

Duvall here seems remarkably perceptive about the perils of celebrity, even on the small scale of a single congregation. (Robert Duvall himself lives on a farm in Virginia and pretty much stays away from the Hollywood scene.) Of course, Sonny gets a lot of adulation on the tent revival circuit that he regularly joins. He's good at preaching, and he likes it, but we cannot be sure it is for the purest of reasons, since this is apparently the source and opportunity of his womanizing. Sonny is more than willing to thrive on the excesses of "preacher-olatry," which means the sincere admiration by those — particularly women — who have found in his charisma a glowing instance of divine speech and presence. Indeed, this danger lurks large in those Protestant traditions where preachers become the primary conduit for grace and revelation in the here and now. It is clear, too, that Sonny has used this assumption in his marriage, claiming a kind of authority and holy purpose to prod his long-suffering wife into submission and tolerance, something that has clearly exhausted her. When he invites her to pray about their strife, she objects that her "knees are worn out" from prayer, all of which seems to have been to no avail in altering Sonny or repairing their marriage. For Sonny, prayer becomes a tool he uses to force his wife to do as he wishes.

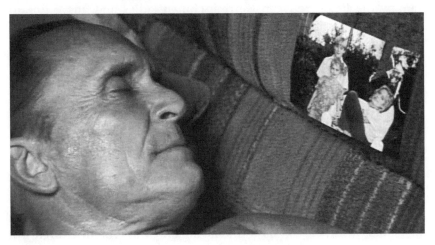

Sonny lies on his couch yearning for his own family.

Finally, of course, Sonny goes too far. Angry and drunk, his manhood offended since he has become a public cuckold, and losing his church amid congregational infighting, he clobbers the mild-mannered youth minister with a bat. Off he goes, alone and desperate, a fugitive and a prodigal, into a "far country." For Sonny, this is an arduous but necessary journey, for he can no longer deny his own evil, though he initially jokes about it with his devoted friend Joe (singer Billy Joe Shaver). Director Duvall catches this retreat from the world perfectly as he shows Sonny, a fellow who seems to run everywhere, progressively slowing down, until he comes to a complete dead rest in a poor man's pup tent.

In contrast to his life as the always scrambling, get-ahead fellow, this is quite a reversal. First Sonny drowns his car, vanity plate and all, and walks away, slowly; then he slows still further on a bridge to toss his wallet with all of his identification into the river, and finally we see him, his shirt sweat-drenched, even more slowly approach the one-legged fisherman, from whom he begs lodging and food, retreating to that tent to fast and pray. He has finally come to a dead stop — both physically and religiously. From there, after fasting and prayer, he emerges to baptize himself anew as the "Apostle E. F.," a new version of the man he once was. Perhaps.

The work he does thereafter is a night-and-day contrast to his previous ministry. Now his congregation is a mere handful of the poor and outcast, and though his church grows slowly, Sonny shows uncharacteristic humility and patience. Instead of discord, he sows peace, taming the feuds between warring church ladies and, more importantly, calming the angry racist who wants to flatten the biracial church. He even initiates a marriage seminar, something he could have used a steady dose of himself in his previous life. Instead of the slick and powerful Chrysler with the vanity plates, he now drives a laughable hand-painted old van converted into a church bus. And instead of wanting to run the whole show, he happily submits to the spiritual guidance of retired minister Charles Blackwell (Beasely), whose ill health has forced him to give up preaching. The issue is even more charged because Blackwell is black, and he really doesn't trust this new "Apostle E. F.," who comes wandering into his life one day with a plan to revive what's left of Blackwell's congregation. The obvious sign of the new Sonny is his attire: no more sunglasses in the pulpit, only a plain black suit, white shirt, and tie. And he not only works at the church, but as a mechanic, cook, and soda jerk. When he runs now, it is not in behalf of his celebrity and aggressiveness, but only after he has anonymously dropped off boxes of food at the homes of the needy. And there's a whole lot more, most of it visual, that serves as counterpoint to what Sonny revered in his life "before."

That is not to say that some of the old Sonny does not hang around. When the "troublemaker" (Billy Bob Thornton) first comes by, Sonny's solution is again violent, beating the stuffing out of him. Only later, when his combatant shows up with a bulldozer, does Sonny try loving persuasion, a course that redeems the angry racist. And then there's Toosie (Miranda Richardson), the radio station secretary who is separated from her husband, a woman on whom Sonny pours the charm as soon as he sees her. And he is persistent in his attentions (and desires), though he does desist — dramatically quitting his job — when he sees her dining with her estranged husband. He does not seem to want to get in the way; perhaps he recalls the brokenness of his own family.

Most of all, though, he finally confesses his crimes to his new friend, the Reverend Blackwell, and when the police do finally show up (alerted by Jessie, who has heard Sonny preaching on a distant AM radio station), he goes quietly, even willingly, leaving all he has to the church and his new friend, Sam (Walton Goggins), on whose couch Sonny sleeps. Clearly, by the end, Sonny's new self and work has transcended the old narcissism. At one point he sits in the dark by himself looking at his little falling-down church, and he quietly thanks God for it. For him, it is now enough to love his flock — and quite a ragtag bunch they are — and to give them promises of God's love. And for Sonny this will not stop, for in the credits we see him leading a prison work crew in a gospel-blues work song.

Post-viewing Questions

1. What, if anything, happens to Sonny Dewey? Yes, he murders a man (second-degree murder or manslaughter, depending on the sympathies of the prosecutor, but it surely is murder, though we are never told the exact charge). And he loses his wife, his children, his church, his mother, and so on. But is he a different person at the end than he was at the beginning, and what in the film shows that?

2. We perhaps see those changes more than we hear about them. Sonny still runs wherever he goes, but now when does he run? He's running from something (the law and himself, mostly), but he also has now started running for other purposes. And before he runs again, he slows to a dead stop, as we once again see.

3. Duvall found a wonderful cast of actors for his film, many of them nonprofessionals. And he also has notables working for little money, such as Billy Bob Thornton, who does a nice job of playing the racist on the bulldozer. But the larger question remains: How much does this subplot add? Does it tell us anything significant about Sonny?

4. What images seem to best encapsulate what happens internally to Sonny Dewey?

5. The loss and pain of Sonny's own state of error and exile seem to instill in him a new measure of understanding. Do any scenes indicate the distance he's traveled?

Critical Comments

As the scores on Rotten Tomatoes suggest, reviewers were agog with praise for Duvall's film. For the hard-nosed, skeptical critic of *Slate*, David Edelstein, Duvall's performance was "glorious" and his movie was "the most vivid and radiantly made of 1997." Its chief virtue is Duvall's accomplishment in both writing and portraying a genuinely ambivalent character. Edelstein observes that "if, as an actor, Duvall gets drunk on Sonny's megalomania, as a director he keeps the character soberly in focus, so that we're simultaneously swept up in Sonny's good while recoiling from his evil . . ." (Jan. 25, 1998). David Denby, one of the country's best film reviewers, simply proclaims *The Apostle* "the best movie ever made about a man of God — which is to say, the most honest and morally the most ambiguous." Though Sonny is "egotistical and manipulative," and also a "con artist, brawler, and womanizer," he is also a "gifted, sometimes inspired preacher who rounds up isolated and demoralized people and forges them into a community" (*New York Magazine*, Jan. 12, 1998). Janet Maslin links Sonny to Elmer Gantry, Sinclair Lewis's portrait of a preacher as scam artist. But in the end what we have is far more complex, "a full, fiery, warts-and-all portrait of Sonny without reducing him to any kind of stereotype." Instead, audiences find an "exhilarating, touching Sonny," a preacher who is "earnest about his mission" (*The New York Times,* Oct. 9, 1997).

Other Notable Films Starring Robert Duvall

Open Range (2003)

A Civil Action (1998) (Academy Award nomination, Best Supporting Actor)

Lonesome Dove (1989) (Emmy award for outstanding lead actor in a miniseries)

Tender Mercies (1983) (Academy Award for Best Actor)

The Great Santini (1979) (Academy Award nomination, Best Actor)

Apocalypse Now (1979) (Academy Award nomination, Best Supporting Actor)

The Godfather (1972) (Academy Award nomination, Best Supporting Actor)

IV. Facsimiles of God:
The Whys and Whos of Incarnation

"Let me tell you a story. Once there was . . ." And so it goes endlessly, over and over, humankind's insatiable hunger for story, partly for the pleasure of escape, partly to derive light for living, and also, perhaps, for a dose of meaning and even joy. And every guru has a story to tell, a metanarrative, whether the evolutionary biologist, the street-corner evangelist, or the fan of the Chicago Cubs — and all souls in between. Indeed, we all scramble as best we can amid generally harried lives in humdrum technological worlds.

Humanity seems to be the everlasting story-loving animal; perhaps that, more than anything else, constitutes both humans' uniqueness among all of earth's creatures. And so we tell stories and hear stories, and with cinema we show and see stories — lifelike, large, and up very close. Movies are the hypertechnological medium for storytelling, but what they do is as ancient as what the first cave-dwelling taletellers did.

Just about every story is a metaphor of sorts, suggesting that the constructed world it presents, whether in documentary or fiction film, is an apt and true rendition of the way things in general really are or, if not that, should or could be. Even the most far-fetched science fiction or fantasy movie has its own plausibility structure that it implicitly asks audiences to buy into — at least for as long as the film lasts. If you stretch that too thin or make it too outlandish, audiences are likely to head for the exits.

Storytelling does have its limits, as do all the arts, especially when it tries to describe the divine. How can one portray God on the screen, or in a symphony, or on a canvas. The divine is, by definition, something beyond the human — perhaps even beyond human understanding. Poet Emily Dickinson suggests that while the divine is indeed "too bright for our Infirm Delight," artists may still tell the truth by telling it "slant," approaching truth by indirection, obliquely, easing its sharp realities for the oversensitive or the obtuse. To this end, metaphor fortunately leaps at the possibilities of "slantness" and has distinct benefits: metaphorical stories can fabricate compelling protracted hypotheses for what God might be like. In the New Testament these are called parables, a strategy Jesus constantly used in trying to explain the hardest and deepest truths, making his point not via a theological proposition but via a story, using the imagination to get at truth: "The kingdom is like this. Once a man went . . ." — and endless variations on that.

Some of the most popular films in film history are in fact parables, seeking in their slantness a portrayal of heavy-duty religious possibility, namely, the possibility of Incarnation. And some of them seem to accomplish the difficult task of transmitting what that would look and feel like. The first of the parables in this section is Steven Spielberg's *E.T.: The Extra-Terrestrial* (1982), the seriocomic story of a bereft boy whose father has run off with his secretary. Elliott (Henry Thomas) finds a gentle alien creature who possesses miraculous powers, including healing, and who encompasses the boy with his love, transforming his world and his flagging hope. It was not until well into the shooting of the film that screenwriter Melissa Mathison, a Catholic school product, recognized just whose story she was telling.

A similar thing happens in Richard Donner's *Superman* (1978), a dead-serious comic take on Jesus as both clown and superhero. The enormous surprise everyone feels at the emergence of transcendent power and delight that seeks to befriend and defend a bedraggled humanity plays on the pervasive human hunger for rescue. And this hero is elegant, masterful, and certainly compassionate, something to which the ambitious reporter Lois Lane surrenders her hard-bitten self in nothing flat. And so do audiences, as the filmmakers use high comedy to mediate the utter seriousness of human hope.

A third film in this section, Danny Boyle's *Millions* (2004), is again about a bereft young British boy, only this time it is his mother who has left (died). Young Damian (Alex Etel) has taken up communing with saints (rather than a kindly alien); he wants to ask them if they have seen his late mother in the heavenly precincts. And it is not just that

Damian studies and communes, but he actually has "in the flesh" conversations: the saints enter his world for a good chat. And that is just the beginning of remarkable events, specifically millions of dollars descending from who knows where. In the end, this playful "what if" parable clarifies what makes a genuine miracle and what marks divine presence.

"Slantness" has its uses, especially in telling and showing the invisible, for by this obliqueness we can approach — pilgrims that we are — the mysteries of Light.

E.T.: The Extra-Terrestrial

Director	Steven Spielberg (Academy Award nomination)
Writer	Melissa Mathison (Academy Award nomination, Best Original Screenplay)
Cinematographer	Allen Daviau (Academy Award nomination)
Music	John Williams (Academy Award, Best Musical Score)
Editing	Carol Littleton (Academy Award nomination, Best Editing)

CAST

Henry Thomas	Elliott
Dee Wallace	Mary (Elliott's mother)
Drew Barrymore	Gertie
Robert MacNaughton	Michael
Peter Coyote	Keys

Rotten Tomatoes	98

- -

General Comments

An odd but perfect pair they are: the lonely little boy and the odd green fellow from some unimaginably distant place. If durability — standing the test of time — makes a classic, then *E.T.: The Extra-Terrestrial* (1982) surely ranks as one. It is as eminently watchable today as it was when it was first released, almost thirty years ago. Seen in high definition, it is visually dazzling, thanks to the quietly vibrant and luminous cinematography of Allen Daviau. And even after repeated viewings, the story does not lose its capacity to entice and move viewers — sometimes deeply. The freshness of the plot, which is full of surprises and wit, has gathered up the best of the science fiction tradition, including Spielberg himself, and carved out remarkable new depth. Though it was pitched as a film for kids, adults seemed to enjoy it far more, reacting with both laughter and tears.

When Spielberg made *E.T.,* he was still the wunderkind of Hollywood. His first feature, *The Sugarland Express* (1974), did well enough for him to secure enough money to make what would be the enormous smash hit *Jaws* (1975, based on the best-selling Peter Benchley novel), which was released when Spielberg was all of twenty-nine years old. And then success after success followed, with nary a flop (well, maybe just one, his World War II comedy, *1941*), including *Close Encounters of the Third Kind* (1977) and *Raiders of the Lost Ark* (1981), both sensational filmmaking and innovative storytelling. Only in his mid-thirties, Spielberg made *E.T.* from a screenplay by Melissa Mathison.

Given that history, *E.T.* arrived with more hype and anticipation than the Second Coming, a comparison that Spielberg himself did not discourage. In fact, the poster art for *E.T.* mimicked Michelangelo's image from the Sistine Chapel ceiling of the finger of God the Father reaching out to touch humankind, except that this time the finger that reaches toward humans is decidedly green and nonhuman. Nothing quite like shooting for the moon — or heaven itself!

Spielberg's previous sci-fi venture was the epic *Close Encounters of the Third Kind,* a rapturous spectacle of immediate and personal contact with visitors from another place. One very ordinary man, Roy Neary, a power lineman, finds himself compelled, along with a lot of other people, to travel from across the country to Devil's Tower in Wyoming to encounter these otherworldly visitors. In Spielberg's hands (and in the hands of the original — but uncredited — storywriter, Paul Schrader) this fast becomes a Moses tale, the story of a wanderer who climbs Sinai to meet the supernatural — with the emphasis on *super.* Spielberg infuses these aliens with enormous power (look at the size of their ships), fearsome music, and the blinding bright light. With painstaking and loving care, Spielberg manages to bring off the majesty of splendor and might, which is a very difficult thing to do in the movies. Efforts at that usually come off as bluster or silliness, and they soon sputter out, like DeMille's *Ten Commandments* (1956) or, more recently, Danny Boyle's mediocre *Sunshine* (2007). However, Spielberg seems to have a deep intuitive sense, at least in part, of what makes the holy *holy*.

The cinematography by the late master Vilmos Zsigmond and the remarkable score by John Williams helped a lot, but it is Spielberg who made the film as he did, overseeing location, production design, special effects, and, of course, all those reaction shots of countless actors to the coming of the quasi divine. Though the film has its problems in articulating a coherent portrait of the nature of this supernatural reality — in other words, its moral substance — Spielberg achieves a dazzling display of what the supernatural might look, sound, and feel like for ordinary people. Most of the scientists, of course, have quite a different view of things, but they've until now lost their capacity for wonder and awe, with the exception of LaCombe (played nicely by famed French director François Truffault).

To come right to the point, *E.T.* shows Spielberg's greatness as a filmmaker — though also as an inconsistent one. Everything here clicks — and dazzles, too — in a story that is full of pathos, humor, splendor, and throughout a kind of playfulness. Spielberg conveys all these ingredients in camera work, lighting, editing, and so on. Especially telling are the images themselves, not only for their technical wizardry but for their revelatory clout. Chief, of course, are those images associated

The mother ship in *Close Encounters* descends as if it is itself the very majesty and radiance of God.

E.T.'s glowing finger not only lights up but heals.

with E.T. himself: the finger that glows when he wishes to heal and the glowing red heart, that foremost emblem of the creature's "supra-humanness" and compassion. Or the image of E.T. that emerges from the back of the package van the boys have stolen to whisk away the liberated alien. Everyone seems to have a favorite. Hardly has any film been so "posterized" (so many different shots ending up on posters), which says something about the potency of this seeming kid story and about the aptness of its images.

E.T. is also the fruition of a long preoccupation that shows up regularly and prominently in Spielberg's films, one that will recur again front and center years later in *A.I.: Artificial Intelligence* (2001), another film title of initials that deals with a small boy and strange creatures. This preoccupation is Spielberg's "lost boy" focus on children, specifically boys, who suffer significant absence of some sort — usually one or both parents. That is young Elliott's plight in *E.T.:* his father has run off to Mexico with his secretary. And Elliott, far more than his two siblings, seems bereft. Into his world comes another lost and abandoned creature, the green, stretchy-necked E.T. In their relationship, specifically in its depth and purity, we glimpse the deepest human longings for intimacy with some other being beyond ourselves. And Spielberg at his best, which *E.T.* surely is, shows the depths of fulfillment of those longings.

Things to Look For

- Many people have commented on Spielberg's worried view of science, not so much for what science discovers, but the means by which it acquires knowledge and the toll that it takes on people. Specifically, Spielberg seems to fear a lack of appropriate reverence in the poking and probing science undertakes simply for the acquisition of more data (this goes back a long way in Western culture, at least to eighteenth-century British poet William Blake). In this regard, he essentially repeats the posture and idea of scientists from *Close Encounters*. Be alert to how Spielberg handles this ambivalence in *E.T.*

- Much the same sort of ambivalence characterizes Spielberg's portrayal of suburbia, in terms of what it does to people and also to nature. Nature looms above and beyond the burbs in *E.T.* The question is whether Spielberg resolves the nature-suburbs question.

- It is not just that E.T. possesses remarkable powers; but Spielberg makes it clear that his powers are of a particular kind for a particular purpose. In that lies a crucial question about divinity: What makes some thing or some person divine, holy, or worthy of veneration? Here the question is whether Spielberg has progressed very far beyond the razzle-dazzle of *Close Encounters*. Is it power and miracle alone?

- Spielberg — or at least screenwriter Mathison — mines both the Old and New Testaments for all kinds of events, imagery, and concepts. Find those if you can.

- John Williams's Oscar-winning score virtually becomes a character in the script, a kind of presence that both explains and greatly amplifies the delight and pathos of the drama. Indeed, how often does it "stretch" the narrative to another domain?

- A special kind of symbiosis seems to develop between Elliott and E.T. (E.T.'s initials even mirror the first and last letters of Elliott's name). Spielberg first treats this comically, but the connection takes on more weight later in the film. One has to wonder toward what territory Spielberg is pushing.

Post-viewing Comments

Poor Elliott. He lives more or less abandoned amid the cookie-cutter sameness of a suburban sea of little boxes. Dad has left, his newly single mom has work and three kids, and his brother's buddies — well, they just love to hassle Elliott. In that featureless monotony of the suburbs, with their insistent emphasis on the rightness of cheeriness, Elliott is not likely to find either solace or hope, let alone understanding.

There are, however, the forested hills beyond and above the suburban sprawl, a fully natural, unspoiled place, remote yet filled with refuge and the unknown. Anything can happen there, at least in contrast to the smothering sameness of suburbia. And from that remote and natural place — indeed, beyond it — comes the abandoned creature, lost and needy, whose friends have also left him behind, whether responsibly or not, in their necessity to escape the pursuit of overcurious scientists, who want nothing more than to turn them all into specimens for analysis. Alone and desperate — and thanks to Spielberg, we feel the terror of E.T.'s near capture — this forlorn creature ventures to the fringes of the homes below, and by chance — or through providence, as the film suggests — he happens upon a like soul, an echo of his own forsakenness. That should ring some bells for those on the hunt for Christ figures.

Elliott takes pity on the homeless fellow, sensing in him someone

This visitor from another place knows rejection and forlornness.

like himself, and, in addition, perhaps something magical, a capacity that will become apparent once they get to know each other. In short, this is no ordinary, mundane alien. This abandoned creature, looking so helpless and forlorn, is supernatural, or at least far beyond earthly nature. He has telekinesis, which is pretty impressive; but it pales next to what he can do with that glowing finger: heal cut fingers and resurrect dead flowers. Indeed, this marvelous creature, both wondrous and gentle, is shocking not only in his unexpected arrival and bizarre appearance, but more so in the powers he wields. That goes for the ends toward which he wields them as well, especially in contrast to the harsh world of the adults, particularly the scientists among them, who are trying to control everything that is natural. They are a cruel and heartless lot who see the dying E.T. as a splendid research opportunity.

Elliott does what the scientists cannot do for E.T. — and E.T. for Elliott — and that is the most vital thing in the world, on earth and far beyond. The thing that makes all these worlds go around, no matter how different and far-flung, is love, and in *E.T.* that love gets theologized — made into Love with a capital *L* — in very big ways. To put the matter simply (and without symbol-mongering, as so many critics like to do), the character E.T. is a very richly drawn Christ figure. And when we think about this possibility, we may find it helpful to regard the film as a kind of parable: "Once upon a time, a small lonely boy. . . ." From his mysterious arrival, to his healing powers, to his resurrection (by the power of love, shown by both Elliott and E.T.'s fellow aliens who are coming to fetch him), his aerial escape (walking on water), and his ascension (there on the mountaintop and in his farewell words), the story tracks the arc and substance of the biblical Christ story.

And this, as I have suggested in my earlier comments, comes preeminently in images. Perhaps the most telling is the emergence of E.T. from the back of the stolen package van, which is a lifelike rendition, borrowed from popular Christian art, of Jesus emerging from the tomb, grave-cloth over his head amid a cloud of white smoke. In fact, it is the climactic moment, the pivot, showing viewers what love can do and that all will be well. We need this reassurance because the medical scenes of E.T.'s near-death experience are very scary, and viewers cannot guess how E.T. will escape death. The surprise and splendor with which he emerges from the back of that van astounds the boys (now his disciples, though they were skeptics before), and their response cues and shapes the viewers' response, as if they needed it.

E.T. emerges from the van, somehow resurrected from the dead.

And to the wilderness mountaintop from whence he came, which has echoes of the places where figures such as Moses and David and Jesus met God the Father, E.T. returns to rendezvous with his compatriots. In that sequence adults kneel as E.T. addresses his followers, essentially echoing Jesus' own words of farewell. E.T. enters a ship that is full of light, divine light in its own way, and the ship itself becomes light as it streaks across the sky, leaving a rainbow light trail, that age-old sign of hope. Significantly, E.T.'s last words to Elliott promise a continued presence in him and, presumably, among others who knew him. As his finger approaches Elliott's forehead, it bursts into light to accentuate the words that follow: "I'll be right here," suggesting a continued kind of indwelling in the same way Jesus promised the coming of the Holy Spirit, the very spirit of God, to dwell in those who believe and love. That message simply repeats the eucharistic exchange that Elliott and E.T. have on the gurneys: each is willing to die for the other.

Thus, *E.T.* amounts to a kind of riff on the Jesus story, a potent retelling that allows sufficient distance for even those who think they already know it all to regrasp the source material all over again, especially those explosive kinds of recognitions and movements of the soul, including emotion, that should be standard fare in the Christian community. This is about transcendent love coming down to dwell among people, consoling and transfiguring all the brokenness of the world. That it is something that most don't want is clear enough, mainly because they're too busy and/or blind to see, or, in this current techno-culture, too deluded and bedazzled by all the gadgets. The doors of perception are difficult to open, though we sometimes find the key in the darnedest places.

That this is a legitimate interpretation was confirmed a few years ago by screenwriter Melissa Mathison, who confessed that midway through the shooting of *E.T.*, she suddenly realized, good Catholic schoolgirl that she was, just what story she was telling. Those nuns and priests apparently did a really good job, for even when Mathison was not thinking about any religious meaning, she was in fact thinking about it — and rather profoundly at that. She jokes that when she told Spielberg the recognition that had just dawned on her, he said something like, "Don't tell me, I'm Jewish!"

A resounding tale it is, portraying what it feels like when God shows up incognito among a weary and bedraggled humanity. And it does make Christian people wonder if they'd do any better recognizing God in their midst than their ancestors did the first time. Or it makes them wonder how wrong they might now be, thinking that they have perhaps already figured out this God thing — all probed and codified and overanalyzed, just like science. The virtue of films such as *E.T.* is that they show how much we humans don't know about what God looks like and where and how God shows up. Indeed, if we're lucky, amid those necessary, searching tears of sorrow and gladness, we may get just a glimpse, even though it's refracted through a kid's tale of a lost alien.

Post-viewing Questions

1. With that glowing, miraculous finger, we see E.T.'s powers on full display. While that image has gotten a lot of attention, ending up on playbills and the like, is it really the best symbol of what the alien visitor E.T. is really all about?

2. Spielberg uses light and light imagery, from the glowing finger to the departing spaceship that carries E.T. home, in strategic ways in this film. How effective is this? What would we miss dramatically without this strategy? There is that New Testament statement that "God is light, and in him there is no darkness at all." How far does the movie go in its visual display in dramatizing such a statement?

3. The film clearly ends with an ascension. E.T.'s last words to the principals in the story — while some of the adults actually fall to their knees — parallel the farewell words of Jesus to his disciples before he ascended. The references to this New Testament sequence are rather plain at the same time that they are cloaked so as not to be too obvious. Does this allow religious people to experience the strangeness of this event — and many others in the film — freshly, as if encountering them for the first time, either within historical time or imaginatively in the present.

4. How much theological truth can be contained in a fairy tale, the form *E.T.* probably most resembles? What is that form's proximity to parable, another vehicle that displays unlikely, if not quite fantastic, endings?

5. Films such as *E.T.*, in their own ways, pose questions to viewers about the limits of the possible. Early in his career, Spielberg talked about the likelihood of extraterrestrial life; later that seemed to fade to the background as he moved to personally embrace a form of historic Judaism, thereafter focusing far more on the burdens and mysteries of real human history in such films as *Schindler's List* (1993) and *Munich* (2005) and his documentary Shoah project. Reportedly, Spielberg will return to questions of space and superreality in a 2011 film, *Interstellar*. How do these two strands blend within Spielberg's religious imagination, if indeed they do? In other words, what do the messes of history have to do with hope for some divine presence?

Critical Comments

The re-release of *E.T.* on video in 2002 occasioned another enthusiastic chorus of reviews, and perhaps a bit more perspective of some of the central elements of its appeal. While Don McKellar simply declared the film "a dog movie," much like standards such as *Lassie Come Home* (*Village Voice*, Mar. 19, 2002), *E.T.* remains, for Owen Gleiberman of *Entertainment Weekly* (Mar. 20, 2002), "a sublime modern fairy tale, a movie that, if anything, looks subtler, darker, and more intimate now than it did when originally released." The forlorn Elliott yearns deeply for some measure of intimacy with something, making the film, "a ticklish and yearning poem of wonder . . . a great movie." Anthony Lane, in

165

a rapturous review, says: "*E.T* is the most enduring love story in recent cinema. . . . Elliott and E.T. are not lovers, but they are literally star-crossed, and each is wrapped up in the fate of the other. . . ." And that makes for a mystery. Lane wonders what its enormous success says about a culture's "thundering waterfall of yearning and grief" that finds solace in "the rapport between a small boy and an amphibious dwarf" (*The New Yorker,* Mar. 23, 2002).

Other Notable Films by Steven Spielberg

Munich (2005)
A.I.: Artificial Intelligence (2001)
Schindler's List (1993)
Empire of the Sun (1987)
Close Encounters of the Third Kind (1977)

Superman: The Movie

Director	Richard Donner
Screenwriters	Jerry Siegel, Joe Shuster,
	Mario Puzo, David Newman,
	Leslie Newman, Robert Benton,
	Tom Mankiewicz
Music	John Williams
Production Design	Geoffrey Unsworth

CAST	
Christopher Reeve	Kal-El/Clark Kent/Superman
Margot Kidder	Lois Lane
Gene Hackman	Lex Luthor
Ned Beatty	Otis
Jackie Cooper	Perry White
Marlon Brando	Jor-El

Rotten Tomatoes	93
Metacritic	88

- -

General Comments

The best known of all comic-book myths — and in a way the original —
is the Man of Steel, the Caped Wonder, Superman, a.k.a. Clark Kent,

faster than a speeding bullet, able to leap tall buildings in a single bound, more powerful than a locomotive, and so forth. A bigger wonder than the comic book origins is that anyone would risk a full-blown big-budget movie on that too-often-told story, especially in the 1970s. By then the United States had been through the tumult of the 1960s, the decade that had begun in hope and had ended in despair, by which time the body politic as a whole had come to ask hard questions about — in the lyrics of protest singer Pete Seeger — "where had all the soldiers gone," not to mention such leaders as Martin Luther King, Bobby Kennedy, and President John F. Kennedy. Indeed, where had hope, idealism, the summer of love, and flowers in the hair gone? The rhetorical questions persisted because so much had been lost so quickly. "Love" soon came to look like old-fashioned human self-indulgence. For whatever reasons, the aura of all that sweet hopefulness was smashed, and a sober, chastened climate took its place.

In hindsight that shift of mood seems obvious, especially in a raft of remarkably groundbreaking movies that, for all their cinematic dazzle, were testaments to quiet despair. The American cinema of the 1970s flourished in extraordinary ways. It was one of the great brief eras in Hollywood cinematic history, but its stunning achievements were not of a cheerful kind: Francis Ford Coppola's *The Godfather* (1972) and *The Godfather: Part II* (1974), *The Conversation* (1974), and *Apocalypse Now* (1979); Martin Scorsese's *Taxi Driver* (1976) and *Raging Bull* (1980); Roman Polanski's *Chinatown* (1974) and *Tess* (1979); and Stanley Kubrick's *A Clockwork Orange* (1971), *Barry Lyndon* (1975), and *The Shining* (1980).

Into this dark array came, improbably, *Superman: The Movie* (1978), an unassuming but brilliant film, cited by *Newsweek* critic David Ansen as one of the best of the titanic decade of the 1970s. However improbable its timing was, the filmmakers put their own unique spin on the Superman story, consciously playing off the well-known 1950s television series that starred George Reeves, who played Clark Kent as a very bland, ordinary guy. In the movie remake, Christopher Reeve plays Kent seriocomically and gleefully straight, covering his super-identity by making Kent into a sweetly dweebish bundle of ineptitude. From the oversized glasses that always slide down his nose to his sloping shoulders and to his too-short trousers, Kent bumbles through his world, though he knows full well exactly what he's doing every minute. Perhaps the most remarkable part of Reeve's performance is the physicali-

Superman **contrasts with the dour mood of the most celebrated time for movies.**

ty of his portrayal of the mild-mannered reporter. And he looks great as well. The casting people had a hard time finding a proper Clark Kent, and they kept coming back to a tall (6-foot, 4-inch) and skinny fellow whose work was in television soap operas. When they finally decided on Reeve, they promptly sent him to work out in the gym, a regimen Reeve maintained throughout production. Rumor had it that the actor put on over twenty pounds of pure muscle, so much muscle, in fact, that by the end of the shoot some scenes that were shot early had to be redone for the final cut. Indeed, this new "Supe," in contrast to older renditions, was distinctly muscular and "built," which made the task of concealing his Clark Kent identity all the more challenging.

On the other hand, viewers all know — as those around Clark Kent do not — who this fellow really is, and we're very much in on the joke as the Kent persona comically exaggerates his clownish inadequacies to mask the superperson he really is. That goodness and power are clear from the start when we see the young Superman, soon to be Clark Kent, plummet to earth as a toddler — though already very super — doing good before he's so much as toilet trained.

And there is also the existence of evil, the malignant genius Lex Luthor (Gene Hackman) and his oafish clown sidekick Otis (Ned Beatty). While Hackman plays the role comically enough, he also laces it with an undercurrent of callous greed of the kind that cares not a whit about what happens to those who get in his way (though this may sound far-fetched, think of greedy banks and the credit debacle). A glance at the other Luthors in the long line of Superman films — in-

In this incarnation, Clark Kent becomes a dweeb.

cluding, most recently, Kevin Spacey — quickly highlights the complexity of Hackman's portrayal. As for his cohorts, we are never quite sure why he keeps the likes of Otis around, except for the fact that he's completely unthinking and enormously servile, and Lex does indeed like to feel like the top dog in every possible way. Valerie Perrine, a former *Playboy* centerfold subject, plays Luthor's girlfriend, Eve Teschmacher, hitting all the notes of the ditzy but tender-hearted blonde. Later she'll prove to be the one who saves Superman and millions more from utter destruction.

While the acting is smashing, including Margot Kidder as Lois Lane and Jackie Cooper as Perry White, the wonder is that *Superman* is as good as it is, given its history as a project, specifically its crew of successive screenwriters. The Internet Movie Database lists four, starting apparently with Mario Puzo, the novelist who wrote *The Godfather*, as story source and screenwriter for *Superman*. Then, apparently, came the husband-and-wife team of David and Leslie Newman, to be followed by distinguished writer-director Robert Benton *(Places in the Heart)*. It is, of course, hard to know who did what to which version of the screenplay to provide this or that kind of magic to the tale. But the final product is a deft weave of story and humor, simultaneously playing the *Superman* story line dead seriously while playing the rest for comedy, if only to deflate the ominousness of its disasters. In the end it is a delicate intertwining of high and broad comedy with poignant, inspiring selflessness.

Ultimately, for people looking for belief, it offers great insight — along with a kind of triumphant glee — into the nature of the Incarnation. Though not recognized as such by most religious folks, *Superman* is a dead-on dramatization of the Christ story. It is the genius of the film that this plays out in such a way that while religious viewers enjoy it mightily for all the right reasons — what it is like to experience an incarnation and a supernatural "friend," as Superman responds to Lois Lane's question, "Just who are you?" — they generally fail to recognize what stares them straight in the face for two hours and twenty minutes.

Things to Look For

- Production design plays a big role in the film. Metropolis, the city, is somewhat predictable, but that is not the case with the Kent farm in Kansas, especially during Clark's farewell to his mother and Superman's "fortress of solitude." Visual surprise is a major element in the success of many of the great films from this era, ranging from *Close Encounters of the Third Kind* to *A Clockwork Orange,* and *Superman* seems to fit into that mix.
- The blockbusters of the era all have John Williams writing and conducting their scores: *Jaws, Star Wars, Close Encounters, E.T., Indiana Jones,* and so on. In *Superman,* Williams's short coda comes at pivotal moments to convey an elusive aspect of this super-man. Of all of Williams's movie music, none perhaps works so well as the music for *Superman,* developing a mood and a thematic.
- The one thing young Superman is forbidden to do by his father, Jor-El (Marlon Brando), is to "interfere with human history," though exactly what that means is not clear, because anything he does somehow does change things that might have otherwise happened differently. But the prohibition certainly does not include literally reversing time itself in order to bring Lois back to life (a variation on the Lazarus miracle in the New Testament). In any case, it is a bold insertion into the story insofar as it extends the film's meditation on the nature of an incarnation.
- What is it that attracts Clark/Superman to Lois anyway? She is self-centered and egotistical and a little hard-bitten, willing to sell her soul for a Pulitzer Prize in journalism. They are clearly opposites, and that allows for considerable humor, but the extent of their differences perhaps detracts from the plausibility of their re-

171

lationship, especially since this is one of the few elements in the film that the filmmakers seem to play straight.

- The film is loaded with multiple visual and verbal references, usually seemingly incidental and low-key, that push its Incarnation theme; for example, Perry White's suggestion that whoever gets an interview with the mysterious caped wonder would have the most important interview "since God talked to Moses," which is a pretty accurate assessment. These abound; find some more of them.
- Perhaps this is a lighthearted and "fun" retelling of the Christ story, and we sometimes wonder whether that humor adds to or detracts from the "holiness" of the source material. Or perhaps that perspective comes closer to the reality of the gospel than the bland and dour pablum that usually proceeds from pulpits.

Post-viewing Comments

There he is, as plain as can be. The heart-leaping joy that everyone feels in rescue catches the jolt that the Incarnation should give us if folks could only see it clearly in the great surprise of its soul-splitting love. Instead, sadly, that "good news" gets mired in politics and sentimentality these days. Again, the wonder is that more did not get the great surprise, or, to quote Frederick Buechner, the joke that is "too good not to be true," the possibility that there is help for confused, desolate humankind. The screenwriters and filmmakers freight the tale with an ample storehouse of clues, some visual and some verbal, and writer-producer Tom Mankiewicz simply declares that the screenwriters set out to tell a Christ story.

First off, there is Father Jor-El back there on Krypton, dressed in dazzling white and possessed of a voice like God's, intoning to his "only son" whom he's sending off to earth (the original comic-book version had Jor-El sending son Kal-El off into space in general) in a desperate attempt to save him from Krypton's destruction. He has no idea where the boy will end up.

"The richness of our lives shall be yours," says Jor-El. "All that I have, all that I learned, everything that I feel, all this and more, I bequeath to you, my son. You'll carry me inside you all the days of your life. You will make my strength your own, see my life through your eyes, as your life will be seen through mine. From the son comes the father, and the father the son."

This is the language theologians use to talk about the mutual indwelling, the co-beingness, of the Trinity, the Christian God. After his three years' ride through space, Jor-El advises his son — in terms that are a dead giveaway to the audience — Kal-El will come to earth to help its befuddled humanity: "They can be a great people, Kal-El. . . . They only lack the light to show the way. For this reason . . . I have sent them you, my only son."

All is done in a knowing, high-comic glee. So when Kal-El's capsule crash-lands in Kansas, the modern equivalent of the backwater known as Galilee in the ancient world, those who find him are a childless couple named Martha Clark Kent and her husband, John, the two biblical names closest to Mary and Joseph, which would have been too obvious in the whole grand joke. And when he surprises them by lifting up their truck to replace the tire, not only does his strength and kindness dazzle them, but it prepares them (and us) for how special this little boy really is. That's also true when young Clark is an adolescent and, when restless, has to restrain his power, playing the class nerd instead of achieving sports fame, even though when he is alone he outruns trains and kicks footballs into orbit. To console the perplexed young man, his earthly father, John, tells him that, for whatever reason he has arrived here in Kansas, it definitely "was not to score touchdowns."

The death of his earthly father, John Kent, follows but a few film minutes afterward, and those last words echo throughout the rest of

Father Jor-El seems to glow, sound, and talk a lot like God, at least in some popular conceptions of the godhead.

the movie. Sometime later, when he is about eighteen, Superman-to-be follows the call of the green crystal buried in the barn floor, a kind of techno Holy Spirit. He leaves his beloved mother — in what is perhaps the film's most moving (and beautifully shot) scene — to move on northward to what Jor-El calls a "fortress of solitude." There he is tutored by a holographic image of his father, Jor-El, in all known knowledge, scientific and historical, including the curious ways of the human heart. This is a long novitiate, roughly twelve years, until Clark Kent is prepared to be the "super man." Only at the very end of this sequence do we glimpse this presence of the powerful, elegant, and playful figure as he soars in flight toward the camera. Those twelve years of his solitude and training correspond roughly to the "lost years" in the life of Jesus; and, as was the case with Jesus, Clark Kent begins his "work" on earth at the age of thirty.

From that image of the airborne Superman, resplendent in red and blue, basking in his power and purpose, the scene abruptly shifts to Metropolis — Any City, U.S.A. — and the newsroom of the *Daily Planet,* where Clark Kent has just landed a job as a reporter, and where Superman goes to great comic lengths to conceal his identity. First the costume: collar too high, suit too small, pants too short, glasses too large and sliding down his nose, flat hair — and on it goes. In demeanor, his voice almost squeaks, his body is stiff and clumsy, and he is physically oblivious to the world around him, as he walks into revolving doors, closing elevators, and even the women's restroom. Smitten though he is by the gumption and savvy of Lois Lane, Clark keeps himself cloaked, though he has a good deal of private fun while earnestly protecting her. This is obvious when he knows the contents of her purse after the mugging that he interrupts to save her life (by literally catching a bullet). In another attempt to protect his identity, he coolly feigns a faint.

And can there be a more heart-leaping moment than when we finally see Clark "break forth" into Superman in order to do what he is supposed to do, whether that be to rescue Air Force One, to apprehend petty crooks, to save little girls' kittens in trees, or to catch falling helicopters and female reporters. Here, finally, that lilting tune we've heard throughout the movie bursts into jubilant splendor, as he answers Lois's question, "Who are you?" by saying, "A friend," and he is no longer the nerd reporter who faints at the merest threat. Instead, it is Lois who crumples in a faint. This is something her cynical heart never

In his triumphal moment of declaration, the bumbling Clark rips open his shirt on the way to rescuing Lois Lane.

dreamed possible: a radiant and powerful lover of kindness, truth, and justice, a "friend" and savior of humankind, a "light to show them the way," as his father, Jor-El, dreamed.

The great accomplishment of *Superman* (and of *Superman II* as well) was to impart what the reality of the Incarnation should feel like: surprise, wonder, elation, relief, gratitude, and postures of response to God-in-flesh, Love-come-here that the church has pretty much forgotten, as it either damps those feelings down or mushes them up. The sheer wonder and amazement concerning the mere possibility of such a figure has largely gone missing. Radical and implausible as it all may be, viewers glimpse in Superman — unaware though they may be, even stalwart church people that they may be — the wildness of the messianic love propounded in the Jewish and Christian traditions. *Superman* makes their deepest core clear and close as it prods bedraggled souls to leap and laugh.

Post-viewing Questions

1. Clearly, there is a lot of humor in *Superman*, but what about poignance? That happens a lot in Clark's life with his family, from the moment that Martha and John first find him, to his father's death, and then to his farewell to his mother. And it occurs again with Lois. What do these segments provide for the story as a whole as they mix with the suspense and the hijinks?

2. The special effects in the film, particularly the very natural-looking flight of Superman, received much praise and set a standard for subsequent films of comic-book superheroes such as Spiderman. How big an accomplishment is this?

3. Christopher Reeve's physical acting in the film, from his feigned clumsiness to the manipulation of his voice, really carry the film. After all, the film hinges to a great extent on making plausible the notion that this bumbling reporter really is superhuman. Look at similar attempts to do Superman, including Bryan Singers's *Superman Returns* (2006), and that point becomes all the more clear. Or is this overstating matters?

4. What moments work particularly well as cinema, specifically those that are nonverbal, when image, acting, and music collaborate to convey emotion and/or meaning?

5. How effective is the film in conveying the experience of what an incarnation feels like? That, after all, is what metaphor and parable seek to do: to make clear by example the inmost character of something that seems alien and incomprehensible.

Critical Comments

As usual, Roger Ebert came right to the point: "*Superman* is a pure delight, a wondrous combination of all the old-fashioned things we never really get tired of: adventure and romance, heroes and villains, earth-shaking special effects, and — you know what else? Wit," meaning "an intelligent sense of humor about itself" (*Chicago Sun-Times*, Dec. 15, 1978). Judith Martin fixed on Reeve's work in creating two very different characters of "authentic sweetness," both "earnest, good and loving; to do this in a way that is charming, rather than corny, is no simple feat" (*Washington Post*, Dec. 15, 1978). However, not everyone bought that. Pauline Kael, who had called *E.T.* a "bliss" of a film, found *Superman* — though she admired Christopher Reeve's performance — "cheesy-looking," especially with John Williams's score, which she said "transcends self-parody" (*The New Yorker*, Jan. 1, 1979).

Other Notable Superhero Fantasy Films

Ironman (2008)
Hellboy (2004)
Spider-Man II (2004)
Spider-Man (2002)
The Lord of the Rings (2001-03)

Millions

Director	Danny Boyle
Screenwriter	Frank Cottrell Boyce
Cinematographer	Anthony Dod Mantle

CAST

Alex Etel	Damian
Lewis McGibbon	Anthony
James Nesbitt	Ronnie
Daisy Donovan	Dorothy

Rotten Tomatoes	88
Metacritic	74

General Comments

From the opening credits to the end, Danny Boyle's *Millions* (2004) is as fresh, funny, and poignant as any recent film in just about any genre, perhaps excepting Boyle's own highly acclaimed *Slumdog Millionaire* (2008). In *Millions,* virtually every scene surprises the viewer in some way or another — in premise, plot, characters, camera angle, editing, or lighting. None of this seems contrived for the mere sake of innovation or "artsiness"; it is pure and exhilarating moviemaking pizzazz. Indeed, when it comes to cinematic storytelling talent, adapting to genre after genre, there's hardly a match for Boyle, and he seems to do all the better when he's hard-pressed for funds. Indeed, *Slumdog*, the winner of multiple Academy Awards (for best film, director, cinematography, editing, score, song, and best adaptation) cost a mere $15 million to make. That stands in stark contrast to the bloated, self-important, gimmicky, and very expensive films Hollywood usually places in Oscar competition, films that run between $50 and $100 million each (and a whole lot more in the case of James Cameron's *Avatar* [2009]).

In short, director Boyle's work, especially in recent years, can be vastly entertaining. This is not to say that Boyle has not made some royal clunkers, such as the recent *Sunshine* (2007). His first movie, *Shallow Grave* (1996), is the macabre story of a bunch of nasty yuppie roommates who dispose of a new roommie's body (dead of an overdose) in order to keep his unforeseen bag of cash. Style over substance, said critics: it was enticing and bold but, like its title, shallow. The same might have been said for his second film, the one that made him famous, *Trainspotting* (1996), an antic, scabrous romp about heroin addiction told, for once, from the inside out. Based on a popular Irvine Welsh novel (and then a stage play), it is about a bunch of Glasgow laddies whose favorite diversion, when not scrambling for dope, is watching trains. Catching both the bliss and bane of "H" (heroin), the film's ambidexterity rather awed viewers. Still, something about that premise — that we should suffer these blithe, amoral dimwits gladly — annoyed the moralist in most all of us. The savvy critic Janet Maslin, in the *New York Times*, much irritated with herself, found the film "perversely irresistible" because of its rambunctious, "inexcusable merriment" in point of view (the film is guided by a voice-over narration by the main character).

Boyle's first real stumble came with *The Beach* (2000), a desert-island romance with *Lord of the Flies* overtones, starring Leonardo DiCaprio (his first role since *Titanic*). Like DiCaprio as an actor — and the character he plays — the film aspires to both the pretty and portentous, and as that odd pairing suggests, badly muddles whatever it was after. The same is true of the more recent big-budget venture *Sunshine* (2007), an arduous sci-fi adventure in which planet Earth sends another crew (after the first has disappeared) to reignite a dying sun. Again, it is interesting the way *Sunshine* plays with notions of light; but that proves to be ironic, for darkness triumphs. The sets are lovely, the visual scheme stunning, but toward what end? The film echoes masters of the visionary space tale, such as Tarkovsky, Kubrick, and even Spielberg, but never remotely coalesces into an intelligible thematic something.

In between those we have had Boyle's *28 Days Later* (2002), the story of PETA activists blithely liberating a bio-engineered virus that instantaneously (a mere twenty seconds after infection) turns normal folks into raging, blood-crazed monsters before they die a gruesome and horrifying death. The film is chilling and brutal, and in the end, its message seems to be that, given what people can do, maybe zombies are not so bad after all. At the same time, much of it is strangely poignant as Boyle steadily laments the frailty of life and civilization. This first comes out in the ethereal soundtrack, starting with the faint strains of "Abide With Me," as the protagonist, awakening from a long coma, finds London empty and destroyed. And the story is about what makes life meaningful. There is new maturity, says A. O. Scott, and even a kind of "curious sweetness" about Boyle.

Fortunately — very fortunately — that note of sweetness is fully evident in *Millions* (2004), a film that is both "life affirming" and "spiritual," as Boyle himself puts it. It surprised just about everyone, including the cynical band known as the critics, and especially since it came after that gruesome zombie horror flick. *Millions* follows a eight-year-old British boy who quite by accident finds a huge duffle bag of cash that seems to have fallen from the sky, as if dropped by God on this particular boy. For young Damian (Alex Etel), that explanation is not at all im-

Director Danny Boyle in full-blown horror mode in his film *28 Days Later*

Young Damian converses casually with Saint Peter.

plausible. After all, Damian not only believes in saints, and he knows their dates and biographies inside and out, but he speaks to them in very immediate, palpable reality. And we get to see them, too, saints both famous (e.g., Peter) and obscure (e.g., Clare); soon enough these saints are so present and human that we also believe in them — sort of, at least for as long as Damian does, as long as the movie lasts. That is no small filmmaking feat, and Boyle pulls it off with ingenuity. And who's to say that Damian doesn't have it right, that he sees what few others can sense? The noted Estonian Orthodox composer Arvo Pärt offhandedly confesses that he senses angels all around and that they mysteriously inform the unique musical innovation that abounds in his work. Well, if not Pärt, then who else might know what most people very dimly intuit?

In fact, Boyle pushed screenwriter Frank Cottrell Boyce to amplify those saints and visions. Boyle is pitch-perfect throughout, providing much visual wit to lighten what could have turned cloying really fast. For one thing, he takes the boy's visions matter-of-factly, just as M. Night Shyamalan treats the kid who sees dead people in *The Sixth Sense* (1999), or the one who wants to find God in *Wide Awake,* to which *Millions* bears a certain kinship. In both of these latter movies, a young boy is desperate to know that a dead parent is okay. In *Millions,* young Damian has the added problem of figuring out what to do with millions in cash that has dropped into his lap. He thinks it's from God because, after all, "who else would have that kind of money?"

In any case, the film is adept, funny, bracing, and hopeful, a tale of deep human hunger that finds a lovely kind of this-worldly fruition. Implausible, surely, but this antic yet dead-serious showing of an eight-year-old's visions of the saints he loves and whose lives he studies plainly seduces just about everyone. Even critics.

Things to Look For

- One of the feats of Boyle's film is that it convincingly brings viewers into an eight-year-old's head. And at the same time Boyle very much keeps an adult perspective on the exploits of the boy. Note scenes where this seems to be particularly effective.
- Another difficult balancing act comes in the film's tone, and it is not very easy to define. On the one hand, we have a potentially mournful tale of a lonely, motherless boy who talks to saints; on the other, there's the funny story of a boy who finds an enormous fortune. Blending these is no easy trick.
- The question of Damian's "spirituality," for want of a better term, runs throughout the movie. Inescapably, viewers compare it to their own — or the absence thereof. Here questions of plausibility and cogency challenge the film. But if the famous composer Arvo Pärt says he senses the presence of angels everywhere, why can't that be true for a sad and motherless — but deeply hopeful — boy?
- One of the more humorous aspects of the film lies in the stark contrast between Damian and his older brother, Anthony. One can hardly imagine that they come from the same gene pool, and viewers usually end up siding with one or the other. And there are parallels to the contemporary "neoatheist" debate on the "God question."

Post-viewing Comments

What happens when a boy who believes in and communicates with saints comes upon millions in loot? That's the question. Like Anthony, Damian is in a hard place, though neither of the boys will quite admit it. The audience doesn't even really know, at least not for a while, the sad reality the brothers share: the death of their young mother, the warm and wise Maureen (Jane Hogarth). However, father knows best, and since he wants to do the best thing for his boys, he guesses that the boys would respond well to a change of scene. So he removes them from their old surroundings, an urban rowhouse. Beneath the opening credits, Boyle jauntily allows the boys to sketch a new house in a new development and, presto, there it is. Boyle does this sequence with the kind of zest, wit, and craft that make him the remarkable filmmaker that he is. With his megaspeed photography of the house going up, shots of the boys on bikes and in fields of flowers, Boyle imbues the film with a joyful but delicate emotional texture, a tone that meshes perfectly with its own representation of the divine.

The boys' glee in sketching — and seemingly moving into — their new home dominates the first part of the film, as they get to know their new world, especially school. And then comes the mysterious bag of cash that is soon to be worthless, which only complicates and reveals who they are. Anthony uses the dough to buy himself into a social set of boys and girls, to buy gadgets, and, since he's a shrewd boy, maybe to invest. In no time at all come friends, an adoring blue-sunglass-sporting crew of admirers, including admiring girls. The kid is a hustler in the making. All this he does while warning Damian not to be "conspicuous" with the money, especially when he sees Damian giving it away, which is ridiculous in Anthony's eyes.

Brother Anthony uses the heaven-sent dough to achieve panache and gather friends around him.

For Damian, giving it away is a natural impulse, so unselfish is he. Furthermore, he's encouraged in his charity by all those saints he meets when he's dealing with the larger matter of his absent mother. At the beginning, though, Damian is mainly interested in saints, even reporting about them in class. Part of the reason he's so glad to see them is that they may offer a way to determine the whereabouts of his mother, who, he is convinced, must also be a saint by now. Who better to confirm this hunch than the saints themselves? Perhaps they have glimpsed her up above in saintland? So he seeks confirmation, asking those visitors if they've noticed any new saints named Maureen in the celestial neighborhood. The first saint to show up is fun-loving, cigarette-smoking Clare of Assisi, the weary patron saint of television. And unconventional she is! When Damian wonders about her tobacco habit (she blows halo-shaped smoke rings), she happily answers, "You can do what you like up there, son." As for his mum, well, Clare has not seen her, but says, "Then again, it *is* infinite up there — absolutely, bloody infinite," with distinct gusto for the dazzle of it all.

And so come others, most notably the grumpy, profane, Scottish-sounding St. Peter, a ring of keys on his rope belt, who cautions Damian, as the boy sends off cash to aid organizations, not to ask for more information from the recipients of his largesse: "For Christ's sake, don't check those little boxes . . . you'll be besieged, man, I'm telling ya." The greatest measure of practical help to Damian comes from St. Joseph the Worker, the father of Jesus, who during the school play manages, first, to foil a would-be thief who is after the dough and, second, to take over for Damian as he heads off with his phony donkey in tow to stash the cash in his old house. They all seem glad that Damian has the money, because they know he'll give it away. St. Nicolas (fourth century) provides timely encouragement as Damian stuffs bills through the Mormons' mail slot. Indeed, as the money tumbles toward Damian's cardboard hermitage by the tracks, Saint Clare hears the music that accompanies a revelation of the divine. "Listen," she says. And we should listen indeed.

That's the world of Damian, of which no others so much as get a peek, but in which he moves effortlessly, even when the likes of Saint Francis come to tell him that he need not kiss the feet of lepers, as Francis did, but "just help the homeless." And this he does indiscriminately, eagerly buying meals for half-phony panhandlers, giving wads of it to the rather-too-venal young Mormon missionaries, and slipping a thousand-pound wad to the school's penny drive to build wells in Ethiopia. For Damian, all of this *means* something, though he tends to get very literal about things, being but eight years old. He's not yet good at ambiguity and complexity, not good at seeing gray instead of black and white, nor is he adept at rationalization, as grownups conveniently grow to become. And always there's his brother accusing him of seeing saints and of bringing "her" (dad's new girlfriend) into the house, of being "a loony."

Nor does Damian get much help from his father, who is bitter about the death of his wife and how hard he has to work, though he is always, to his credit, upbeat around his boys. When Damian invokes God as an authority for giving all the money away, his father advocates a rather hard-nosed, even corrosive realism: "Look around, Damian. . . . No one is looking out for us, so we're looking out for ourselves." And he's even more acidic about his wife: "She's dead. You'll never see her again, and neither will I." Telling without words, Boyle turns the camera away from the father to dwell on poor Damian's stricken face.

Thus it's no wonder that, even after the cops have caught the very serious thief, Damian decides to burn what is left of the money, given the family mess it has caused. He does so just to be rid of it, for it seems to be a never-ending curse, and they will never have any peace about it. Logically enough, Damian hauls it out to the tracks from whence it came. This is perhaps his greatest act of heroism, for, as his visitor will tell him, "Money makes it harder to see what's what." Once again, nature provides some help, namely a strong wind to fan the flames and then a high-speed train to scatter it all. Through the swirling cloud of bills, Damian sees his mother: she has come to console and encourage him, to explain to him (about his brother and his father), and to enjoin him to take care of others, for she knows well enough the depth and mettle of this small boy. As for Damian's lingering question concerning the riddle of her whereabouts, she gently tells him that she is among the saints. A smart and intellectually honest boy, Damian poses the hard criterion: "You do have to do an actual miracle" — that is, in order to qualify to be a saint. By which he means, "What certifiable miracle have you done, momsie?" Maureen responds, mildly incredulous at his blindness, with a question of her own: "Don't you know?" And the answer is plain enough, just in case we, like Damian, haven't gotten it ourselves: "It was you."

Indeed, Damian does seem too good to be true, and so should we

Damian has a long-awaited chat with his mother.

all be. And that is at least part of the point. Yet, more than that, Boyle has pulled off something really remarkable, making the religious plausible without sounding or looking hokey, without seeming cooked up and paltry, which is the way a lot of self-consciously religious films feel — at once clunky, gooey, and heavy-handed. Here the playful, festive, even joyful mood in the smartness and humor of Boyle's storytelling, even in the dark parts, works brilliantly. In fact, what Boyle pulls off in tone and antic humor here perhaps comprises the most trenchant aspect of its rendition of the God questions: not only whether there is a God, but what that God is like. Here Boyle manages to capture the same high spirits of the parables about latecomers to the vineyards and kindly Samaritans as well as some of Jesus' more impractical utterances about "suffering the little children" and washing feet.

And Boyle saves the best for last: the new family, new mother and wife included, in a perhaps actual visit to Ethiopia, as villagers enjoy the first water from the new well. It's not exactly new wine in old skins, but it comes pretty close.

Post-viewing Questions

1. One of the more charming aspects of the film is its production design, especially at the beginning as the two boys envision their

new home, laying out its blueprints, after which the audience sees it speedily come into being. And Damian makes his own house as well, those cardboard chambers by the railroad. Symbolically, this film sees a lot of house-building, or is it really about building *homes*, which is something else altogether?

2. As a director, Danny Boyle roams over a huge number of genres, from horror and sci-fi to children's stories and, remarkably, a Bollywood success tale in his highly awarded *Slumdog Millionaire* (2008). Indeed, part of the fun of filmmaking seems to lie in the creation of these many kinds of cinematic worlds. Boyle seems always able to impart his enjoyment to viewers. What specific kinds of pleasures does *Millions* deliver, both for director and audience?

3. A couple of critics rather savagely attacked the film for what they thought was a sentimental and exploitative depiction of a young boy talking to saints, thinking that this was only to encourage delusion and wishful thinking. Keeping things polite and mannerly, how might one respond to them?

4. Damian ends up returning the money to the spot where it seemed to drop out of the sky — in order to send it back, so to speak. And there he burns it. Why exactly, and what does it say about this young saint-in-the-making?

5. There is the very real question of Damian's religiousness (what some might call "spirituality"). Indeed, how does one test out the authenticity and healthiness of very personal religious apprehensions? All people have a host of longings kicking around in them — for relationships, for beauty, for play, and even for what we label God. And sometimes those longings find satisfaction in credible reality, or so it seems. The difficulty is knowing that the longings themselves, however profound and fitting, have not manufactured a "reality" of their own making.

6. In a delightful and insightful end to the film, Damian again meets his own mother, who gives him that telling answer to his question of what miracle she has done. His mother's claim that Damian himself is her verifiable miracle startles him, for it is a fresh (though really very old) way of looking at the nature of miracles and the stark reality of the people (and world) all around us. Or is this just New Agey sentimentality?

Critical Comments

Roger Ebert thought this obscure British kids' movie "a miracle" and "one of the best films of the year" (*Chicago Sun-Times,* Mar. 18, 2005). Lisa Schwarzbaum found it "sparkling" (*Entertainment Weekly,* Mar. 9, 2005), and Kenneth Turan was startled by a "lively and most unlikely film, a sweet-natured fable told with a whimsicality all its own" (*Los Angeles Times,* Mar. 11, 2005). Deeson Thomson perhaps came closest to locating its charm in a "fascinating mix of textures: realistic, bold, comic, fairy tale-ish and devotional," calling it an "an extraordinary experience" that is "not only engaging but enriching" (*Washington Post,* Mar. 18, 2005).

Other Notable Films by Danny Boyle

Slumdog Millionaire (2008)
28 Days Later (2002)
Shallow Grave (1994)

V. The Feast of Love

The grandest ritual in the Christian tradition is what Roman Catholics call the Eucharist and what most Protestants call Communion. The early Methodists referred to it as a "love feast," and that term probably comes closest to catching its essence and purpose. At its heart lies the hope of reconciliation wrought by the comprehension and practice of love. It is done in commemoration of the Lord of Love, who on the night before his sacrificial death shared a meal with his friends and asked them all to remember what he was about by — fittingly — sharing a meal together. It has since become a symbol of the final destination of history, when in the full realization of holy love all will reconcile into one human family. Over the centuries some have suggested other symbols that do the same thing, such as dance or play or the lamb lying down with the lion. But all evoke the festive consummation in which the fullness and purity of divine love is made real and light envelops the earth. Enemies reconcile, swords are transformed into plowshares, brokenness is repaired, creation heals, and Eden comes round.

It's simple enough, and given the immense brokenness of this world, we know well enough in our bowels and souls the nature of humankind's deepest aches and longings, and none greater than the hunger for the restoration of intimacy and delight in all the earth. This is the New Jerusalem, the Second Coming, the return to Eden — all of them suggesting a new creation that fulfills the intentions of the first. In his book on preaching, *Telling the Truth,* Frederick Buechner retells the parable of the prodigal son, a somewhat elaborate tale of a young man who demands his inheritance from his father and soon squanders it all on booze and women, much to his father's sorrow. While the tale is often cited as a warning to profligate young men, Buechner puts the emphasis on the father's response when the lost son, now dead broke and homeless, returns to beg for the old man's forgiveness. More than happy to see his son — for he was once lost but is now home again — the father tells the servants to kill the calf, open the kegs, and invite in friends, family, and neighbors for a welcome-home party like no other — a love feast.

The three films in this section go a long way toward sketching out the centrality of human community and the nature of the healing for which humans thirst. *Places in the Heart* (1984), written and directed by Robert Benton, is set during the Depression in Waxahachie, Texas. Newly widowed Edna Spalding (Sally Field in an Oscar-winning role) finds herself hard-pressed to take care of her son and daughter; the economic times are bad, and her farm has a huge mortgage. Desperate, she takes on some unlikely help, and that practical gesture leads to events she couldn't have imagined, even after tragedy strikes again and again. While much of *Places in the Heart* seems to spin a Hollywood formula, it also works hard to shatter those formulas, especially in its unforeseeable conclusion, one that drove some critics mad but presents one of filmdom's most striking renditions of the Love Feast.

Lawrence Kasdan's *Grand Canyon* (1991) is culturally set about as far from rural Texas as one can get, namely, in contemporary, very urban Los Angeles. Amid the disparate and desperate lives of an array of Angelinos — fancy lawyers and tow-truck drivers, male and female, white and black, young and old — Kasdan seeks a thread of commonality and connection. Then again, it is still much the same: tragedy looming, race conflict, cheating spouses, the blind and the lame, and so on. Kasdan explores how concord and solace might displace the discord and sorrow that so conspicuously thrives and blights so many lives. The means are strange indeed, and once again a filmmaker provides a fitting and memorable end with a sharp narrative turn and startling camera work.

The film here that has do with an actual feast is the classic Danish film *Babette's Feast* (1987), an Oscar winner for best foreign film, which is about a fabulous meal prepared by a mysterious refugee cook in remote Jutland in the latter part of the nineteenth century. The film is based on a short story by Isak Dinesen (the pen name of Karen Blixen, author of another famous text that was adapted to film, *Out of Africa*).

Writer-director Gabriel Axel deftly dramatizes the lives of two spinster sisters in a tiny seaside village, daughters of a famous minister whose flock has withered to an aging remnant. One stormy night they take in a refugee sent their way by an old acquaintance, and twenty years later, to everyone's lasting surprise, characters and audiences alike, things change radically. Alas, the sisters had no idea just who it was they took in, and for them she prepares a "real French dinner," as she innocently puts it. And what a feast it is!

So feasts can happen, ones that satisfy humanity's deepest needs and longings. And meetings and friendships happen, marvels to savor, of which the feast of the Eucharist offers a fitting symbol and a culmination of the journey toward mutuality for which humans were made in the first place. That is where intimacy and love play a song of appetite and delight, a hymn of reconciliation and trust.

Places in the Heart

Director	Robert Benton (Academy Award nomination)
Writer	Robert Benton (Academy Award winner, Best Original Screenplay)
Cinematographer	Nestor Almendros

CAST	
Sally Field	Edna Spalding (Academy Award winner)
Danny Glover	Moses
John Malkovich	Mr. Will (Academy Award nomination, Best Supporting Actor)
Lindsay Crouse	Margaret Lomax (Academy Award nomination, Best Supporting Actress)
Ed Harris	Wayne Lomax
Amy Madigan	Viola Kelsey

Rotten Tomatoes	100

- -

General Comments

Places in the Heart (1984) is one of those blockbusters nobody wanted to make. Screenwriter Robert Benton, though highly regarded in Hollywood (especially for his work on *Bonnie and Clyde*), could not find a studio willing to invest in his tale of a struggling widow and mother in

Depression-era Texas. Only when Sally Field signed on to play the main character, Edna Spalding, for which she would win the Oscar, did studios cough up the dough to fund the project. Even then it did not become a costly project, which was reflected in the rest of the cast: Benton chose mostly unknown and struggling actors whose work before that had been in television. Thanks to *Places in the Heart*, which turned into an enormously popular film, both John Malkovich and Danny Glover catapulted to prominence and celebrated film careers. And the movie also helped to solidify the reputation of Ed Harris, who had the year before starred in *The Right Stuff* (1983).

The reluctance of Hollywood to fund *Places in the Heart* was to some degree understandable. The question, of course, was about who the potential audience might be — meaning plain old box office (also known as profits). For most studios, this kind of story — a solitary woman in Texas in the 1930s — seemed to have all the appeal of soggy popcorn. It is possible that old-fashioned sexism or regional bias influenced Hollywood's thinking, so that neither widows nor Texas had a great deal of appeal to producers. And there also may have been more than a bit of perplexity occasioned by the film's cryptic ending. Hollywood folks were as mystified by the ending as many American reviewers would prove to be. In fact, that ending made a few reviewers sputtering mad.

In most ways, *Places in the Heart,* its title dripping with sentiment, is at once a deeply conventional film and a very surprising one that repeatedly bends expectations just in those critical places where viewers think they know what will come next. That is nowhere more obvious than in the film's opening sequences. While the credits roll, director Benton, at the helm of his own screenplay, lovingly provides a lengthy montage of life amid the rural agriculture (cotton) of Waxachie, Texas, circa 1935. In the distance lies a town with the courthouse spire rising above the trees, and then the fairgrounds, outlying farms, diners, windmills and empty roads, hobos praying over their handouts, and African-American families praying over their meals. Over it all is a choir singing Fanny Crosby's well-known hymn "Blessed Assurance." The second line of the hymn, "O what a foretaste of glory divine!" captures the gist of all we've seen, for this town does indeed seem like a precursor of heaven itself: it is picturesque, kindly, and — despite glimpses of segregation — altogether harmonious. Indeed, it all looks too good to be true, especially given its locale and time.

The town of Waxahachie in the distance, circa 1935

That sense of harmony only heightens when we get our first glimpse of the Spalding family gathered over Sunday dinner: a manly father, Royce (Ray Baker); the world's cutest mother, Edna (Sally Field); twelve-year-old son Frank (Yankton Hatten); and, of course, the world's cutest little girl, Possum (Gennie James). There are prayers over the meal, good manners, and polite conversation. Those who feared the sentimentality of the film's title seem to have a point, for all this, like the prologue, seems rather too homey and treacly, a kind of live-action Norman Rockwell painting.

That idyllic still life does not last long, however, or we wouldn't have much of a movie. Evil rears its head — even though it comes as an accident — and a whole string of other woes follows for the Spaldings. Indeed, what makes the film singular is how much of the "unexpected" Benton slips into it. At the beginning, and then for a long time in the middle section, *Places in the Heart* looks and feels pretty formulaic, and it seems as though the ending will be as clear and certain as the sun shining on the Texas prairie. Just when it all seems to be going according to sweet expectations, all hell breaks loose. And then comes the ending no one could foresee — the remarkable conclusion that drove critics crazy — and it is wild and strange and unforgettable and profound. There's nothing else like it anywhere in film: the apparent outlandish impossibility made immediate and utterly rapturous.

Things to Look For

- The film works hard to achieve the look of period realism, and it does feel like a bit of time travel. Try to look for what Benton uses to achieve this.
- For all of its seeming cheeriness, this movie is pretty hard-nosed in enumerating various kinds of evil that beset the Spaldings and bystanders. It is perhaps useful to keep a back-of-the-mind inventory as the film progresses.
- Benton also sneaks in a lot of seemingly random elements that may carry disproportionate weight as we try to understand the film, such as hymn lyrics and homeless women. The incidental elements may seem to be just that, incidental, but that rarely proves to be the case.
- Benton chose cinematographer Nestor Almendros to shoot the film, and it is lovely cinematography throughout. Keep a list of particular shots or sequences by Almendros that seem especially effective.

Post-viewing Commentary

Evil does erupt in that tranquil world, devouring the good and the young, fathers, wives, and children, white and black. For no good reason, and from no ill intent, young Sheriff Royce dies. The young black man, Wiley, does not mean to kill him, believing that the gun was empty (the preceding trigger pull had hit an empty chamber). The accident stuns everyone — Wiley, Royce, and the viewers. The young sheriff arrives home to lie cold and dead on the table where he had eaten his Sunday dinner minutes before. What happens to Wiley — brutalized, exhibited, and then hung in the vile lynching tradition of the South — soaks the horror of death in malice. Wiley deserves punishment, but not for murder. However, no black boy may be allowed to kill a white person with impunity, let alone a sheriff, regardless of the innocence of the circumstance. And thus the Klan brazenly rears its ugly head, not even bothering with the cover of sheets or darkness, to maim and murder.

Evil also comes in other kinds of relationships, specifically the brokenness in the marriages of Margaret (Lindsay Crouse) and Wayne

Lomax (Ed Harris) and their best friends, Viola (Amy Madigan) and Buddy Kelsey (Terry O'Quinn). In one way or another, evil visits everyone in the community, leaving no one alone, afflicting and devouring, no matter how pristine Waxahachie looks. Behind its beguiling surface run currents of destruction and death, spectacularly in the deaths of Royce and Wiley, and in a smarmy way in the affair of Viola and Wayne.

Not many Hollywood films quite sock it to the viewer's sensibilities so quickly and with such "real-world" force. Having done that, after a deft and moving funeral sequence, it quickly turns to the new widow's efforts to support her family. In this Benton continues his stalwart realism, for women in the 1930s had few options — either by training or social encouragement. No matter how smart and brave she is, Edna has no workplace skills of any kind, except for those of being a mother. She doesn't know the size of the mortgage on her family's house, or even how to write a check. Her sister, Margaret the hairdresser, cannot take her on because she barely makes enough to support herself and her shiftless husband. And Margaret dismisses Edna's idea about opening a gift shop in her home. This *is* the Depression, after all.

With her prospects looking that poor, the bank is more than eager to grab her house and land. In fact, banker Denby (Lane Smith) advises her to sell it all to the bank and to send her kids to live with relatives, a prospect the widow simply cannot abide. This advice raises her ire and resolve, which prod her to take outlandish risks that will ultimately bring her to triumph. By virtue of a time-honored Hollywood formula, viewers know right away that, through calamity and distress, the conspicuous pluck of the widow will eventually win. Through the storm and the race to bring in the first harvest of cotton, Edna relentlessly pushes, at one point even threatening to consign her helpers "straight to hell" if they falter. Here Edna looks and acts like John Ford's memorable Ma Joad (Jane Darwell) in his film version of John Steinbeck's *The Grapes of Wrath* (1940). What we expect — and get — at this point, and for quite a while through the long middle section of the film, is a pretty stock Hollywood movie about a courageous widow who triumphs over great odds.

While that is indeed what the film does, Benton works hard to change the insides of the success formula. First, he changes the means by which Edna succeeds: that is, her embrace of a very unexpected and unusual crew of helpers, because running that farm is not something

The new sheriff brings Moses and the silverware to the widow.

she can do by herself. First comes Moses (Danny Glover), the itinerant African-American farm laborer who comes around looking for work. We first see him on the night of Royce's wake, when he knocks on the Spaldings' door to beg a meal. Edna feeds him and then her sister shoos him off; but in the morning Edna wakes in her rocking chair to the sound of wood being chopped. Moze has hung around to make himself useful, hoping that the widow will offer him some work. He even suggests planting cotton on her unused twenty acres. No luck, says the widow, and she sends him away after giving him breakfast. (A black stranger doing as much as hanging around a widowed white woman was in itself dangerous in this community in the 1930s.)

But what a difference a day makes. Visits with her sister and the banker shift her perspective to something like economic desperation. So when the new sheriff, previously her husband's deputy, shows up that night holding Moze for the silverware he stole from Edna, she covers for his misdemeanor and forthwith takes him up on his offer to raise cotton. A more kindly and earnest fellow would be hard to find, and he fast becomes a kind of surrogate father to young Frank, sharing a mutual love of the practices of superstition. Nonetheless, as the film soon makes clear, his presence there helping the widow is an affront to the vehemently racist white power structure, and that eventually ruins the success that is coming.

And then comes the blind war veteran, Mr. Will (John Malkovich), foisted on Edna as a boarder by his brother-in-law, the banker Denby, who wants to move Will from his own home to anywhere else. At first taciturn, approaching misanthropic, Mr. Will loses his cold edge through the kindness of those around him, and slowly he melds into the life of this makeshift extended family. While Edna and Moze labor in the fields, he becomes chief cook and bottle washer; while they are rushing to bring in the first bale, he delivers food and news by means of strung clothesline. He even shares the record player he prizes as the crew works through the night to harvest the crop. Most of all, he becomes a friend to Edna: the pair comes to rely on each other for support. One of the significant things Benton accomplishes in the film is to show what a "blind" world might look like. Will likes Edna for who she is, not for her cute-as-a-button looks; and Will becomes Moze's dear friend despite the latter's black skin.

Benton makes quite clear just how much has changed for everyone in this new kind of family — for that is what it has become — midway through the movie, in the long, wordless storm sequence. The carefully choreographed rescues show it all: the radical care and mutuality, how they all risk everything to protect each other. And against all odds of place and circumstance, that is what they have found in one another: shelter amid life's "pitiless storm," as Shakespeare calls it in *King Lear*. Benton slowly dwells on each individual, seeing each in his or her fear and aloneness; but he also shows the group as a whole and

The reluctant Mr. Will has his first visit with the widow.

The family finds refuge — and one another — as they escape the "pitiless storm."

single entity, suggesting the strange kinship of all people to have and hold each other. This is exactly what this ragtag bunch is about — the outcast, the blind man, the widow, and the fatherless — finding shelter in one another, and looking a lot like the new community that Jesus announces in his very first sermon.

Just when we expect it to end, as it would within the confines of a Hollywood formula film — the widow and her new family of friends triumphing and living happily ever after — Benton upends his own ending. In cold-blooded honesty, he pulls the story away from Pollyanna-land back to hard reality, and he then proceeds, in a wholly unexpected gesture, to transfigure the tale into remarkable, even transcendent filmmaking.

Of course, whatever new "family" the Spaldings have found soon smashes into bits, as evil again rears its devouring head. In the midst of the community's harvest celebration, the Klan shows up to murder Moze, because a black man's success in helping a white woman doubly offends them. Exactly how much Moze means to Will appears in the extreme measures the latter takes to rescue him, risking his own life. But it is to no avail, for the Klan will return, as the white-hooded mill owner tells Moze. In the aftermath, in one of the film's most affecting scenes, Moze weeps in the dirt as his friend Will holds him. For a very long moment of film time, Benton's camera listens and watches, letting it all seep into the viewer's awareness. As much as he's gotten "attached" to this place, Moze must go into exile.

Then comes the most unusual church service in the history of cinema, if not in the history of the church. Benton deftly conflates and plays all kinds of ecclesiastical elements. The scene starts normally enough in the church, with the Spalding family seated near the front just behind Aunt Viola and her wandering husband. During the minister's reading of 1 Corinthians 13, St. Paul's rapturous hymn to love, Viola reaches over to take her husband's hand, and in that simple physical gesture, as in Will's embrace of Moze, she bestows abundant love. (My guess is that the whole tawdry adultery subplot was there to justify that sequence, and it is worth it.)

Then comes that communion, as it is usually called in Protestant churches — the Lord's Supper, the holy Eucharist itself — and things get a little strange. The elements of communion proceed down along the pews as the minister reads the words of instruction, while the choir sings over his words, and as the camera follows the bread and wine (grape juice), the Spalding family, who previously always sat in front, is nowhere to be seen. That is, they are unseen until — oddly, even miraculously — we see the exiled Moze receiving the elements and then serving the blind Mr. Will. This is quite startling, for not only did Moze have to flee town for his life, but this is no place for a black man at all: in a white church amid the deep segregation of Depression-era Texas. As Will passes the tray of grape juice on to the children, Frank says to himself, before he drinks, "the peace of God," inserting a new element into the ritual, and so does his mother, Edna. The transcendent jolt comes when Edna passes the tray to the person next to her, who turns out to be her dead husband, Royce; the latter then passes the tray on to the next person — saying "the peace of God" — to Wiley, the young black man who shot him, who returns the peace to him. With a final lengthy two-shot of that pair looking straight ahead, and the hymn proclaiming "the joy we share as we tarry there," the film ends. In terms of what Benton pulls off with his own bit of holy "shock and awe," that music might as well have been Handel's "Hallelujah Chorus."

Probably no other shot in cinema so deeply captures the crux of what the whole Christian venture is all about, namely, renewal and reconciliation: for "God so loved the world. . . ." It is for these bedraggled folks to be redeemed from what life has done to them, a holy intimacy with others that is the fullness of the blessing of God. Nor is this a mat-

Peace

ter of slick moviemaking happenstance. Benton took weeks to construct the elaborate apparatus that would allow the camera to shoot the entire sequence in one long take (there are no cuts or edits in over two minutes of tricky filming) that would follow the trail of the blood of Christ. That last shot of the killed and killer displays the boundless end for which Christ's blood was shed in the first place. One person told me of his seminary liturgics professor's claim that, after hosting Benton in his class, the depth of meaning in that cinematic Eucharist gets closer to the purposes of the Eucharist than two millennia of ecclesiastical wrestling.

Post-viewing Questions

1. Does Benton succeed in uncovering the deepest purposes and meaning of the celebration of the Holy Communion? How does the last sequence strike you? Is it an apt representation of the inmost character of God?
2. A point that some theological critics might raise focuses on the question of relationship, specifically whether the kinds of communion that take place in the film are merely human or somehow hint at divine presence. How might they be one and the same?
3. Needless to say, the film is very much about family — about

"places in the heart." How does it do in covering the "territory" that identifies those notable places?

4. How well does Benton's double subversion of Hollywood formula expectations work? The first delivers a jolt, but what about the second one — the coming of the Klan to murder Moze?

5. The history of Mr. Will is provocative and perhaps suggestive of the path that everyone has to take sooner or later. There is his initial haughtiness and self-pity, but that morphs into quite another attitude. Where does that show itself most fully, and how would you characterize it?

Critical Comments

A lot of reviewers simply did not know what to make of *Places in the Heart* — and particularly of its ending. An exception was Vincent Canby, who thought the film "a tonic, a revivifying experience right down to the final images, which, like those at the end of Luis Bunuel's *Tristana,* carry us back to the very beginning of the cycle of these particular lives" (*The New York Times,* Sept. 21, 1984). Roger Ebert did not see it that way: he thought the film simply could not support the grandeur of the conclusion, "a dreamy, idealistic fantasy in which all the characters in the film — friends and enemies, wives and mistresses, living and dead, black and white — take communion together at a church service." Unfortunately, though that was "a scene of great vision and power," it was simply "too strong for the movie it concludes," whose story largely excludes most of those located in town (*Chicago Sun-Times,* Jan. 1, 1984). As good a critic as he is, Ebert might have missed the gist of that conclusion, one that pictures a reconciliation that transcends locale, race, and social class. Frederic and Mary Ann Brussat, in their journal *Spirituality and Practice,* got that just about right: "As the camera slowly pans the congregation . . . we recognize all the characters — those living and dead and departed for other places. It is an image in which the lambs and the wolves, the wronged and the wrongdoers, the betrayers and the betrayed, are all together as one."

Other Notable Films by Robert Benton

Feast of Love (2007)
The Human Stain (2003)
Nobody's Fool (1994)
Kramer vs. Kramer (1979)
Bad Company (1972)

Grand Canyon

Director	Lawrence Kasdan
Writers	Lawrence Kasdan, Meg Kasdan
Cinematographer	Owen Roizman
Music	James Newton Howard

CAST

Kevin Kline	Mac
Danny Glover	Simon
Mary McDonnell	Claire
Steve Martin	Davis
Alfre Woodard	Jane
Mary-Louise Parker	Dee
Jeremy Sisto	Roberto

Rotten Tomatoes	75
Metacritic	64

- -

General Comments

Lawrence Kasdan's *Grand Canyon* (1991) came very much out of his own experience. Kasdan and wife Meg found themselves talking about a sense of the strangeness of life in general and especially in their own immediate experience and that of their friends. The result was a film unusual for its time, but one that clearly paved the way for more popular — though not necessarily better — films, such as *Crash* (the 2004 Oscar winner for best picture) and *Babel* (2006), a tale that moves over the entire globe. If not for Kasdan's own prominent position in Hollywood, his fresh, innovative film might not have gotten made, so peculiar was its story and structure in 1990. Around the movie industry for a long time, though by no means elderly, Kasdan had enough industry credibility that anything he really wanted to make probably would get made, though his record has not been without bigtime expensive flops, as was the case with his epic retelling of the legendary Western hero, *Wyatt Earp* (1994), another movie that showed the acting limitations of Kevin Costner. At barely thirty years of age, he co-wrote the screenplay for *The Empire Strikes Back* (story by George Lucas), the second installment of *Star Wars*. From there he moved on to write and direct his own noir film, *Body Heat* (1981), an elegant and downright shocking tale of murder and deception, starring Kathleen Turner and William Hurt (with quiet financial backing from Lucas, who didn't want his name associated with this very graphic, very grownup picture).

Kasdan's career flourished. With the stories shaped by others, he wrote the screenplays for both *The Raiders of the Lost Ark* (1981) and *The Return of the Jedi* (1983). More directing came in the form of his own screenplay for the cult classic *The Big Chill* (1983), the story of 1960s college friends who have been reunited for the funeral of their leader. Its large ensemble cast and rock soundtrack set new patterns for Hollywood. The immensely popular *Silverado* (1985) embraced western movie myths in his story of a random bunch of cowboys who come together to defeat a ruthless cattle baron. After those came *The Accidental Tourist* (1988), a moving adaptation of an Anne Tyler novel about a grief-stricken travel writer whose only child has died. For two of the three central roles in the film, Kasdan turned to the stars of *Body Heat*, William Hurt and Kathleen Turner. All these films — *The Big Chill, Body Heat,* and *The Accidental Tourist* — are stories of tragedy and friendship among strangers, and they forecast the kind of story Kasdan would tell when at last he turned to contemporary life, namely, survival in Los Angeles at the end of the twentieth century. As a helicopter traffic reporter says about halfway through the film, just in case viewers have missed the point, "It looks like hell down there."

As one might guess from the kind of stories Kasdan likes to tell, things don't start out well in *Grand Canyon*, even though many of the central characters live privileged lives. Shot in a kind of muted sepia, the opening credits play over a street-corner basketball game played by black men; in the background, drug deals are taking place. Still, there is the fun and glory of the game. As the ball bounces indecisively on the rim, the camera cuts to another ball, now in full color, bouncing indecisively on the rim during a Los Angeles Lakers game in the old Forum during the heyday of Magic Johnson (an editing device called a "jump cut," or "form cut"). In the front row courtside is a restive Mac (Kevin Kline from *Silverado*), who is at the game with his friend Davis (Steve Martin), a flamboyant, Ferrari-driving producer of graphically violent B-grade crime flicks, and his sultry girlfriend. As the friends bid farewell in the parking lot after the game, Davis, in his typical blowhard way, reminds Mac that fear thrives in the city, and soon enough Mac will find out just how true that is.

To avoid the postgame traffic jam, Mac shortcuts through an unlovely neighborhood only to have his fancy Lexus suddenly conk out. As he waits in his stranded car for a tow truck, a gang of gun-packing youths accost him. Things are threatening to get dangerous when a whirling yellow light shows up with tow-truck driver Simon (Danny Glover, also from *Silverado* and still wearing his cowboy boots). Simon proceeds to rescue not only the Lexus, but — with some gentle persuasion of the gang leader — Mac as well. At the service station afterwards, the two talk about life in Los Angeles and about life in general. Indeed, given what can happen in L.A. — notably, traffic, gangs, smog, urban decay, earthquake, and Santa Ana brushfires — it is a wonder, as Mac comments, that there's "anybody alive at the end of the day." And while Simon is a very generous and thoughtful fellow, he is not an optimist: he reflects that the world is a painful Darwinian mess of the strong preying on the weak amid the general indifference of the universe. Indeed, at its heart the film seems to be testing that proposition: Is the world a random struggle for survival, or might there be some superintending providence that we do not see because we aren't looking for it?

And from these two middle-aged men, different in so many ways, spins a whole web of characters. The prosperous immigration lawyer Mac lives in the affluent Brentwood area of L.A., with his wife, Claire (Mary McDonnell), and his teenage son, Roberto (Jeremy Sisto), who is named after the famous Pittsburgh Pirates baseball player Roberto Clemente. Simon, on the other hand, lives alone, his deaf daughter

Simon and Mac philosophize after Simon has come to the rescue.

clear across the country in Washington, D.C., attending the famous school for the deaf, Gallaudet University. But Simon's sister lives nearby, a single mother trying to raise her teenage son and young daughter in the midst of gangs and drugs. The workplace worlds of Simon and Mac differ substantially, too. If Simon is the night-shift Lone Ranger, Mac enjoys a comfortable day job with splendid high-rise views from his posh office and an adoring — in fact, too adoring — secretary, Dee (Mary Louise Parker). Dee has her good friend in the workplace, the equally single and equally lonely Jane (Alfre Woodard). What might happen amid this diverse array of people? — that's the question. The acting throughout the movie is fully convincing, especially as these diverse characters attempt to wend their way through the increasingly perilous world of Los Angeles. Their honesty helps enormously in giving plausibility to the philosophical riddle at the center of the film. Events provoke wonder at the mystery of being and fate. Grownups like Mac and Simon and Claire ponder what might be the reasons, if any, that things happen the way they do. Thanks to Lawrence Kasdan's fertile cinematic imagination, deft editing, haunting images, and suggestive camera work, we get a picture of what happens — and why.

Things to Look For

- Kasdan does a lot in this film with aerial photography. It is, in fact, one of his chief editing devices. There are also a lot of shots of and

207

Friends Jane and Dee discuss the perils of romance during a coffee break.

from helicopters, and these become a stylistic signature in the film and add significantly to its thematic questions about the possibility of a meaning-filled world.

- Another crucial strategy lies in his use of flashbacks, especially for Mac as he tries to understand different moments in his life. The first occurs in the cab of the tow truck as he and Simon make their way to the service station; more will come when he has breakfast with Simon. Mac wonders just what these flashbacks are trying to "tell" him, especially as he seeks to thank Simon — and then get to know him.
- The film is full of connections of various kinds, some new and some old, some emerging and some fading. Altogether these go a long way to develop and clarify a kind of answer to the central questions Kasdan poses throughout.
- The film is set in Los Angeles, so the title is not readily applicable, though we do come across several references from different characters to the Grand Canyon in the course of the story. These all relate, as does the film's ending, to Simon's initial appraisal of the meaning of human existence and perhaps provide a potent indication of how experience influences human understanding.
- Sports also play a big role, as they do in American culture as a whole. There are the opening basketball games described above, and at one point Mac and Simon talk of their love of both baseball and basketball. And near the end, Simon and Mac shoot baskets together. Perhaps Kasdan suggests something about what sports can tell humans about how to live and what to live for.

Post-viewing Commentary

So what exactly might these rescues mean — these unforeseeable and undeserved incidents of being pulled from the jaws of calamity — especially as they come to Mac? But Mac is not the only one to experience strange encounters and instances of being saved. For most of the others in the story, various kinds of rescue do indeed come, unbidden and full of grace, though certainly not in the spectacular, uncanny ways that Mac experiences. Peculiar "interventions" — miracles, says Claire, the clear-sighted one — happen all the time, though we poor mortals are often ill equipped to see them. Humankind's dimness of vision is especially true in places like Los Angeles, a frantic and lonely land full of peril and despair.

For Mac, Simon seems to be evidence of a kindly force of some kind or other that intrudes into the messiness, sometimes sheer danger, of ordinary human affairs, a realm that usually runs by strict material causality. The surprise of Simon's arrival and intervention is strange enough, but the matter is further complicated when Mac connects that rescue with an earlier occasion in L.A., in which another total stranger kept him from mortal harm. What do such events say about this world, and for what reasons do they happen? In this regard, Mac is very much like everyone, sensing that such rescues, mysterious as they are, must have some purpose. Since the viewers get the whole story, so to speak, they perhaps see connections and outcomes far better than the limited perspective of any one character in the film, as each one bumbles along trying to make sense of the seemingly meaningless. Beyond the characters' perplexity, viewers enjoy a kind of omniscience, though by no means Godlike, that provides an overview of the strange ways of Providence.

Mac, of course, is at the center of this question. It is Simon who rescues him, showing up in the nick of time, just as the young thugs are getting very threatening. And while his truck is by no means a chariot of fire, Simon himself comes with yellow lights whirling, in a sunny-gold T-shirt and cowboy boots (highlighted in the camera angle as he exits the truck), carrying not a six-gun but a tire iron. Nonetheless, the sequence works. It is Simon, the wise one, who talks the gang leader into letting them go. For Mac, Simon's arrival recalls in brief flashback that time years before when a stranger grabbed his shirt collar to keep him from absent-mindedly stepping to his death in front of a roaring bus.

209

It is this second occasion of rescue that prompts Mac the next day to look up his rescuer to buy him breakfast. In their small talk over coffee they find they have much in common: a love for sports in general, but especially a love for basketball and the baseball great Roberto Clemente, who died in a 1972 plane crash while attempting to deliver relief supplies to Nicaraguan earthquake victims. Simon explains that Mac owes him nothing because he probably was not in all that much danger from the gang; but that claim inspires Mac to tell the tale of his first rescue.

Here Kasdan freights the story with clues about its significance that Mac himself seems not to pick up, but the audience certainly does. On his way to a meeting in the part of Los Angeles known as "the Miracle Mile," near the Mutual Benefit building, the hand that snatches Mac from death belongs to a middle-aged woman in a Pittsburgh Pirates baseball cap, who promptly walks away and replies, "My pleasure," when Mac tries to thank her. Mac finds this unusual: a woman in a baseball cap of his favorite team who just happens to be on Wilshire Boulevard in the early morning to save his life. He felt as though he never got to thank her properly, and now he tracks Simon down to make sure he does the proper thanking this time. "Who" or "what" exactly did the rescuing — putting that woman there — and what that means seems a bit foggy to Mac, who apparently does not recognize the fittingness of where it takes place: on the Miracle Mile by (and for?) Mutual Benefit.

In this case, Simon, much as he does with the gang leader, offers a counterview, one that essentially repeats the grim perspective con-

On the "Miracle Mile," Mac tries to thank the woman who has saved his life.

tained in his late-night Darwinian gas-station musings. Here he offers the story of his father, "a black man in Los Angeles," whose life was hard and to no apparent purpose. His face looked like a "beat-up old suitcase," and he buried his wives and most of his children, and in that Simon finds nothing good, let alone splendidly miraculous. Simon's a realist, and when Mac offers to see if he can find Simon's sister a better place to live (mutual benefit) because her family has experienced a drive-by shooting, Simon has the honesty, guts, and realism to ask Mac whether his present generosity derives from white liberal guilt. He is not nasty, bitter, or condescending when he says this. He simply understands pretty well that people don't amount to much and accepts the fact and is determined not to let it dictate his behavior, for he seems to be a gentle man.

Plainly, though, things of "mutual benefit" do come out of this "miracle." One is that Mac fixes up Simon with a blind date with Jane, a vivacious secretary in his office building, and that date seems to start up a flourishing relationship. We know that it will when the camera, looking straight down, sees Simon arrive in his bright golden Camaro — the film's signal color — and shows their good-bye after the date to be one of the tenderest, and best-played, romantic scenes in recent film. Still, Jane's good fortune in meeting Simon emphasizes the loneliness of Dee, Mac's secretary. She and Mac have had some kind of very brief romantic relationship: Dee has been the aggressor, despite Jane's sage advice to stay away. By the end, though, in a kind of summary sequence, Dee seems to emerge from her isolation when she is rescued from an ugly road-rage incident by a charming young policeman. Again, good comes out of near-tragedy.

That is nowhere more clear than in the case of Claire, Mac's energetic but mildly anxious wife, who is the clear-eyed one, the one who sees and knows more than the rest. She is the one who most clearly articulates the husband-and-wife Kasdan writing team's cautious musing about the strangeness of life. Out jogging one day in the lovely streets of Brentwood, she hears an infant's cry from a copse of bushes. She enters it to find an abandoned infant, for whom she feels a sudden deep attachment and obligation, one that mystifies Mac and causes some tension in the marriage. Claire clearly senses the wonder of it all, muttering "surprise, surprise" as she sits poolside in her backyard with the child in her arms. Her resolve to adopt the child becomes steadfast one day, as she is running down an alley, when a homeless man — in a trenchcoat, with hair and beard long and unkempt, whom viewers have seen earlier raving incoherently — mutters, "Keep the baby — you need her more than she needs you." The comment causes Claire to whirl around in gaping wonder, an expression the camera dwells on as the scene fades not to black but stark white.

It is no wonder, then, that she later explains to Mac that such events as Simon's rescuing him and her rescuing the baby are "miracles" that we do not see because we do not look for them. Miracles of this kind, she contends, happen all around us. The term "God" never comes up, but it is clear that Claire sees a caring providence threading through the mysteries of their lives, a providence that not only conspicuously rescues the lost and imperiled but pushes people to connection, trust, and friendship, those elements for which the world was made.

On the opposite side of Claire's view is Davis, the gaudy producer of films of graphic violence. He looks and seems the perfect narcissist, the cynical counterpoint to Claire's hopefulness, and it is strange that he and Mac would be friends. Early in the film Davis gets a dose of his own medicine, so to speak, when he is shot in a random holdup on Rodeo Drive, Hollywood's super-tinseled shopping strip (he's stepping out of his Ferrari dressed in white pants and purple suede jacket). We see the grisly horror of actual crime: the camera looks straight down on Davis as blood and urine soak the leg of his white trousers. He barely survives, and in the aftermath he experiences a religious epiphany as he watches in awe as dawn rises over downtown Los Angeles, which he sees through his hospital window. The buildings and Davis are both bathed in intensely golden light, and the light in Davis is just as obvi-

Claire stares in astonishment after receiving counsel from a homeless man.

ous. He's grateful to be alive and — for a while at least — he turns kindly; he even pledges to stop making his luridly violent but profitable films. The feeling wears off, however, and Davis recedes into his old blustery self, frustrated by the bad limp left over from the shooting. In the audience's last view of him, at the huge doors of a studio warehouse, he enters a deep darkness as the gates of hell itself, it seems, slam shut.

That contrasts starkly with how the story ends for most of the other characters. At some later date, Simon goes to Mac's house because he wants to thank Mac for introducing him to Jane. As the two shoot baskets under lights in the driveway, Simon has a proposal. In the last sequence of the film we see one character after another get out of a rented passenger van into warm golden sunlight: Roberto, Jane and Simon, Simon's nephew Otis, Mac and Claire, and the baby. Claire adjusts a Pittsburgh Pirates cap on the head of the child she found in the bushes on her morning jog. And then the camera moves from character to character to catch their reaction to what they are looking at — what the audience cannot yet see. Those responses range from delight to surprise, especially as it registers on the grumpy demeanor of Otis, who clearly is not happy to find himself with this crew. Mac asks Simon what he thinks, to which the latter replies, "It's not all bad," indicating a stark shift in his views from the bleak estimate of the Grand Canyon that he offered in their gas-station talk at the beginning of the film. Because what they are looking at is indeed the Grand Canyon, and we see it as they do: in an elegant crane shot that moves from a view of the collected group to up and behind so that the audience can finally see what the group sees.

And what a strange route it has been to arrive here at the Grand Canyon. As Claire said at the pool to the abandoned infant in her arms, "Surprise, surprise!" We are surprised, too, as the camera sails through those canyons with the sound of a full-throated orchestra carrying us along. Like love itself, jubilant and wild and, as Frederick Buechner says, "Too good not to be true."

Post-viewing Questions

1. Might there be other meanings for Simon's comment at the Grand Canyon, "It's not all bad"? That seems to be a pretty grudging ad-

mission, even as he has his arms wrapped around his new love. Then again, Simon is a man of considerable understatement — such as in his story about his father — and is not given to melo- drama, even when he falls in love. And that stands in stark contrast to his very grim Darwinian reading of the Grand Canyon at the film's beginning, when he and Mac are sitting under the lights of the gas station. So what is the gist of the statement in this closing?

2. What is the gist of all those downward-looking and helicopter shots? Might they give us the sense that there is a vertical dimen- sion to life, or even an all-seeing something that connects us all, especially as that surveillance helicopter carries us from one scene to another? But even as a suggestive metaphor, is it one that perhaps should not be pushed too hard?

3. The film is perhaps not entirely successful insofar as it weaves so much into the tale that viewers sometimes wonder what could possibly come next. A good example is Roberto's experience at camp and his efforts to learn to drive. They seem not only to in- trude on the other prominent story lines but to offer nothing new to the story's thematic thrust. Is this a fair criticism? Could the movie as a whole be maybe twenty minutes shorter without los- ing too much?

4. Claire seems to "get" things more than others in the story. Simon sees the world darkly, pretty much excluding the possibility of much good or happiness, especially with an absent wife and im- paired daughter. Mac is confused, and Davis is the cynical egotist. Claire, though, seems open to hope and love in such a way that she ends up with a measure of some kind of faith. Characters ar- rive at different places by virtue of their life experience, their rela- tionships to one another — and just maybe, "miracles."

5. And what about Davis? He seems to see the light, in fact claims that he does, and that it is transformative; but then he seems to go back to his own overwhelming self-concern and old habits: chas- ing women, making bad movies for a buck, and seeing himself as a great filmmaker. Kasdan seems to seal that view in providing our last glimpses of Davis as he limps away from Mac's golf cart into a dark and cavernous soundstage, on which the doors slam shut. Why has he lost what he thought he had? Claire never seems to take him very seriously, even when he's in his grateful-and- good stage.

Critical Comments

An "offbeat and innovative film," declared Janet Maslin, one in which "the viewer truly has no idea what will happen next and many reasons to care." Within that perplexity of events, the film highlights "the ominous and the miraculous in everyday events" in an effort to understand "the intricate exchanges and equations that make up our destiny" (*The New York Times,* Dec. 25, 1991). Louis Black picked up on the same theme, going so far as to conclude that *Grand Canyon* is really about miracles "that settle quietly on the lives" of six characters (*Austin Chronicle,* Jan. 17, 1992). So moved was Roger Ebert that he declared that "[i]n a time when our cities are wounded, movies like *Grand Canyon* can help to heal" (*Chicago Sun-Times,* Jan. 10, 1992).

Other Notable Films by Lawrence Kasdan

Mumford (1999)
The Accidental Tourist (1988)
Star Wars: Episode VI — Return of the Jedi (1983) (screenplay)
The Big Chill (1983)
Body Heat (1981)

Films with Similar Thematic Concerns

Babel (2006)
Crash (2004)
Amores Perros (2000)
Magnolia (1999)
Hannah and Her Sisters (1986)

Babette's Feast

Director	Gabriel Axel
Writers	Karen Blixen (short story),
	Gabriel Axel (screenplay)
Music	Per Nørgaard
Cinematography	Henning Kristiansen

Babette's Feast won the Academy Award for Best Foreign Film (1988)

CAST

Stéphane Audran	Babette Hersant
Bodil Kjer	Filippa
Bergitte Federspiel	Martina
Jan Kulle	General Lorens Löwenhielm
Jean-Philippe Lafont	Achille Papin

- -

General Comments

Babette's Feast seemed an unlikely film to ignite an international craze. The film follows rather closely a short story written by a baroness, the famous Danish writer Karen Blixen (1885-1962), whose pen name was Isak Dinesen. She also wrote the source material, *Out of Africa,* her second book (1937), for another narrative that became a well-known film (1985), a memoir of her years in Africa running a coffee plantation and of her long romance with the famed English adventurer Denys Finch

Hatton (Meryl Streep and Robert Redford starred in the late Sydney Pollack's film adaptation). "Babette's Feast," the short story, first appeared in 1953 in *The Ladies' Home Journal* and was then collected with other Dinesen stories in *Anecdotes of Destiny* (1958).

None of this quite prepared viewers for this offbeat film and the remarkable response to it. As the title suggests, the film *Babette's Feast* (1987) is about a meal, not a likely source for engrossing filmmaking at the time (it was produced long before whole cable channels were devoted to everything for "foodies"). Moreover, the film takes place in a spot as close to nowhere as is perhaps humanly possible: a remote and tiny fishing village on the harsh Jutland coast of Denmark, really no more than a small collection of huts and small houses. And the folks who inhabit these homes and eat this meal are not an exciting group; rather, they are the aging remnants of an ascetic religious sect. In fact, the two leaders of the group are elderly spinsters ominously named after the Protestant reformers Martin Luther and Philip Melanchthon. Their father, who has been dead for decades at the time of the meal, founded the group and won notoriety for his conservative religious writings. Now, however, the aging remnants of the group barely limp along, soon to disappear as its members die off one by one. The celebration of the founder's hundredth birthday looms more as a valedictory than as a celebration. And it is for that sober occasion that Babette's surprising and stupendous feast arrives, much like a lush oasis in a parched desert. Or, in its own right, as a miracle of plenty, beauty, and healing.

In this obscure fringe of the world, that meal will be prepared by a refugee chef, Frenchwoman Babette Hersant (Stéphane Audran), whom the aging sisters, Martina and Filippa, took in during a fierce storm decades earlier. And Babette has stayed with them ever since, living quietly (and distantly) in an upstairs room and working tirelessly for very little, if anything at all. The cook, it seems, sought the sisters out because she was referred to them by a well-known Parisian opera singer who had passed through the village on a vacation many years before, and had gotten to know the devout sisters. For most of the film Babette seems to be a person with no past: we know little of her, save for the quiet devotion with which she serves the sisters, bargains for food with local merchants, and greatly improves the charitable fare prepared for the village's infirm and impoverished members, a task the sisters had taken on — not too successfully — before Babette's arrival.

The feast that will be

The story itself is full of events that are not only surprising but peculiar, ones that are marvelously rendered in the spare and elegant storytelling of Gabriel Axel, a Dane who spent his filmmaking career in France. Perhaps because of his limited budget, Axel allows the story to speak for itself, and it is most notable visually in its early parts for its representation of a muted, even drab world, as befits the climate, setting, and the austere religious and moral culture in which the two sisters reached maturity. The sun does shine, but it falls on a grayish world. It is only in the second half of the film, with its abundance of interior shots, that Axel begins to stoke the film's color register with a host of lamps and candles. Indeed, the prevailing sense one takes away from the film is of a profuse luminousness, a dark and harsh world that nonetheless has within it a warm golden light. And there's music too: first the hymns the sisters sing in early church scenes, and then later — in their shared spinsterhood — around the piano. Both of these provide an exacting delicacy of thoughtfulness and feeling to the film, a kind of counterweight to the severe world in which they dwell. When those elements are mixed with the precisely calculated lighting scheme, viewers feel transported to quite different realms that are seemingly far away from the tiny hardscrabble village on the Jutland seashore.

For a foreign film — in the Danish language, no less — *Babette's*

Feast became an enormous success, winning the 1988 Oscar for best foreign film. So captivated were the folks who watch foreign films, largely urbanites, especially in the days before Netflix, that the very menu of the feast Babette prepares in the film soon became a featured option in many restaurants in large American cities. Fortunately, long after that culinary groundswell evaporated, the film has remained a favorite of audiences all over, especially among religious film viewers, for its unique blend of the carnal (all that food) and the spiritual (all that God talk). Neither the setting nor the film itself seems a likely place for revelations, but here they abound in a place where the carnal becomes holy and the soul finds a rapturous elation in the unfathomable gift of being alive with others. Even wholly secular critics were taken with the film. The then dean of American film critics, Vincent Canby of *The New York Times,* called the film "swift, clean, witty, and elegant," "a spectacular feast." And David Denby, now of *The New Yorker,* got it exactly right when he called *Babette's Feast* "a triumphant sunburst of sensual and spiritual delight, a supreme banquet harmonizing body and soul." Indeed, it is an appetizing journey in numerous ways.

Things to Look For

- The enigmatic founder of the pietistic sect, the father of the two sisters, seems an ambiguous figure, especially concerning the kind of influence he must have had on his very admirable daughters. Was his role in their lives ultimately bane or blessing?
- Pay close heed to the mood and lyrics of the hymns sung throughout the sisters' youth, and how they help construct a conceptual frame for the story all around them.
- One of the most peculiar images of Jesus ever found in film appears when the camera dwells on a crucifix on which hangs a broadly smiling Jesus. One interesting possibility for its significance in the film lies in its "summary value," insofar as that image significantly catches up the mood of the film.
- Palette and lighting play a large role in constructing both mood and thematic in the film, especially in the latter half as the story moves between the interior of the dining room and the kitchen. Track the changes in both and what kind of effect they might have on viewers.

- Without symbol-mongering, look for scenes and/or shots that seem to summarize the gist of the film or push its meaning beyond the literal telling of the story.

Post-viewing Comments

Martina and Filippa are unusual sisters, and their lives have suffered from the strange behavior of their pious and very problematic preacher-father, who subverted budding romances for both of them with considerable calculation and delight. Though it is undoubtedly difficult for liberated twenty-first-century postmoderns to sympathize with his behavior, he may very well have done exactly the right thing in arranging for the departure of their very dubious suitors: neither man seems particularly well suited for the preacher's lovely, pure-spirited girls. One is a spoiled wastrel of a soldier who seems just recently to have finally cleaned up his act; the other is a Parisian bon vivant and opera star who seems to have no restraint whatsoever in his wooing of an innocent country girl — mostly, it seems, to exploit her voice. These judgments may seem harsh, but they are nonetheless entirely reasonable. Exactly how long would Lorens Löwenhielm stay on the wagon? And would Achille Papin actually make an honest woman of his new romantic and musical conquest?

There is enough in the film to suggest that odds of success for either would not be good. And fathers, bless their protective hearts, are a suspicious lot. No wonder, then, that the preacher smirks when he contrives Papin's departure. The very best that can be said for the fellows is that they were eminently flaky, and the likely truth might be that they were a good deal worse. At the same time, it is reasonable to see the father as a repressive control freak who would not relinquish his daughters to anyone, let alone allow them to determine their own lives.

If we do acknowledge that, the daughters in their spinsterhood do mourn their lost opportunities, though how much they do is not entirely clear. At one point, one does ask the other if she ever thinks of the young man, to which the former answers a poignant yes. Nonetheless, they seem to have found a measure of contentment in their adult lives. They try to sustain the small flock of followers whom their father had attracted, though there has clearly been attrition and now, in old age, quarrelsomeness among the survivors. The sisters also sustain the work of charity by tending to the town's sick and poor: they both visit and provide daily meals that they cook and deliver themselves. For themselves they read and play music and host the dwindling flock. Thoughtful and meditative, they doubtless brood on the meaning of it all, though that conclusion lies more in the mood of the film than in anything overt in script or action.

Nor does the coming of their cook much alter their lives. They do not so much hire her as give her refuge, though they have no idea how very badly she needs it. She certainly needs simple escape from the fires of revenge, but perhaps she needs even more a kind of harbor where she can heal her lashed soul in the aftermath of losing her art, her husband, and her son. So Babette stays, decade after decade — at least content, if not fully happy. And then comes the improbable lottery win, the ten thousand francs, an enormous sum by humble rural standards. And here is where the film gets really interesting.

And surely the biggest shock in the film is Babette's choice of how to use all of that lottery money. Like the sisters, viewers expect the servant cook Babette, now with resources and changed political winds in Paris, to be gone on the first boat out of that solitary place. Instead, she asks to prepare a meal — an honest-to-goodness real French meal —

Babette asks the sisters' permission to prepare a real French meal to celebrate the 100th birthday of their long-deceased father.

for the "flock" on the occasion of the founder's one hundredth birthday, a prospect that just plain horrifies the ascetic daughters. As she heads off by boat for a few days to gather the ingredients, it becomes clear that she intends to prepare an elaborate meal.

The term "exotic," at least for these sisters, does not begin to do justice to what Babette intends to bring back: live turtles and live quail, boxes of wine, all looking delectable and very dangerous — enough to cause nightmares of perdition. By happenstance — that is, visiting his ancient aunt — the once-young suitor Lorens Löwenhielm, now a well-traveled general, will attend the dinner. That is a good thing, because he is the only guest with any idea of just what they are all consuming. It is his astonishment, recollection, and gusto that cue viewers into the assorted miracles of the feast. The foremost surprise is the explanation of who Babette really is. At last we get it, though the general never seems curious enough to inquire about who's in the kitchen cooking up all this wonderful food. The further surprise is that Babette would lavish all her skill and money on these humble people, who fail to recognize just how special their feast really is. But that is who Babette is, the humble one who clasps her necklace cross as she requests permission of the sisters to present the meal for the flock.

And then comes the meal itself, a lustrous visual and culinary display. The cutlery and tableware and candles transfigure the modest

The astonishment on Löwenhielm's face as he tastes a rare wine

222

dining room, all gorgeously filmed by Axel. This is an unusual domain for beauty to show itself. Yet, if the splendor of landscapes can make glad the heart, cannot food do the same in its exquisite, sensuous variety? The full array, including the benefits of various wines, has its way with the guests. Magically, quarrelsomeness gives way to joy, gratitude, confession, reconciliation, and renewed affection. Finally, in one of the film's loveliest sequences, the guests toast one another, and then the little flock moves outside to sing under the stars an old song that has been made new and meaningful by the eucharistic meal they have shared. Like the original love feast, the agapic art of this feast has been given to them in love.

The inmost dramatic structure of *Babette's Feast* reenacts the primal Christian story: the master chef of Paris becomes the lowly cook for the lowliest, using her skills and art to display the reality of light and love. The gesture is at once an expression of her indebtedness for the sisters' shelter and welcome *and* a savoring of the craft that celebrates the enduring goodness of creation. It is a token of the supreme love-fired blessing of humans that they should live in such a place and enjoy such a heart-gladdening feast.

The fullest expression of divine presence amongst these lives is that when Babette wins the lottery and again has the chance to display the fullness of her art (it does take money), she eschews fame and wealth, both of which she could have enjoyed abundantly had she returned to Paris, where her fame persists still. Instead, she simply gives it all away, lavishing her magnificence on those who took her in when she was outcast and desolate. She returns the favor via a bedazzling and transforming performance of her art.

In the last scenes, viewers enter a world full of meaning and a quiet but dense gladness. It is there in the last conversation between Martina and Lorens, in the hymn that is sung around the well (a fitting image itself), and in the exchange on art between Babette and Filippa. A cascade of surprise followed by wonder, all profound and mysterious, has come to these people in this obscure place. The film perhaps evokes the Christian notion that the most remarkable events come out of nowhere and transpire in obscure places, places like a stable in Bethlehem — and even Gethsemane and Golgotha. Amid the thicket of mystery in which these people live out their days comes a full measure of light and warmth and also mystery. They only know that they have seen it — and so have the viewers.

The once quarrelsome members of the little flock now sing and dance under the stars.

Post-viewing Questions

1. General Löwenhielm seems to be the only one who really understands the extraordinary culinary magic of what those gathered for Babette's feast are consuming. And he is also the only one who understands how odd it is that they should be eating what they are eating, where they are eating — in the harsh Danish outback. Throughout the film it is he — as the one genuine sophisticate in the group, the one who has been around — who time after time cues viewers' responses to the splendors of the meal. Of course, viewers are already in on the joke, having seen Babette import all those materials for the meal. How much does the general help us understand the sense in which this is a "love feast"?

2. The shared meal, prepared as both gift and expression of the artist's inmost character, echoes in significant ways not so much the specific doctrinal details of different Christian theologies but the existential heft of the event itself. What does it really mean in human terms? Is it transforming or transfiguring? And in what ways?

3. Perhaps the biggest surprise comes when the sisters, after the meal, discover that Babette, first, will not be leaving them to re-

turn to Paris to start over in a new Café Anglais, and that, second, she has spent all her winnings, all that she is worth, on this meal. Her view is, after all, that a meal for twelve at the Café Anglais would cost 10,000 francs. The big question, of course, is the simple but inescapable "why?"

4. One of the more remarkable — though mysterious — scenes in the film is the parting exchange between Martina and Lorens Löwenhielm. Though the two still clearly love each other, though they have been and ever will be apart, what is the mood in this scene? How do we understand Lorens's comment that, despite that perpetual separation, they have always been together?

5. The film ends curiously, with the snow falling outside the candlelit window before the candle itself extinguishes. It is a lovely and potent visual image and seems to exude some sort of symbolic meaning — but of what?

Critical Comments

Opening to critical raves, *Babette's Feast* spurred a culinary craze, one that was — strangely — at odds with the spirit of the film. And most critics did focus on the feast. Roger Ebert called it "one of the great sensuous sequences in contemporary films" and the film as a whole "a small but wonderful treasure" (*At the Movies*, Mar. 4, 1988). Deeson Thomson pointed to the significance of the feast but did not quite grasp its eucharistic significance: "As we watch this magnificence being eaten we are seeing Babette's substance consumed" in "a willing and wonderful sacrifice" (*Washington Post*, Apr. 8, 1988). Vincent Canby waxed eloquent — and religious — in proclaiming the film "an affirmation of art as the force by which, in the words of the old pastor (who never quite realized what he was saying), 'righteousness and bliss,' otherwise known as the spirit and the flesh, shall be reconciled" (*The New York Times*, Oct. 1, 1987).

Other Memorable Films About Dinner and Food

Julie and Julia (2009), in which Meryl Streep plays the person most responsible for the contemporary exaltation of cuisine.

Eat Drink Man Woman (1994), the film that put director Ang Lee on the map.

My Dinner with Andre (1981), Louis Malle's film of two New Yorkers (Wallace Shawn and Andre Gregory) having dinner together, the screenplay written by the actors themselves.

VI. Signs and Wonders

This world is a strange place, and one of its stranger questions inquires about the meaning of events and how they might be connected to others — or are they random? The hounding enigma of *fate*, as the Greeks called it, or *providence*, as some Jews and Christians call it, simply does not go away as people of all ages and beliefs try to make sense of the contours of their lives. Even secularists look for design or meaning in the flow of events, finding something benign — even serendipitous — in the course of evolutionary biology.

The great American playwright and novelist Thornton Wilder, whose work is now undergoing a long overdue reappraisal, wondered in his novel *The Eighth Day* (1968) if life was indeed capricious, whether we are thrown into existence "like dice from a box," or whether life more accurately resembles a tapestry whose design we don't see because we see only its ragged underside of loose ends.

That question becomes a lot more difficult when it is placed within the context of misfortune, especially when the good or innocent suffer or die horribly. What sense there is to be made of cruelty — practiced by people or the gods — tests just about everyone's optimism. Earthquakes and tsunamis hit and are devastating in scope and frequency. That stalwart champion of belief Saint Paul acknowledged that we see much of life as through a dim glass. The best he could do when facing the question of theodicy was to suggest that evil inflicted by the malice of the principalities and powers might someday, somehow, turn toward goodness. In short, evil may indeed devour goodness in the short run; but in the long run, the evil that is suffered may be transformed to goodness. That the world is a tragic place, evil outside and in, remains a given in the Jewish-Christian scriptures. Evil works its persistent, insidious way despite the sundry protestations of the health-and-wealth schools of thought, those who turn divine providence into a rabbit's foot or a juicy portfolio.

Two recent remarkable and very surreal tales hold out the hope that pattern, design, and purpose do abound, though their reality often remains hidden to the beneficiaries — that is, the people involved. Paul Thomas Anderson's *Magnolia* (1999) tracks the disparate lives of nine people who end up intersecting in curious ways that both judge and redeem. In a zany prologue, Anderson posits up front the seemingly outlandish possibility that this world is indeed stranger — and more meaningful — than we think. Along the way, the viewers are given a tour of the woe and self-destruction people suffer, until — finally, unforeseeably — miraculous events befall them all.

The last film is a fitting one with which to end these discussions: *Heaven* (2002), a Tom Tykwer film of a Kieslowski-Piesiewicz screenplay, starring Cate Blanchett in her best-ever performance. A young British-born schoolteacher in Turin, Italy, sets out to even the score with a "respectable" drug lord whose product has killed her husband and some of her students. In her attempt at justice, everything goes horribly wrong; then, abruptly and strangely, everything goes right — or so it seems. There is a peculiar intervention that transfigures Philippa Boyen's sense of the world and the purpose of life — and ours, too. Beautifully shot and told, the film incrementally moves viewers into a different frame of understanding, wherein they also become pilgrims ascending to Light itself.

The perplexing and haunting riddle is that of one's own life and the role of the divine within it — especially with respect to other lives. Both Anderson and Kieslowski-Piesiewicz-Tykwer offer perspectives that see light and reconciliation emerge amid chaos and darkness. From the darkness new dawn may come.

Magnolia

Writer	Paul Thomas Anderson
Director	Paul Thomas Anderson
Cinematographer	Robert Elswit
Editor	Dylan Tichenor
Production Design	William Arnold and Mark Bridges
Music	Aimee Mann and Jon Brion

CAST

John C. Reilly	Jim Kurring
Tom Cruise	Frank T. J. Mackey
Julianne Moore	Linda Partridge
Philip Seymour Hoffman	Phil Parma
Jason Robards, Jr.	Earl Partridge
William H. Macy	Donnie Smith
Jeremy Blackman	Stanley Spector
Philip Baker Hall	Jimmie Gator
Melora Walters	Claudia Wilson Gator
Melinda Dillon	Rose Gator

Rotten Tomatoes	**85**
Metacritic	77

General Comments

A relatively recent and wholly distinct genre of Hollywood movie is called the "network narrative," which refers to films that have a multitude of characters and also, typically, a multitude of plot lines that weave in and out of one another. Woody Allen mastered this in films such as *Hannah and Her Sisters* (1986) and *Crimes and Misdemeanors* (1989); Lawrence Kasdan followed with *Grand Canyon* (1991); more recently, Paul Haggis won the Oscar for best picture with *Crash* (2004). The late Robert Altman had dipped into this kind of storytelling a generation ago with *Nashville* (1975) and then *Short Cuts* (1993). With plots and lives aplenty weaving through the narrative, the questions that usually emerge for audiences focus on what possible connection all these disparate characters might have with one another.

The boldest — and probably best — of these sprawling network narratives is P. T. Anderson's *Magnolia* (1999), a film that is zany from start to finish, always very deeply wrenching and propulsive, and finally — after a long slog through unforgettable misery and guilt — triumphant. As both writer and director, Anderson was working mostly with his favorite crew of actors, and thus *Magnolia* is fairly pure auteur filmmaking, singularly originating from within the zesty and wildly creative imagination of young Mr. Anderson. (His recent *There Will Be Blood* [2007] is a stunning example of cinema at its best, especially Daniel Day Lewis's Oscar-winning performance.) If most filmmakers comfortably work within the conventions and limits of the medium, Anderson yanks the medium around to encompass in *Magnolia* his vision of the way things are. There are simply no precedents for what he does — bold, transfixing, and always surprising.

Magnolia follows the lives of a diverse lot of people, nine central characters in all, in a three-hour submersion into pain, confusion, psychospiritual desolation, death, and — at long last — an exultant kind of epiphany. Throughout the interwoven narratives the film grabs viewers by the scruff of the neck, so to speak, and evokes frustration, tolerance, sympathy, credulity, and, finally, relief. Two hours into my first viewing of it, I concluded that if things did not soon take a new turn, I was heading for the exit. That was not because the film was boring or bad; it was because it was all too enveloping, and I wasn't sure whether I could much longer take what was happening to its multiple desperate characters (this was the part of the film that the DVD labels "meltdown").

At the very beginning, for example, as an example of Anderson's wonderfully off-kilter imagination, we are confronted by a very bizarre — and very funny — prologue to the film proper, an anecdotal investigation of crazy coincidences, all of which make viewers feel as though they have been thrust, willy-nilly, into the whacky late-night TV terrain of space aliens or conspiracy theories. Anderson first disarms and then grabs the viewers, and finally he pitches the most overwhelming question of all: Is life an accident, or could there be some meaning amid the apparent randomness of events? This is a question he will pose again in voice-over at the very end.

Nor do any of the characters in the story bear any resemblance to any others anywhere — even less in the way we meet them. First comes Los Angeles policeman Jim Kurring, wonderfully played by Anderson regular John C. Reilly: this cop is a far cry from Clint Eastwood's Dirty Harry or Mel Gibson's half-lunatic but lethal cop in the *Lethal Weapon* series. Kurring is at the opposite end of the spectrum: an officious, lonely, and marginally competent officer with whom none of his fellow officers want to partner. This seems to be the guy about whom the first Aimee Mann song in the score was written ("One is the loneliest number . . .") — though it could be the song about just about anybody in this narrative, as we will soon find out. In fact, Kurring is so lonely that he immediately falls for an attractive young addict he meets while investigating complaints about a loud stereo. So befuddled and hungry for attention is Kurring that he does not see what is obvious to all: this woman is a serious druggie and is presently as high as a kite.

The young woman is Claudia Gator (Melora Walters), the estranged daughter of television's longest-running quiz-show host, Jimmy Gator

Jim Kurring, the inept policeman

(Philip Baker Hall). She is also kind of an amateur hooker, partly to abate her loneliness but mostly to earn money for her habit. Her father, whose last name proves telling, has his own sizable problems. Jimmy hosts a quiz show that features precocious children pitted against ordinary adults. The star of the current kids' team is Stanley Spector (Jeremy Blackman), a very bright young boy who learns facts as a refuge from and antidote to his cruelly exploitative father, himself a full-gown child who dreams of someday becoming a star. Given his circumstances, Stanley seems headed for the same fate as the most famous contestant of all, "Quiz Kid" Donnie Smith (William H. Macy), who made piles of dough (for his parents) as a child but cannot pull off life as an adult. He works now as an appliance salesman who is obsessed with getting braces on his teeth so that he can attract the attention of a muscle-bound bartender.

The Gators, Stanley, and Donnie have all depended on the largesse, such as it is, of "Big Earl" Partridge (Jason Robards, Jr.), a daytime television magnate who lies on his deathbed for the duration of the film, tended by his hospice nurse, Phil Parma (Philip Seymour Hoffman), and intermittently by his distraught trophy wife, Linda (Julianne Moore), who seems to have a potent prescription drug habit.

As he dies, Big Earl turns confessional; and well he should, because he carries a trainload of guilt, all of which he exposes in torrents of shame and vitriolic self-loathing. It is a candid and brutal trip. The chief manifestation of his sins is his son, Frank T. J. Mackey (Tom Cruise), an entrepreneurial self-help guru and an abominable example of predatory sexual exploitation. What we hear from him fully matches his father in violent, rancid diatribe, though its function is just the opposite.

Linda Partridge bids farewell to her dying husband, Earl.

This is a miserable bunch, and that is the point: a cohort of pretty ordinary people who carry around with them their own unique brands of brokenness, some self-inflicted and others inflicted on them by other people. Human transgressions are destroying lives and relationships and any chance for intimacy, no matter the status of one's success or failure. As the narrator says at the beginning of the narrative, "Is this really all just an accident?"

So be warned: *Magnolia* is not for the faint of heart, either in substance or film style. It bluntly shows people at their worst, morally and emotionally, and it pulls no punches. For the first two hours, it feels as though viewers are right there in the ring with the characters, getting pummeled by life's biggest and toughest woes. At the same time, the cinematic storytelling is exhilarating, and the stories swirl one upon another, all of them sustained by the songs of Aimee Mann, exceptional editing, and bravura performances. And as the periodic weather reports inform us, wear a raincoat — and maybe body armor, too.

What to Look For

- While *Magnolia* by no means depends on them, the songs of Aimee Mann (a line from one of them actually inspiring the whole of the film) perform many functions throughout the course of the film. So listen carefully!
- And there are those occasional cryptic weather reports that seem to have little function. Or do they?
- At times the film goes just plain surreal, especially as it pivots toward its conclusion. A couple of specific events break the intense emotional realism of the story, and these two conspicuous departures dramatically reshape viewer understanding of what's afoot here, especially with respect to the voice-over commentary on chance and the characters' mounting despair over the direction of their lives.
- For all of its sensationalism — and much of this film goes places few films have gone — all of these characters do make, for better or worse, a "transit" of sorts, moving from one place to another. Their destinations suggest a lot about the human condition shared by everyone.

- Of course, the story as a whole finally focuses again on those initial suggestions about luck, chance, and ultimately providence (in religious terms).

Post-viewing Comments

When P. T. Anderson entitles one section of the DVD edition of the film "Meltdowns," he isn't kidding: characters keep reaching their breaking point and showing it. Jim Kurring, in the ultimate cop mistake, loses his gun, making him more of a buffoon than ever among the other policemen. Claudia Gator, again coke-blitzed on her couch, just plain despairs as she takes another snort. Frank T. J. Mackey, finally confronted with the real truth about himself and the imminent death of the father he hates, first walks out of a media interview and, soon after, out of his macho-guy seminar. His father, Earl, moments before he dies, vents his scathing self-recrimination. His wife, Linda, full of guilt and loss, drains her prescription meds as she sits wrapped in fur in her Mercedes sports car. And Stanley Spector considers just giving up. In the words of Aimee Mann's song, and indeed as all the characters come to realize, "It's not going to stop, till you wise up." But then the question surely is, for them as for the viewers: How exactly does one do that?

No wonder, then, that the whole desperate group soon, one by one, join in the singing of "Wise Up," which will take some doing all right, especially for Linda, who is already comatose in a lonely, rain-soaked parking lot in her Mercedes. Also comatose, her husband, Earl, clearly needs help as well, given what we've heard of his stupidity and malefactions; but that will have to be in another world, so close is he to death. Jimmy Gator, Earl's TV vassal but the very opposite of a "host," alone seems beyond rescue, given his egregious crimes — particularly against his daughter — crimes he can't even remember because he was so soaked in booze. Jimmy will die in a fire, as though hell itself can't wait to get its hands on him.

And "so it goes," as the narrator says over and over again: the inexorable and inescapable human impetus to destroy others and ourselves, unceasing and crass, even when we know better. Strangely, success, wealth, and fame seem only to exacerbate the evil appetites and impulses. Those who should know, however privileged and bright they are, just don't. In the end, the Bible has it right: in the Fall, in Ecclesias-

"Quiz-Kid" Donnie Smith joins in the singing of "Wise Up" before going out to rob his employer.

tes and Lamentations — and in what the dying Earl Partridge realizes in his last moments — is the cogency and finality of love.

Thank God, then, for the frogs, the book of Exodus sign of judgment on the Egyptian slavers and of liberation for the enslaved, which is just about everybody. That is the radical intrusion that begins the reversal of the towering wrongness of things, except in the case of Jimmy Gator, as if Anderson wishes to say that, in his case, simple suicide was too easy an exit for him. There is, after all the woe depicted, help for human desolation, which is the state where most of us end up before the falling of the frogs. It is wonder and amazement, a radical sign that life is not fatally foreclosed, that anything can and will happen, just as the narrator contends. And it ignites enormous change for all the characters, a remarkable intrusion that proves, in different ways, salvific for them all.

Something like this is simply not coincidence. The storm rains those fat, gloppy, splattering frogs down on Angelinos, some of whom think very little of it, as if it happens every day, just another annoyance in the land of brushfires, earthquakes, and endless traffic. However, it does miraculously hasten what we least expect. It is not just that something strange is happening here, another freak of nature, but that this storm belongs to a certain kind that we expect even less — and that is *reconciliation*. Rose and Claudia Gator cling together in terror — both because of the storm and, as Rose now knows, because of the sexual abuse Claudia has suffered at the hands of her father. Frank pivots from fury at his father to forgiveness and a hope that his father may survive.

The roads that are slick with frog innards cause the wreck of the ambulance carrying the nearly dead Linda Partridge to the hospital, where she will receive a visit from her estranged stepson, Jack, formerly known as Frank T. J. Mackey.

But the most significant turn of events, and the clearest indication of what Anderson aims to do in this film, is the fact of the suddenly intertwined fates of "Quiz-Kid" Donnie Smith and the cop Jim Kurring. Donnie has decided, after stealing money from his former employer, to return it, which he tries to do. But he discovers that, in his hurry to leave the store, he has haplessly broken off his key in the lock. He is climbing the drainpipe when he's spotted by the equally hapless Kurring, who is on his way home from his disastrous date with Claudia.

Always the dutiful and moral cop, even when he's off duty, Kurring turns his car around to arrest the "dummy" climbing up to the roof of the store. But then the frogs begin to plop down and goo up the streets, and Kurring struggles to rescue Donnie (who has taken a frog right in the face) by pulling him under the roof of a service station. The heretofore hyperlegalistic Kurring then does something exceptional for him: he helps Donnie, now bloodied and toothless from his encounter with the falling frog, to return the money, explaining in a voice-over that sometimes one has to deviate from the rules to help another person. The storm has accelerated his recognition of the fact that he's too judgmental and that people need compassion, not judgment. It seems as though Kurring and Donnie have actually found a friend in each other.

So here the lawbreaker and the law-enforcer have moved within the newfound realm of mercy, the undreamt-of land of reconciliation, the only route to what will indeed "save me." In fact, Anderson leaves no doubt whatsoever about what he's after when Kurring's lost gun becomes visible among the dead frogs that have fallen from the sky. Good work, Jim; you are now fully worthy of the gun.

The only one who really understands the marvel of the frog storm is Stanley Spector, who, in the middle of the storm, is bathed in a kind of ethereal, beatific light. The young boy, who has broken into the school library late at night, reads a book about wunderkinder like himself. Only Stanley seems to comprehend what has befallen him and all those around him: it is nothing less than a wild breaking out of the divine, above all, that gives him hope. This is so true that he will rebuke his greedily exploitative and utterly domineering father by telling him, "You've got to treat me better." If only Donnie Smith, as smart as he is, had had this measure of hope about the openness of human history — that things can indeed change — when he was young, he might not now be heisting appliance stores for braces to make himself attractive to muscle-bound bartenders. More than that, the young boy Stanley realizes deep in his bones that the world is a strange place, so strange that the divine may at any time — in astounding, wildly mysterious, and merciful ways — break into human affairs to do the unforeseeable works of love that retrieve the lost.

In the epilogue, we see the toll of ill-lived lives: Earl's body being carted off and the fire department at the Gator house. But best of all, we see the emergence of hope and reconciliation. Frank/Jack goes to visit Linda in the hospital, Stanley tells his father to behave, and Jim visits Claudia, now lovingly tended by her mother. In the closing shots, though we cannot hear all of what he says, Jim assures Claudia that he will be there for her and that the two of them can work together toward some sort of relationship, at the end of which we see, in the last shot of the film, Claudia actually breaking out in a joyous smile.

In *Magnolia,* Paul Thomas Anderson stokes up an enormous amount of cinematic inventiveness and storytelling energy to present a whirlwind tale of multiple woe-stricken lives that are headed toward even greater misery. Many of them have reached the end of their rope, but they are then willing to let go of the guilt and remorse that unremittingly consumes them. None of this is pretty, save for the filmmaking, which is downright dazzling — in the music, editing, narrative, language, point of view, and surrealism. Anderson melds all of these together into a kind of aria-like cry of the soul for succor and hope, where *Magnolia* ultimately arrives after a long and arduous trip. Help and

Stanley Spector sits in wonder at the coming of the frog storm.

hope pull these people — at least the survivors — out of the swamp of their brokenness and despair.

Post-viewing Questions

1. One of the wonderful accomplishments of *Magnolia* is the deft way in which this multistranded story effortlessly weaves its way through the distress of these many characters. How does Anderson accomplish this?
2. The only character who gets a voice-over presence, and then a very considerable one, is Jim Kurring, the policeman. Why is that the case, and what does it allow us to discover?
3. The frog storm is, needless to say, one of a kind in the history of movies. What was your initial response, and did it make any more — or any final — sense by the end of the film?
4. Anderson does provide several hints about the approaching story by sprinkling the text with the numbers eight and twelve, which is the chapter and verse citation for the plague of frogs in the book of Exodus. Any luck in finding any of those?
5. The film's language is extreme, both profane and obscene, and some have raised a fuss about whether quite so much of that continual diet is necessary. The film surely earned its "R" rating. Is it all necessary?
6. The only adult in the film who seems genuinely likable and admirable is hospice nurse Phil Parma. How does he function with regard to those other characters he knows, and what is the gist of his presence in the film in developing its thematic core?

Critical Comments

Roger Ebert advises viewers to leave "logic at the door" in order to understand the "operatic ecstasy" as "its characters strive against the dying of the light, and the great wheel of chance rolls on toward them" (*Chicago Sun-Times*, Jan. 7, 2000). Peter Travers thought not in terms of opera but miracles, describing *Magnolia* as "a movie of constant astonishments, including a cast sing-along to a ballad by Aimee Mann and a rain of frogs (check your Bible, Exodus 8:8) that serves as a millennial wake-up call" (*Rolling Stone,* Feb. 27, 2001). Rita Kempley correctly sees Anderson not as a cynic but "a bighearted guy who's madly in love with his characters, and even when they're very bad, he can't bring himself to sneer at their shortcomings. Punish them, yes, for the filmmaker believes in a just God and the pop aphorism that what goes around comes around" (*Washington Post,* Jan. 7, 2000).

Other Notable Films by Paul Thomas Anderson

There Will Be Blood (2007)
Punch-Drunk Love (2002)
Boogie Nights (1997)

Heaven

Director	Tom Tykwer
Writers	Krzysztof Kieslowski, Krzysztof Piesiewicz
Cinematographer	Frank Griebe

CAST

Cate Blanchett	Philippa Boyen
Giovanni Ribisi	Filippo
Remo Girone	Father
Alessandro Sperduti	Ariel

Rotten Tomatoes	73
Metacritic	68

- -

General Comments

Written by the famed Polish duo of Krzysztof Piesiewicz and Krzysztof Kieslowski, and directed by German director Tom Tykwer, *Heaven* (2002) plainly suggests the inevitability of a kind of afterlife — and not merely in its title. The film itself appeared posthumously for Kieslowski, who died suddenly in 1996. Two years before his death, Kieslowski declared that he was not going to make another film. What he apparently meant was that he was giving up directing, an all-encompassing and exhausting task — and especially at the pace at which Kieslowski pushed himself. But he did not stop writing screenplays. In fact, before his death, Kieslowski and his longtime writing partner, Krzysztof Piesiewicz, had begun work on a new trilogy of films, a kind of cinematic divine comedy: Heaven, Hell, and Purgatory. News of this drew the interest of North American producers and directors Sydney Pollack and Anthony Minghella (both of whom died unexpectedly in 2008). The screenplay was given to the talented German director Tom Tykwer (*Run, Lola, Run* [1998]) because he seemed to share some of the Polish writers' thematic interests. The other two parts of the trilogy have since been filmed in Europe: *Hell* in Italy (2005) and *Hope* in Poland (2007), though neither one has yet been released in North America, either in theaters or on DVD.

Another surprise is that for a long time through its story, *Heaven* shows nothing whatever of what might connect the story to the film's title, at least in terms of the usual expectations of what Hollywood produces when it gets around to referring to heaven. However, that is characteristic of Piesiewicz-Kieslowski films. *Three Colors,* their trilogy on the colors of the French flag, with the individual films subtitled *Red, White,* and *Blue,* never gets near anything particularly patriotic or French — at least certainly not directly. Instead, the films simply address the values denoted by those colors — liberty, equality, and freedom — and even then it is often difficult to identify which of the three an individual work pursues, though in the end each one of them surely does. So also with their most famous work, *Decalogue* (1988-89), a ten-part Polish television series on the Ten Commandments. There is nothing hokey or overly pious about these probing, incisive explorations of human motivation; but it is often difficult to make out which film segment deals with which commandment, in part due to the different ordering of the commandments in Roman Catholic and Protestant translations of the Bible.

The same can be said of *Heaven,* for the story initially looks and feels much like a very well-done Hollywood thriller — with suspense, bombs, culprits, destruction, and death — and in that regard about as far from heaven as one could get. Indeed, it seems to have set out to defy its title. The opening is so downright gripping in its intricate plotting and crisp editing that it hooks viewers for the duration of the film — long after it has largely left behind those scary, spectacular, and suspenseful elements.

Heaven focuses on two people, with very few other characters marginally important to the plot. At the very center is thirty-ish Philippa Boyen (played by Australian actress Cate Blanchett, in as fine a performance as she has given), who grew up in Italy as the daughter of an expatriate British family and now teaches in the Turin middle schools. And she is a widow whose husband has died of a drug over-dose, just as some of her young students have also died. Philippa is deeply upset about that, as well as about police inaction, needless to say, and the film begins with her response to both. And there's Filippo (American actor Giovanni Ribisi), a fledgling policeman and interroga-tion stenographer who is the son of the now retired Turin police super-intendent (the well-known Italian actor Remo Girone); and the angelic-looking little brother, Ariel (Alessandro Sperduti), who happens to have Ms. Boyen for his teacher. In this film, family and history count for a lot, for they not only shape who we are but forecast our futures.

Full of surprising turns, the story finally morphs from one world to the next, so to speak, although it always dwells within a realistic tex-ture, which is part of its wonderfully baffling appeal. What exactly hap-pens and where exactly the film ends — well, that's the kind of mystery that good art conjures. In this case, it first provokes and even exasper-ates, but then finally it just haunts: in its story, its images, the acting, the music, and the wildly peculiar ending.

Director Tykwer uses a host of cinematic resources, though he

Philippa walks to an office tower to avenge the death of her husband and students.

keeps his bag of tricks from being at all conspicuous. The purely cinematic ones have to do with camera angles, camera distance, the length of takes, filters, palette, and, as always, lighting. To these he adds remarkable kinds of imagery, ranging from hands to all kinds of religious symbols sprinkled throughout the plot. They all function to add atmosphere, a kind of fittingness and even portentousness, to the gist of the story, and they all carry specific kinds of religious meaning. Even casting and makeup play a role in posing opposites: the blonde and lanky Aussie and the dark and solid Italian. Sound is also featured significantly, from the long periods of quiet to the simple and profoundly searching musical score, consisting only of a piano and one violin, adapted from Estonian composer Arvo Pärt's *Für Alina*. As the film moves to its conclusion, the world of words and the sounds of the physical world seem to recede.

Things to Look For

- *Heaven* has a host of down-looking camera shots — from the aerial shots looking straight down on Turin's blocks of apartments to shots of the couple looking up — which are clearly meant to influence the story and the viewer's visceral response to it. Notice who's doing the looking, what he or she is seeing, and why.
- The film is full of different kinds of imagery. Be attuned along the way not so much for meaning as for suggestions of what this might be about.
- Director Tykwer also likes to use large, mostly empty spaces throughout the film. These, too, are intended to have an effect on the viewer. Another way to reflect on this effect is to ask how the film would feel if small, cramped spaces prevailed.
- Makeup and costuming become important as well — and pretty obvious. The very looks of the characters seem to morph into something "other" as the film proceeds.
- For a thriller, this film ends strangely, though in many ways the final elements are typical of police pursuits of runaway evildoers. In departing from the norm of the thriller, Piesiewicz-Kieslowski-Tykwer work hard to push us elsewhere in order to contemplate questions other than who did what to whom. To this end, they

supply markers along the way that the "usual" is not really taking place.

Post-viewing Commentary

Philippa Boyen, the schoolteacher widowed too soon, does the unexpected. She sets out to murder the police-protected drug lord who hooked her husband in college and whose product eventually killed him (and some of her middle school students). She plants a bomb in his office and then makes sure that his secretary will not be there when it goes off, and immediately thereafter she informs the police about the bomb and gives them her name. The surprise is not that this woman chooses to kill the drug lord — though we do not usually think of women as avengers, righteous or otherwise — but what she does afterwards, especially giving her name to the police. Of course, things go horribly wrong: Philippa goes from being a would-be vigilante to becoming a terrorist and mass murderer. She knows that all too well, and she is devastated by the disastrous result of her well-laid plan. All the while, a leading police official, in league with the drug lord, wants her dead, lest her claims of police indifference gain credibility in the police department and spur an internal investigation (the official has managed to bury all her calls and correspondence to the department).

And there, seemingly by happenstance, is young Filippo, police stenographer and son of the retired police chief. A more cherubic-looking attendant would be hard to imagine (he even seems to be wearing lipstick, at least in the early scenes). He ends up translating for her (though she is fluent in Italian, she insists that she be allowed to answer in English, as provided by international law). And he is amazed by her answers as he observes her horror when she learns that the bomb went awry. He attends to her when she faints, and that night, as he falls asleep, he looks at the hand that held her hand. As he tells his kindly father the next morning, he also wets the bed during the night — a sure sign, if there ever was one, that he is, alas, in love.

From that realization is hatched the elaborate escape plot, something they pull off even though the corrupt official has bugged Philippa's cell and knows all about it. He hopes to use the escape attempt to his own ends: to catch her in the act so that the police have cause to kill her. Instead, in a last-minute change of plans, Filippo and

244

Policeman Filippo gets ready to translate the words of the suspect, Philippa Boyen.

Philippa take refuge in the cavernous attic of the police headquarters, a building Filippo knows well from his childhood days of playing there when his father took him to work (the mother has apparently long been absent, though we are not told why). It is in the attic scene that Tykwer starts upping the stakes visually and thematically: the lofty attic, with its circular windows, looks very much like a cathedral, and there the escapees appear for the first time within the same frame (up until then they have never appeared together in one shot). And there also begins their slow movement into one identity: first come the white T-shirts, and then, once they are in the countryside town where Philippa grew up, they shave their heads, making the two look not only unisexual but monkish. This is quite appropriate because, until the last frames of the movie, they never touch, despite their conspicuous caring for each other. Whatever they feel and yearn for in each other transcends the sexual, though the striking images of their eventual union make clear that physical love persists and is even transfigured by the spiritual.

By that time, though, the couple has entered another world. When they emerge from the train tunnel, the camera suddenly sees the landscape in intense off-kilter browns and greens, as if they are in another realm altogether (something like the skewed color in the helicopter simulator that opens the film). More striking still is that strange string of linkages between the two: more than the close similarity of

245

The fugitives stare at the hilltop village where Philippa grew up.

their names, Filippo was born at the very hour of Filippa's confirmation and First Communion. And now it appears that he has come into her life in the nick of time to rescue her, not only physically from the clutches of death, but for something more — as the rest of the story makes clear. Here the story ceases to be about hair-raising escapes and safety, and becomes something else altogether.

A number of events make that clear. First, immediately upon arriving in that mountain town and looking at that hilltop village for the first time, the awed and devout look on their faces suggests that they have seen something akin to the city of God bursting forth in the sky ahead. The first thing they do on their arrival is enter the church, where Philippa confesses to Filippo in one long take as the camera circles around them in the darkened and hushed sanctuary, a confessional booth obvious in the immediate background. And Filippo might as well be a priest: he hears her long litany of error and crime, including murder, about which she is very blunt and for which she expects — even desires — to be punished. Filippo's response is the more remarkable, given her self-knowledge and candor: a direct and simple "I love you," as eloquent a distillation of the words of absolution as might be found. In spite of all the error and the crime, and perhaps because of the obvious remorse, forgiveness flows.

Then follow the haircuts, giving them new looks that blur their individual identities. And after that, the clandestine meeting at the hilltop church when Filippo's father in effect marries them, knowing that this is probably the last time he will see his son alive. This is also where Philippa acknowledges her love for this physical, moral, and spiritual rescuer who has mysteriously come to her out of nowhere. Though she confesses that she no longer believes — a reasonable conclusion, given the evil that surrounds her — the very presence of Filippo works to contradict her despair.

Philippa's redemption and return to belief are sealed in the concluding scenes. In a stable at her friend's farm, golden light pours in on them as they share a simple meal of bread and wine. Then comes their run to the hilltop and that solitary tree — indeed, a tree of life — where they consummate their love, something that now is entirely appropriate, given their troth and the blessing of his father. At the very end, with the film having moved to a wholly symbolic framework, they ascend, redeemed and made whole, untouched by the bullets that fly up at them (despite the constant volley, the firing never seems to hit the plastic bubble of the helicopter). The question of how high one can fly, which Filippo asks in the simulator, now has found both mysterious and wondrous answer. In this peculiar tale, love encompasses and transfigures darkness and its despair, and the Light shines on the couple as they ascend. Before that, though, heaven has come to them: it is realized in love that features forgiveness, sacrifice, and reconciliation.

The two finally embrace under what seems to be a tree of life.

Post-viewing Questions

1. Why, exactly, does Filippo fall for Philippa? It's an unlikely attraction — a policeman and a killer. What points are Piesiewicz and Kieslowski trying to make with it?

2. Director Tykwer comments (in an interview in the "making-of" featurette on the DVD) that the film remains realistic for about fifteen minutes. What does he mean by that, and where do the first signs of departure from realism show?

3. The very first scene in the helicopter simulator was added after the film was finished as indispensable to the plot. Were the filmmakers right about that?

4. The film seems to feature two different schemes of calculation: the necessary legal one that computes crime and punishment, but also a divine economy that trumps punishment with mercy and forgiveness. The latter seeks new life as opposed to paying for the wrongs of the old life, and this radical declaration bothers a lot of viewers. In most ways, this sounds very much like traditional Christian theology, or are Piesiewicz and Kieslowski carrying this redemption thing too far?

5. How effective are the visual strategies of the film — from palette to makeup — in conveying the fundamental "eeriness" of the story and especially of the world that the pair enter into?

Critical Comments

Given its distinguished parentage, namely Kieslowski and Piesiewicz, *Heaven* received the benefit of the doubt, getting a more generous reception than it might have if it had been by a writer with no previous credentials. The ardent Kieslowski fan Stephen Holden praises the film, one full of surprises, such as the "strange opening scene [that] finally pays off in an unforgettable final image of romantic and spiritual transcendence that leaves you breathless" (*The New York Times*, Oct. 4, 2002). Even the *Village Voice*, a periodical not particularly kind toward anything religious, got the point: "The detached patterns produced by the frequent overhead lateral pans suggest a divine perspective, and Tykwer is disinclined to judge his characters. Blanchett grows increasingly ethereal, while Ribisi never loses the open expression of a wise fool." In the end, Blanchett's "avenging angel and her smitten guardian angel escape their earthly bounds to travel by train through Tuscany, across an empty, timeless, 'virtual' landscape. Even before the Bonnie and Clyde finale, the movie has intimations of an afterlife" (J. Hoberman, Oct. 1, 2002). A scholar-critic, Antonio D. Sison, sees the ending reinforcing "the impulse to interpret Heaven as a postmodern re-appropriation of the biblical Creation-Fall account told in reverse." When Philippa and Filippo ascend and disappear into the sky, "spatiotemporal boundaries blur and the open-endedness encourages an eschatological hermeneutic akin to the impact of the celestial denouement of Kidlat Tahimik's *Perfumed Nightmare* or Lars von Trier's *Breaking the Waves*" (*The Journal of Religion and Film*, Apr. 2003).

Other Notable Films by Piesiewicz and Kieslowski

Three Colors, a trilogy inspired by the colors of the French flag: *White* (1994), *Red* (1994), and *Blue* (1993)

The Double Life of Veronique (1991)

Decalogue (1989-90), a ten-part series on the Ten Commandments done for Polish television.